The Soul's Journey:
Guidance from the Divine Within

D0902136

For more information or to contact
Lawrence Edwards, Ph.D. visit:
www.thesoulsjourney.com
or call: 914-241-8510

The Soul's Journey:
Guidance from the Divine Within

Lawrence Edwards, Ph.D.

Writer's Showcase
presented by *Writer's Digest*
San Jose New York Lincoln Shanghai

The Soul's Journey:
Guidance from the Divine Within

Writer's Showcase
presented by *Writer's Digest*
an imprint of iUniverse.com, Inc.

For information address:
iUniverse.com, Inc.
5220 S 16th, Ste. 200
Lincoln, NE 68512
www.iuniverse.com

ISBN: 0-595-12648-0

Printed in the United States of America

Acknowledgement

Beacon Press for excerpts by Robert Bly, from *The Kabir Book* versions by Robert Bly, copyright © 1971, 1977 by Robert Bly, © 1977 by the Seventies Press. Reprinted by permission of Beacon Press, Boston.

Motilal Banarsidass for excerpts by Jaideva Singh, from *Shiva Sutras: Yoga of Supreme Identity*, copyright © 1990 by Motilal Banarsidass Publishers Pvt Ltd. Reprinted by permission of Motilal Banarsidass Publishers Pvt Ltd.

New Directions Publishing Corp. for excerpts by Stephen Clissold, from The *Wisdom of the Spanish Mystics*, copyright © 1977 by Stephen Clissold. Reprinted by permission of New Directions Publishing Corp.

New Directions Publishing Corp. for the excerpt by Thomas Merton, from *The Wisdom of the Desert*, copyright © 1960 by The Abbey of Gethsemani, Inc. Reprinted by permission of New Directions Publishing Corp.

New Directions Publishing Corp. for excerpts by Robert Way, from *The Wisdom of the English Mystics*, copyright © 1978 by Robert Way. Reprinted by permission of New Directions Publishing Corp.

Princeton University Press for excerpts by Joseph Campbell, from *The Hero with a Thousand Faces*, copyright © 1949 by Bollingen Foundation. Reprinted by permission of Princeton University Press.

Spring Publications, Inc. for the excerpt by C. G. Jung, from *Psychological Commentary on Kundalini Yoga, Lectures One and Two*, copyright © 1975 by The Analytical Psychology Club of New York, Inc. Reprinted by permission of Spring Publications, Inc.

Dedication

To the Divine Mother in all Her forms,
Jaya Kali Ma!
Jaya Kali Ma!
Jaya Kali Ma!

The Soul's Journey:
Guidance from the Divine Within

Contents

Foreword

Foreword
by Stephen Larsen, Ph.D[*]

One of Joseph Campbell's profoundest discoveries of the Wisdom of the East[1] was the life and teachings of Sri Ramakrishna, the nineteenth-century Bengali Saint. Ramakrishna had a spiritual opening in which he felt his human life to unfold in the embrace of the Cosmic Goddess, *Kali*, whose effect was to instill divine rapture and love for all beings. Ramakrishna's insights are full of poetry and metaphysical wisdom of an extraordinary depth.[2]

Like Ramakrishna, whom he refers to, Edwards reveals himself in this book to be a *bhakta*, a devotee of the Goddess, she whose Radiance permeates the visible world. He is engaged in a kind of love affair with a Divine Being, with ever-renewing levels of rapture to be attained. In this way, there is no end to the revelations.

Little Lawrence's spiritual life, he tells us, began to unfold at about age three and a half, as a beautiful, luminous woman visited him during a thunderstorm; her gentle light was interwoven with the lightning;

---

[*] *Editor's Note*: Stephen Larsen, Ph.D. is the author of *The Shaman's Doorway, The Mythic Imagination* and numerous other works. He was a close student and friend of Joseph Campbell, editing volumes of Campbell's works and co-authoring, with his wife, Robin, *A Fire in the Mind*, Campbell's authorized biography. The Larsen's just completed *The Fashioning of Angels: Partnership as Spiritual Practice*, published by the Swedenborg Foundation.

tenderness and fierce power present simultaneously. The cry that came spontaneously from his lips is known in languages the world over: *"Mommy! Ma!"* The little boy thought he was calling his mother, but named she who stands behind the maternal human person as well; the Mother of us all. More visions came in a gradually unfolding revelation, and then mythical or allegorical stories began to come to him; offering a kind of guiding or explanatory orientation to the states of ecstasy. These make the book accessible to the general reader, and offer an easy initiation into intoxicating and complex spiritual ideas.

Lawrence Edwards is a modern shaman, but with a Ph.D. in psychology, which he gained to be able to operate on a competent professional, as well as spiritually intuitive level. Combining both qualifies him as a "technician of the sacred," as Mircea Eliade referred to the primordial shaman.[3] The instruction in the spiritual life comes not from a tradition, or an historically elaborated system, but from the universe itself (*herself*).

The world today has many spiritual seekers in it, but they may be interested to learn from one with a personal revelation that is so life-supporting and deeply enriching. Perhaps we need a new faith, and if we are to take this work seriously; it is not to be a *credo*, but an invitation to believe in the living spirituality of the universe. The personalization as a Goddess presented by Dr. Edwards is an invitation to enter the feeling side of divinity through Divine Love—a gateway that, though very ancient, is having a renewed appeal for many of us as a portal to the Transpersonal.

In this newly emerging spiritual approach, as Edwards models it for us, humble openness is to be combined with love and gratitude. One can be spiritually alive and questing with the wholeness of one's being—but on a personal path, not a collective one. Edwards' insights at times approximate the luminous insights of Rāmakrishna, or his modern interpreter, Lex Hixon.

Edwards writes of: "…the Divine Mother who gives birth to everything, who contains within her all that is or ever will be. In this form she symbolizes the totality of our unconscious which contains within it the Light of the Self. Until we are aware of the Self its Light is buried in our unconscious." Here he is evoking the metaphysical wisdom of the *Mandukya Upanishad*, which says that there is an especial quality of consciousness, in which it may learn to penetrate all of its own potential states: Waking, Dream, Deep Sleep, and *Turiya*. It is just beyond deep sleep that our knowledge of Cosmic Consciousness exists. It's here all the time, only we are unconscious of it. The yogi's task is to penetrate that state in order to experience unity (*nirvikalpa samadhi*). Edwards displays a quite sophisticated understanding of the Sanskrit literature, with which he made himself familiar in order to help him understand his continuously unfolding visions. He interweaves three elements: Indian Yogic wisdom, knowledge of both psychology and psychotherapy, and personal experience.

There is useful and felicitously phrased practical instruction in this book for how to align oneself in this approach:

> One way that Consciousness is enabling me to contain even the small currents of Shakti that come into me, is by maintaining the seeming dissociation between the Goddess and myself. This leaves my identity as Lawrence Edwards relatively intact and functional. It allows Lawrence to strengthen that identity by doing what he can to be a better servant and student of the Divine. At the same time, I experience the Shakti gradually shifting my sense of self away from just the mind and body of Lawrence Edwards and into the Divine. This doesn't negate my limited identity as this particular man, but adds to it such an extraordinary vastness of Being that the previous sense of self seems like a droplet of water blown off the crest of a wave, and having enjoyed coursing through the air, it now looks with great joy at the infinite expanse of ocean into which it is about to fall.

The biographical aspects of this work are integrated into a journey of discovery—the hero's journey of Campbell, which Edwards uses as a guidance system. At times he is like a sorcerer's apprentice, getting in over his head in spiritual realities that trip him up. This is the special value of this book, which is surely one of the finest examples of an emerging genre: First hand accounts of contemporary mystics who are plumbing the same depths as historically significant saints and mystics in the identifiable literature of the *Perennial Philosophy*. It is a privilege to have self-befuddlement and personal mistakes so openly disclosed as herein; and it is to be hoped for that our response to such disclosures is to learn from them—just as we do from our own errors. In this way, the lineaments of the once and future spiritual path are discernible. It is a version of Campbell's Hero Journey, a Western version of the spiritual enlightenment Quest of the East, but stretched out over time: a more gradual revelation.

Mircea Eliade referred to *illo tempore*, a sacred revelation from the long ago, which in enactment, puts one in contact with the ancient power: *As it was once, is now and ever shall be, world without end...Amen!*[4] We moderns will madly venerate any sacred revelation from the past—Koran, Bible, *Bhagavad Gita*—which somehow becomes more sacred the more ancient it is regarded to be. But what Martin Buber regarded as a "spiritual exile" from the Holy Land, that afflicts the modern world, and T. S. Eliot called "the wasteland," can be moistened, and sweetened with the nectar of living experience. Thus this account, with its honest self-revelation, agonies as well as ecstasies, tell us the same thing said by the Gnostic Jesus: *The Kingdom of God is spread upon the Earth and Men do not see it!* (one of Campbell's favorite quotes) Lawrence Edwards joins Yogananda and Krishnamurti in contemporary spiritual autobiography. Any contemporary mystic, especially one as young as Edwards, has a chance to show us the actualization that is ongoing in life—"here now, there now, always" as Eliot put it.

The Kundalini material is especially interesting, and Edwards treats this living energy with great respect—while celebrating its own revelatory power—its ability to "clean" the chakras as it arises and infuses the psychospiritual energy system of the body. When this happens, he shows, we are challenged with greater life—greater sensitivity and responsibility. He affirms that we do not have to stay within a traditional spiritual path if we prefer a more spontaneous and open journey—but we must regularly invoke the beneficent, loving, and charitable powers of the universe to guide us.

This book is full of wisdom, revelation and love. Let readers prepare themselves for transformation—and a joyful willingness to engage consciously in their own *sadhana*—their own spiritual path.

Stephen Larsen, Ph.D.
The Center for Symbolic Studies
New Paltz, NY
March 2000

Chapter 1

First Encounters

It would not be too much to say that myth is the secret opening through which the inexhaustible energies of the cosmos pour into human cultural manifestation.

Joseph Campbell[1]

Suppose you were to look at your life as a grand journey. Now ask yourself, really inquire of yourself, where are you going and what you are searching for on your journey? Where are you going? What are you searching for? As you sit quietly, carefully listening to the answers that come to mind, you might just accept them to begin with, sitting with them awhile. And then ask the same questions of yourself again. Each new round of questioning can take you beyond the previous answers to new and deeper layers of understanding. Just that simply, you've opened your mind to discovering profound insights about your life. Staying with those questions, really pondering them, thrusts us forward on a journey of discovery. This is our quest, our great personal mythic journey, and whether we know it or not, we're all on such a journey. To succeed, we must consciously choose full engagement with our quest. Many times along the way we will have to question what we've considered to be true in order to discover what really is true for ourselves.

Joseph Campbell wrote in his brilliant work on the symbolic quest, *The Hero with a Thousand Faces*:

> It has always been the prime function of mythology and rite to supply the symbols that carry the human spirit forward, in counteraction to those other constant human fantasies that tend to tie it back. In fact, it may well be that the very high incidence of neuroticism among ourselves follows from the decline among us of such effective spiritual aid. We remain fixated to the unexorcised images of our infancy, and hence disinclined to the necessary passages of our adulthood.[2]

By examining our life as a mythic journey we discover the deeper symbolic meanings of our struggles, whether our heroic battles are at work or at home, with our spouse, parents or children, or within the domain of the spirit. Connecting with the deeper symbolism of what we are doing allows us to know the significance of our lives regardless of whether the cultural markers of money and fame are present. Discovering the deeper symbolism of our journey, just as it is, also allows us to know and feel that what we are doing is meaningful, or to make adjustments in our lives so they become more meaningful.

I'll be sharing with you meditation experiences and vignettes from my own journey through life thus far. As you read them, themes from your life story may be reflected, possibly in contrast to mine or through similarity with it. The particulars of my life aren't important. The process of discovery and finding the greatest meaning to our individual existence, the meaning that then informs everything in our lives—these are the crown jewels of a person's life. Perhaps by the time you've finished reading this book something about the meaning of your quest will shine more brightly for you.

Contemplation is a key practice on our quest. I wonder in what ways you've contemplated your life. What is your life like? What has your journey through life been like? If the sequence of experiences life has brought you were told as a story, an odyssey, what themes would stand out to the listener of that story? What is the meaning of the tale told by your life story?

Where is your journey taking you?

Who chose the route?

Who chose the destination?

Who or what influenced those choices? In what ways did your family and friends, your culture, and the important situations in your life affect your choices, the twists and turns of your journey's route?

In what ways are you heading toward your chosen destination? What are you doing that takes you away from your destination or delays your progress? Who or what supports you on your quest? Who or what challenges you on your quest or appears as an obstacle? What personal qualities or resources must you access or develop as a result of being confronted by those challenges or obstacles?

You will be amazed by the wisdom that comes from within yourself as you note your reflections on these questions. I hope you'll contemplate in depth these and all the other questions that will occur to you. You may find writing your thoughts about each of them in a personal journal very useful. An easy way to do this is to take a loose-leaf binder and make sections of blank pages for the different questions. As you think about them you write your reflections and insights down. Sometimes you may just write a sentence or two, at other times you might write pages. You may even want to record your dreams or include other things in your book, such as photos from important times in your life that relate to your quest. It will become a treasury of your valued thoughts, memories, and insights about your spiritual journey.

Much is being written about the search for meaning and true identity as men and women question the limitations imposed by definitions of who they are. People are challenging these shallow or distorted definitions given by family and society. In this search some men look to discover the gods within themselves while women search out the goddesses within them. To expand beyond the confines of their inherited identities some men are seeking to understand the feminine within themselves, while some women look to explore the masculine within. The extraordinary interest in the works of Joseph Campbell on myth and the journey of the hero reflect the breadth of this search for meaning in our materialist culture. As the goal of such a journey, many people seek to experience the Divine, or the Self at the very core of who they are, through various forms of meditation and yoga.

When we grow uncomfortable with the limitations and constricted views of ourselves, the world, and God that come from our old "truths" and no longer serve us, we have to summon an inner directed form of courage to relinquish them. Then we've rejoined our quest, our journey of discovery. That's the direction our vitality, our enthusiasm or as Joseph Campbell would have said, our "inner bliss" leads us. I've included views from my continuing journey of discovery with the hope that what you read will encourage you to "go for it" in your own life, while questioning what the "it" is. If the "it" isn't the highest, the most expansive and inclusive, the most sublime and loving, ask yourself: Why should I settle for less?

At the same time, it's important to consider what the many costs of engaging your quest will be. Every great undertaking exacts its due. It's necessary to have a sense of those demands right from the outset. The rewards of fully engaging in our quest are boundless while the demands are limited—significant, but limited. Engaging in our quest releases an extraordinary amount of energy. The universe supports us by sending more energy and creating events, synchronistic occurrences, that further our journey. This brings about change within us and around us. You may find it useful to think about what changes you would like to create in your life and what needs to happen to support those changes. Who besides yourself needs to be prepared to deal with the changes you are creating, and what individuals or groups can you call on to support you on your quest? Personal transformation can stress the families and groups we are members of.

The power of Consciousness that propels us along our inner journey of discovery is given many names in different spiritual traditions—grace, the Holy Spirit, the soul's yearning, *mumukshtva* (Sanskrit for "longing for liberation"), the bond between the lover and the Divine Beloved, the fire of yoga, and divine discontent are some of those names. That power of all-encompassing Divine Consciousness, what we in the West call God, which seeks to reveal the truth of who we are, which seeks to reveal our own true nature and unite us with Itself, is called Kundalini in the yogic tradition. She is spoken of as a Goddess; this may make her seem alien or separate from us, but she is not. She is more fundamentally "you" than you can imagine. In essence She's formless, not a Goddess at all, but pure Divine Consciousness. She's the very power of Grace, one of the infinite powers of the Divine.

In the monistic tradition of Kashmir Shaivism, one of India's most ancient and sublime expressions of the mystical vision of God and the Universe, the Lord is said to have five powers. Everything else in the universe is a manifestation of these five: the power of creation, the power of sustenance, the power of destruction, the power of concealment, and the power of grace or revelation. When God goes to create the universe there's nothing to create it out of other than God. He or She (it doesn't matter which since God is neither *and* both) can't run down to the nearest building supply center for stuff to create it with, so she uses herself. What is God? Pure Consciousness, infinite power or energy that is Divine Consciousness. That's what the universe is made of. Everything is united with God because everything is made of God. God has the power to create all the forms of the universe, the power to sustain the continued existence of those forms, and the power to dissolve them back into the formless Divine. Now in order for God's play of creating, sustaining, and destroying to really work, all the forms in the universe, which are in union with God because they are made of God, have to forget they are one with the Divine. For their individual existence and the world drama to fully evolve they must have their union with God concealed from them. That's where the power of concealment comes in. Our truly unbreakable union with God is concealed, hidden from us by God. It's as if a part of God hides from another part in order to allow the drama of God's creation to unfold. That drama is the seemingly disconnected part of God evolving and beginning to yearn for re-union with God once again.

Imagine a vast deep ocean, calm and still, as the infinite Consciousness of God. God begins to create and a wave forms on the ocean, a form that seems to have its individual existence, yet is still one with the ocean. Now imagine that the wave's oneness with the ocean is concealed from it and the wave is given permission to play at taking on all different kinds of forms. The wave is conscious and experiences itself as a huge wave, then a small wave, a ripple, a tall wave, a fat wave, and on and on. But, as with all activities, this gets boring after a while. The wave has learned all it could from taking on different shapes, and now it's no longer creative or meaningful to continue doing it. The wave has a vague memory of having been a part of something greater and begins to long for something greater. It wants to re-unite with the ocean, with God. This is where the fifth power of God comes in, the power of grace, the power of revelation. By an act of grace God undoes the work of the power of concealment and reveals our true unity with God. The wave delights in being a projection of the ocean. The illusion of separation is dissolved and once again we enjoy the ecstasy of oneness with our Creator.

The poet saint Kabir wrote:

> I have been thinking of the difference
> between water
> and the waves on it. Rising,
> water's still water, falling back,
> it is water, will you give me a hint
> how to tell them apart?

Because someone has made up the word
'wave,' do I have to distinguish it
from water?

There is a Secret One inside us;
the planets and all the galaxies
pass through his hands like beads.

That is a string of beads one should look at with
luminous eyes.[3]

With the bestowal of grace we awaken to the Truth, the truth of our union with the "Secret One." When we wake up in the morning we begin to experience a different reality from the one we were in just moments before while we were asleep. The power of consciousness that begins to operate with our awakening each morning allows us to experience the reality of the waking world around us. Kundalini is the power of Consciousness that allows us to know we are one with God, to know that all others are one with God, and to know that all of creation is one with God. Until that power of Consciousness is awakened within us, we can't know the truth directly for ourselves. When that power of Consciousness awakens, transformation of the highest order ensues. The Kundalini has been called "the face of God." Just as we know someone by his or her face, we come to know God by the Kundalini.

She is fully present in everyone, though inactive, waiting for the great awakening that marks the most sacred event in the soul's journey back to its source. It is this Goddess and Her workings that are reflected in the experiences I (and countless others) have been given in meditation. These experiences have come as gifts from the Goddess, gifts to be shared. Such gifts are available to anyone who wishes to honor and pursue within themselves Her divine presence. Remember, She is the most sublime aspect of your own divine Self, already fully present within you. Literally thousands of people are finding this out for themselves. What unique and beautiful form those gifts will take for you awaits your discovery!

The Kundalini is often depicted in yogic texts as a coiled serpent lying dormant within us, a serpent whose mighty powers become manifest as it awakens. This may sound unbelievable, just too fantastic! But what if I were to tell you it's a well researched fact that within each person there is a spiral form of bound energy that holds more knowledge than the world's best scientists can comprehend. This spiral form of bound energy awakens and begins to unfold its unfathomable wisdom when two halves of the spiral are joined to form a whole. You can't see it, it's so microscopic in size, and yet it knows how to grow an entire human being from a single cell. It guided the development of one infinitesimally small bit of protoplasm into all the trillions of different cells that make up your body. This spiral form of bound energy knew how to transform that one microscopic speck of living substance into your heart, lungs, nerves, brain, eyes, ears, nose, skin, teeth, bones and muscles. It knew how to create all the different white blood cells, red blood cells, muscle cells, and bone cells; it knew where to grow them and when to stop growing them. It lets your fingernails grow but not your fingers, it lets your hair grow but not your ears; it grew your heart in the right place and connected it to your head. It knew where to grow each artery and vein in your entire circulatory system. It knew just the right place to grow the nerve cells that run all the way from your big toe up to your brain and back again.

Does this sound too incredible? Do I really expect you to believe that a microscopic, spiral form of bound energy knows how to do all that? Yes! We don't know how, but we do know that DNA, the spiral form of bound energy which makes up your genes, guides the truly miraculous development of a single cell into the unimaginably complex organization of trillions of cells which we call the human body. If the energy of the universe can be bound in the molecules forming DNA, subtly encoding in it all the information necessary to create from itself the many diverse organs, tissues, and cells of the body and have them successfully operate together, from the biochemistry of your digestive tract to the intricate functions of your brain, what makes you think a little Consciousness couldn't be lying dormant within you, symbolized as a coiled serpent, waiting to propel your awareness back to union with the Creator? The Goddess Kundalini is there within you; perhaps She has already begun to stir from Her slumber!

My first encounter with this divine feminine presence happened when I was very young and totally unaware of the meaning of the event. A booming thunderstorm awakened me in the middle of the night. I could hear the rain beating on the roof overhead. It ran noisily into the old copper gutters and down-spouts outside my bedroom windows. I liked thunderstorms. I could hear my older brother and sister sleeping soundly in our shared bedroom. I was about three and half, maybe four years old.

As I opened my eyes in the darkened room, I saw a beautiful woman standing beside my bed looking over me. Her form illuminated itself against the night as though she were comprised solely of light. Her face was strikingly sweet and loving as she looked over me with great tenderness. I thought this must be Mom. No one else ever looked at me like that and made me feel so secure. I just looked at her for a while. She didn't say anything. She simply stood by me as the thunderstorm boomed on. I noticed that as the room lit up with the lightning flashes she would flicker and fade. Her light mixed with the lightning and she could hardly be seen. It was only in the dark that she was clearly visible. That was very unlike Mom! Was this really Mom?

In a little voice I said, "Ma?" She didn't respond, she just kept smiling benevolently at me. "Ma?" I said a bit louder. Still nothing. Beginning to panic I yelled, "Mommy!" I heard my parent's bedroom door open across the hall from where we were. The "lady of light" stood there looking at me as I heard my mother's footsteps coming toward my room. The instant my mother entered our bedroom the radiant figure vanished. Mom said it was nothing but a dream. I knew better. For years I talked about the "lady of light", as I called her, who visited me during the thunderstorm. I didn't know then that I would see her again many years later.

Children begin life open to the presence of the Divine in all its forms. They see mystery and wonder in even the smallest of things around them. When she was an infant, our daughter, Molly, like all infants, would gaze around the room looking as if she wasn't dialed into this reality at all! With our professional backgrounds (my wife is a pediatrician) we certainly knew the scientific explanations of what she was experiencing, but they never fit the feel of the moment. When Molly would look around with that beatific expression and then squeal in delight at something invisible in mid-air, we created our own theory to explain what was happening, one that many other parents have also created. We decided she was visiting with her angel friends from the realm she just left. Her limbs would flail in delight at their jokes and at other times they would join her in seeing how ridiculous we adult humans can be, especially when we are very serious! We've welcomed her and her angel friends into our lives. She's brought more than a touch of divinity to our daily routines. We've also discovered that many parents have the same secret theory about their infants visiting with angels!

Every Sunday when I was little, my parents dropped me off at Sunday school before they went to the church service. My kindergarten class met in a simple basement classroom. Its walls were clean and shiny, like the well-scrubbed faces of all us kids dressed in our Sunday garb, skipping along holding our parents' hands. Mom would take me down to the classroom. This Sunday seemed like every other Sunday. My kindergarten buddies, Pete and Keith were there. We all sat around one of those long, rectangular, Formica-topped tables, boys seated every other chair with girls between to keep us in line. Deborah and Susan were there. They were too goody-goody for my liking. The teacher stood at the end of the table and was telling us about Lord Jesus. I loved stories from the Bible and Biblical times. They were so alive with the power of God. As she was talking about Christ, I looked over to her left toward the far wall behind her. The cement block wall appeared to have opened and there stood Jesus Christ. I wasn't shocked. After all, He was God. He could do whatever He wanted. He was simply standing there, just as the principal at school would come and stand in the doorway watching the class for a while. What I didn't understand was why the teacher was talking as if he was long gone.

Finally I said, "Why are you talking like that, He's standing right there!" The teacher, unfazed, didn't even look in the direction I pointed toward.

She was so sure that Jesus was dead and gone, she just said, "Oh, Larry you have such vivid imagination," and continued with her lesson.

The muffled giggles of my classmates lasted only a few moments. I was quieted by what she said—puzzled, and vaguely upset too. When I looked back toward where I had seen Jesus standing, He faded away. The unadorned cement wall met my innocent gaze.

I rejoined Mom and Dad outside the church after class. I felt a bit like I had lost something, though I wouldn't have been able to say what. I was still a little upset, but not seriously enough that a game of catch in the backyard with Dad didn't cure it, at least for the moment. Talking about it with grown-ups was out of the question. They still didn't believe in my "Lady of Light."

It wasn't long before I lost interest in Sunday school. Of course I had to keep going. That struck me as a particularly grown-up way of doing things—you just keep doing them for some unknown reason, even though you don't want to anymore. But Keith showed me a trick. We were big enough now that our folks wouldn't walk us to the classroom. As long as they saw you go in the front door, they felt fine. And as long as you met them outside of church at 10:30, like you always did, then everything was O.K. Keith showed me that in between you could do all kinds of unchurchly activities! We would go in the front door with all the other kids, then simply walk through the building and out the back door. We were free! Now the excitement was back in Sundays! I didn't much mind going anymore. I saw Keith get into trouble because he would skip every Sunday. I stuck with skipping out only every third or fourth.

We always had this little offering envelope that we placed in the basket each Sunday. It had a dime in it. Big money back then. Keith would open his and use it to buy candy at the candy store we would skip out to. Horrified at first, I wouldn't do it. Keith was way ahead of me. He said, "Listen. When you put this in the basket what do you get? Nothing. When you put it in Frank's hand you get a piece of candy. It's simple." Sounded pretty good to me, though I was always uneasy about it. I wouldn't do it too often. I kept thinking, "What if there is a God who gets angry?"

My thought processes at eight years of age weren't sophisticated enough to let me know that God gives with great abundance to children as they make their truly wonderful offerings—their open hearts and minds. God responded to my feelings and allowed me to perceive the living presence of Jesus. If adults don't trample or devalue God's gifts to children, then children won't be imprisoned within the confining walls of the adult's beliefs and left desperately looking for ways to be free. Keith and I found a way of escaping, but no way to be free.

In the unremarkable suburban middle class community I grew up in during the late 50's and early 60's, we were all subjected to rampant fears of nuclear war. Bomb shelters, air raid drills, and the Cuban missile crisis all hung over elementary school life, spurring odd conversations among ten-year-old boys about how it would feel to look out of the bomb shelter and have your head vaporized by THE BOMB. I wondered how those few gallons of water in the shelter were going to last for the 50 zillion years they said everything around us would be radioactive. And did they really expect us to play monopoly for that long while we waited for it to become "safe" outside? For a while, nuclear war and the death of masses seemed almost unavoidable. It forced us kids to face death in an abstract kind of way and come to terms with it. We would joke in the nuclear bomb drills at school that when they told us to take cover and put our head between our legs, the only thing to do was to kiss your ass goodbye.

A towering pine tree stood at the corner of our house. Its branches formed a perfect ladder up alongside its trunk. I would climb onto the roof of our house and go to the highest peak to sit and look at the world. I hung out alone there for hours. Everything looked smaller from there. Adults looked smaller. I could see the whole neighborhood. Most of all I liked to just lie on my back and watch the sky as clouds and birds sailed by. It felt so quiet, so immense. It was a place I could wonder about God, about my pet snakes, about why I couldn't hit Warren's fastball and all the other important things in the life of a young boy. Once when I was 12 years old I was lying up on the roof with my mind as expansive and clear as the brilliant blue sky. Suddenly I heard a mature masculine voice in my head tell me quite matter-of-factly that I was going to die when I was 24. I wouldn't live to see my 25th birthday. Though it sounded unalterably true I wasn't particularly shocked or troubled by it. Twenty-four seemed nearly middle-aged to me, and given that we were likely to have a nuclear war, dying was quite possible. Besides, at the time I was much more concerned with sorting out my God and religion problem. It was coming to a head because I was approaching the time for confirmation in my parent's church. I was expected to go through it and I didn't want to.

When confirmation classes began, the intensity of my arguments with my parents increased. I told my folks I didn't believe in the church and I couldn't take the vows they demanded of you in the confirmation ceremony. My parents decided to negotiate a deal. If I went through the ceremony I would never have to go to church on Sunday again. After arguing the absurdity and hypocrisy of that, I agreed, with one addendum that I added privately in my mind. I wouldn't actually take the vows. It was a group ceremony and the "I do's" and "I will's" would be spoken by the group of young confirmees. I simply wouldn't join in. I was only agreeing to place my body in the church during a given hour one Sunday while my mind and being recoiled. It was becoming obvious to me that in the adult world the outer form of things was what mattered most. The confirmation happened as planned and I celebrated being free of the church and my parents on this issue. But I was still troubled by God and what to believe. I had felt a kind of Divine Presence in my life at times, and the memory of the Lady of Light never faded. I also never forgot the vision of Jesus I had in the church when I was little. However, for all the church-going adults I knew, Christ was dead and long gone. I proceeded to get lost looking for answers.

Through my teen years I put my life, health and future in serious jeopardy through drug and alcohol abuse. I was very successful in school and worked a full-time job in addition to school in order to save for college. Drugs and alcohol were my ways of numbing myself to the pain I felt from the spiritual crisis I was in. The prevailing motivators for people I was growing up with—competition, proving yourself and material gain—didn't speak to the needs of my soul for meaning, for leading a meaningful life. Relationships weren't the answer either. I remember struggling, like most adolescents, with understanding love. I was thinking about it one day while I was with my girlfriend and some other kids from my high school. She was talking to someone about how she loved potato chips as she devoured a bag. A few minutes later she told me she loved me, the smell of potato chips still on her breath. My spirit recoiled. I concluded that what most people called love was consumption. They either wanted to consume you or be consumed by you. My soul screamed that this wasn't love and had nothing to do with love. But the questions remained, what is love, what is the meaning of life?

As I looked around the adult world that I was about to enter, nobody had the answers. Too often big business consumed people and the environment, turning both into disposable, often toxic, waste products. The government exhausted our money and wasted precious human lives in the Vietnam War. Religion as I had experienced it was a farce. Drugs didn't assuage my need for answers or meaning, but they were more potent distracters than anything else society offered. I graduated from high school with honors and a full academic scholarship for college, while at the same time I was beginning to think about suicide. At times I would remember the Lady of Light and wonder if she had anything to do with my narrowly missing self-destruction; I felt protected as, more than once, I watched people around me die of overdoses or get busted for dealing drugs. It was around this time that I was introduced to Eastern philosophies, hatha yoga, meditation and mysticism. Those were the days of hippies, peace movements, and the first big wave of gurus sweeping over our culture. By the end of my freshman year of college I had nearly destroyed my mind and my record of academic excellence through drug abuse, but I had discovered something in yoga.

As I completed that first year of college I was terrified by my state of mind and ill health. I left the crowd I was hanging with, transferred to a university in a different state, quit all drug use, and began practicing hatha yoga and meditation. Within two months of beginning the yoga practices I was feeling better than I had in years. Yoga was putting my body back into shape. Meditation detached me from the tyranny of my mind and its self-defeating patterns, while giving me ways to use it more successfully. I was meeting people for whom God was alive and able to be directly experienced. They didn't call it God; using the Eastern traditions' terminology they called it Consciousness—omniscient, omnipotent, all-embracing Consciousness. It wasn't hard to recognize this was God. I really felt graced. I was looking forward to beginning anew as a sophomore. A few weeks before the start of the academic year an amazing event occurred.

I was back living with my folks for a while. They were in their new house in rural Connecticut, far away from where I grew up on Long Island. I used to go to bed early in order to get up at 5 A.M. for yoga and meditation. My father smoked cigars in the living room down the hall from my bedroom. I always kept the door to my room closed in order not to choke on the offensive odor. I went to bed as usual this one night, closing the door tightly beforehand. In the middle of the night I awoke for no apparent reason.

As I opened my eyes and looked past the foot of the bed I saw standing in the doorway my Lady of Light! She stood there just as she had 16 years earlier in our other home. Her radiance was exquisite. Gentle, soft light emanated from her every feature and from her diaphanous, flowing robes. Tender love, enveloping, caring love—beyond measure—poured from her and wrapped around me like a warm blanket. Tears ran down my cheeks. I felt like she had been there guiding me, protecting me, and enabling me to survive the struggles my life included.

Now that I had chosen to engage consciously in my quest through yoga, this was her time to reveal herself to me once again. I took it as an incredibly auspicious sign, assuring me I was headed in the right direction. I couldn't keep my eyes off her as I lay in my bed staring at her. Finally I spoke saying, "I know you, I remember you." She continued to stand there, showering me with her radiant presence. An indescribable joy welled up inside me. No more words were necessary.

Eventually I closed my eyes, sinking into meditation and then back to sleep. I rested in a comfort I had never experienced before. It came with the security of knowing I was protected and guided in a most miraculous way. Years would pass before I learned we all have that protection available to us. When I awoke in the morning the door was ajar. I asked my parents if they had opened it and of course they hadn't. Her visit remained a secret with me. Fortunately, I wouldn't have to wait another 16 years before experiencing Her presence again.

I began pursuing yoga and meditation practices with more and more self-discipline and dedication. They honed my body and mind to such an extent that I maintained straight A's even while working full-time to support myself. I graduated magna cum laude from the University of Connecticut. I was no saint, as anyone who knew me then could tell you, but such is the power of even simple meditation practices done regularly that my slips couldn't undo the progress. During these years I studied under a few of the contemporary gurus on the scene at the time. Usually after following their practices for a couple of years my experience would plateau off and stop or in some way they would show they weren't truly masters. By 1975 I was feeling discouraged by the lack of leadership available to me and feeling quite stuck without it. I was reading St. John of the Cross, the great Christian mystic, and his words about the necessity of having a teacher concerned me. He said a soul "…on its own without a master is like a burning coal which is left to itself; it loses its glow and grows cold."[4] I was in danger. I needed the fire only a real master could bring, but so far all I had found were smoldering impostors.

Finally, I met someone who told me about a great master of meditation, a swami or monk, from India. He was reputed to be able to awaken the Kundalini, a very rare ability even amongst accomplished yogis. In the late summer of 1976 I met Swami Muktananda at an ashram in upstate New York where he was giving programs. My meeting with him wasn't any different from that of tens of thousands of people who had met him during his previous world tours or would meet him in his subsequent world tours. Like most of those people I had no idea of the enormity of the moment or what was to unfold from that almost casual happenstance. After the program, a long greeting line formed with everyone who wanted to meet him or receive his blessings. I joined the "dar-han line," as it is called. When I arrived before him, I could hardly make sense of what was occurring inside me. My mind was saying, "Oh well, here's another guru. I doubt anything will be different from before." Simultaneously, my heart and body were trembling with excitement. My heart was saying "This is it! Somehow he's the one!" His eyes were unlike any eyes I had ever looked into—all at once they were jovial, compassionate and unfathomable. The brush of the wand of peacock feathers he used to greet and bless people was strangely energizing and quieting at the same time. He gave me the mantra that everyone received for meditation, *Om Namah Shivaya* ("I bow to the Divine"). I walked away feeling so light that it was literally as if I was several feet off the ground. I couldn't figure out what happened. I left him to return home, not knowing that this marked the awakening of Kundalini for me. The next day the meditation master returned to India. I put the whole event aside and went back to the Jungian analytic training and the bio-energetic therapy training I was pursuing along with my meditation practices.

Shankaracharya, the eighth century sage of Advaita Vedanta and one of the greatest spiritual masters ever to live, wrote an ecstatic prayer, *Saundaryalahari*, proclaiming the supreme power of Kundalini.[5] In it he states that all knowledge, all wisdom, all inspiration, and all creativity— musical, poetic, literary, artistic, as well as union with the Divine come through the power of Kundalini *alone*. For this reason the awakening of Kundalini is the esoteric goal of all yogas. *Shaktipat* is the term for the descent of grace that awakens the Kundalini. The ancient text, the *Kularnava Tantra*, states that without shaktipat there is no liberation or Self-realization.[6] The descent of grace may happen spontaneously and unexpectedly, or through the power of a master of genuine attainment. In some cases shaktipat is received through contact with a mystic guide who appears in one's dreams or meditation. Often it is awakened through a mantra or the practices learned from an accomplished spiritual teacher. Also, it may have been awakened in a past life and is continuing to unfold in this life. No one person or practice is the solely available means of receiving the descent of grace, the awakening of the Kundalini. The Divine is too generous to put such limitations on its accessibility.

A couple of months after that brief encounter with Swami Muktananda I entered the hospital for arthroscopic surgery on my knees. I was supposed to be in and out the same day. A week later I was still in the hospital; the knee surgery hadn't been done. The screening x-ray showed two fist-sized growths in my chest. The doctors thought I might have lympho-sarcoma, in which case it was likely I would be dead in two to three months. "Very interesting" I thought, as the memory came back of being 12 years old, laying on our roof and hearing a voice from within me speak of my death at the age of 24, only now 24 wasn't old!

I began thinking about my life and the lessons that were being presented to me. I was an avid backpacker and rock climber. Those activities provided the metaphor for life as I saw it. You struggled up to the top of some mountain, enjoyed the view and the accomplishment, went down-hill and began looking for the next mountain. Self-effort and struggle dominated my perspective on life. I had even learned to enjoy them. But now I was encountering situations in which only a kind of surrender and letting go would work. They were very difficult for me. The present illness was the most dramatic situation to arise thus far.

As I lay in my hospital bed one evening, I thought of the meditation master I had briefly encountered. People called him "Baba," which simply means father and is routinely used in India when speaking to any male elders, swamis, or gurus. His image was vividly present in my mind, and I had a conversation with him. I said, "Baba, I don't really know who you are. In fact, I don't think I know *what* you are, but I have no one else to turn to. I pray that you'll be able to help me. I don't have anything to offer you but this life of mine and even that may not amount to much. I gladly surrender it to you. Please show me a way through this."

Within a few moments my mind became very still and I fell into a deep state of meditation. I felt I was in the presence of both Baba and the Lady of Light. The serenity and the feeling of being watched over that I experienced in that moment put all concerns about my future out of my mind. It felt as though a powerful energy was washing through my body, leaving it very relaxed and refreshed. I came out of the meditation knowing everything would be fine, without knowing what "fine" would look like. I knew I would be at peace regardless of what happened. I offered a prayer of thanks to Baba and my Lady of Light before falling asleep in my hospital bed.

After several more days of testing and exploratory surgery, the doctors changed their diagnosis to a disease called sarcoidosis, not cancer, and as one doctor crassly said, "this one might not kill you until you're in your fifties!" I knew I had nothing to worry about. Within a few months all traces of this disease disappeared too.

A year later I left my job, my fiancé, and everything else to fulfill my inner promise to offer my life to Baba. I had never told him anything about what had happened. In fact, my only contact with him had been that brief moment on the greeting line 18 months earlier. As a result of Kundalini awakening, I was having many powerful meditation experiences that further inspired me to detach from the world and look for a way to live a life of the spirit. It was difficult for me to leave everyone and everything I loved, but my soul demanded it of me. I told family and friends I was going to India to become a monk. My fiancé did her best to understand, but couldn't escape the pain of my leaving her. She was crying in the airport as I boarded a plane for Bombay, never expecting to return.

I made it to Swami Muktananda's ashram in rural India, thoroughly exhausted from a 36-hour flight, 11-hour jetlag, and the attendant ordeals of traveling for hours through the Indian countryside in a three-wheel motorscooter. In my bedraggled state I was immediately brought to Baba. I told him I had left everyone and everything because I felt that in order to really give myself to God and a life of the spirit I had to renounce everything, become a monk, and spend the rest of my life in service. I was terribly serious. Fortunately Baba wasn't. He was humorously serious. Baba looked at me warmly and laughed, saying I could have them both, the worldly and the spiritual life. He paused and waited for that to sink in. The look on my face must have been something to behold, I felt like massive stone curtains were crumbling and falling away from my mind and vision. He continued, saying the worldly and the spiritual are not opposed; there was no reason to give up my life in that way. His words opened my heart again. I was ready to explode with joy. I left his presence with a lightness that nearly had me flying back home. I was so excited by this turnaround that I felt I should leave immediately and return to my fiancé and career. I started packing again the next morning. Luckily, a friend brought me back to the ground and pointed out that since I had traveled halfway around the world to be with this great master it would be best if I stayed a few weeks to learn all that I could. There was no hurry; my boss, a Jungian analyst and mentor to me, had said I could have my job back if it became apparent that monkhood wasn't my path.

When I did arrive back in the States I returned to my previous position at a Jungian psychiatric treatment center. A few months later I was married. My wife had to endure my living like a monk for several years and one more episode of my being inspired to become a monk two years after we were married! Eventually my spiritual preceptor helped me to see that the obstacles I wanted to remove from my life through renunciation were actually the very aids I needed in this life to fully experience God's love and to learn to be an instrument of God's love. From then on my wife and I have continued our journey together. Others have likened her to the mythic Queen Chudala, whose husband, the King, wanted to renounce the world and live the life of an ascetic in the forest. She had the wisdom and patience to stay with him, helping him to learn that true renunciation is an inner state of freedom. Once he learned that, it allowed him to be a great and righteous king while embodying the highest spiritual attainment.

Over several years I watched with amazement as the transformative process of meditation unfolded in my life by the grace of the awakened Kundalini. The changes I experienced and the ones I saw in countless others who had experienced Kundalini awakening led me to do my doctoral research thesis on the dimensions of psychological change and spiritual growth that people experienced through their practice of a Kundalini-based yoga.[7] The research study was the culmination of my Ph.D. studies in the Department of Psychoeducational Processes at Temple University.

In the spring of 1986 I was working on my dissertation and faced the task of writing about the Kundalini as a part of my thesis. Suddenly I confronted the fact that I really knew very little about the Kundalini. Despite practicing a yoga based on the awakened Kundalini for a decade, despite experiencing profound states of meditation, and despite hearing numerous lectures on the Kundalini, I couldn't say that I truly understood her or knew how this Divine power worked. For the most part I simply felt awed by the transformations wrought by her in myself and others. I was reminded of a story my high school physics teacher liked to tell about the discovery of gravity. He said it used to be that people thought there was a mysterious power of attraction that made objects draw close to the earth. Now if someone asks why a ball falls when you throw it up into the air, we say that's just gravity, dismissing it without a second thought. However, if someone asks what is gravity, we'd have to say it's a mysterious force of attraction that exists between objects. We know a few ways to describe the manner in which the force works, but its essence is just as much a mystery as it ever has been. The term gravity has become quite familiar and the scientific theory on the "law of gravity" has become so accepted that we're no longer even conscious of it being just a theory. By naming phenomena and accepting an authority's (scientific, religious, yogic, etc.) explanation of them we demystify them, even if they really are still a mystery. Kundalini had become familiar, but as I approached the task of writing about it, I was once again aware of what a mysterious power it is.

C. G. Jung wrote that "when you succeed in the awakening of Kundalini, so that she starts to move out of her mere potentiality, you necessarily start a world which is totally different from our world: it is a world of eternity."[8]

Into that mystical world our quest leads us.

Chapter 2

Ascent to Union

Mother of Ultimacy,
unspeakable and unthinkable,
who can comprehend your countless revelations?

Sometimes you remove every veil
    to be known by enlightened sages
as the formless Mother of the Universe,
the transparent presence who dwells secretly
        within every atom, every perception, every event.
Other times you manifest as Mother Kundalini,
the evolutionary potency
        coiled at the root of the subtle body.

Ramprasad[1]

There I sat staring at my computer screen, wondering how I was going to write an explanation of the Kundalini that would be appropriate to a doctoral thesis; on a deeper level, I wondered what I truly knew of her divine nature. It was May of 1986, and I began by reviewing what I had learned about the Kundalini. Through years of study and meditation practices I had gained both theoretical knowledge of the Kundalini and numinous meditation experiences that revealed some aspects of her mysterious nature. The yogic system of psychophysiology gives a fascinating description of what is called the subtle body. It is within the subtle body that the energy form of Universal Consciousness known as Kundalini resides. Once activated from her resting-place in the subtle body, the awakened Kundalini begins her work of transforming and purifying the subtle and physical bodies. The ensuing experiences and shifts in consciousness constitute the seeker's unfolding spiritual journey.

The subtle body is an energy body that interpenetrates our physical body. You may have heard of it without knowing that it was the subtle body being referred to. What is often described as one's "aura" is a visible manifestation of the subtle body. Acupuncture is a form of medical treatment that works on the energy flowing through the subtle body. This body is subtle compared with the gross body which we experience very concretely through all the physical sensations our sense organs make available to us. The subtle body is the "body" of our mind, our thoughts, feelings, emotions, intuitions, and other less commonly identified forms of energy. It's a subtle realm that is very real to us, even though science can't verify the existence of any specific thought or feeling we might be having.

Science deals with the gross physical realm and can only detect physical correlates to thoughts and feelings, correlates such as brainwave patterns, respiratory rates, or galvanic skin response. A researcher using the most refined instruments attached to your skull may be able to give you data about neuro-muscular activity, but only you know that at that instant you are recalling a tender moment of being held in the arms of a loved one. That kind of memory is not at all subtle, yet the rich content of it goes far beyond the ability of the most sensitive scientific instrument of measurement to detect. However, you already possess the most subtle and powerful instrument capable of apprehending such memories and even subtler phenomenon: that instrument is consciousness. Your conscious attention is your power of apprehension. It can be developed and refined through meditation and the awakened Kundalini.

During ordinary waking-state awareness, our consciousness is almost entirely identified with the physical body. In waking-state consciousness our experience is dominated by body awareness and things related to it. We're aware of various sensations, feelings, and thoughts about ourselves that are rooted in the gender of our body, the shape it is in, and the functions or roles it is performing in our family or society. We think of ourselves as man or woman, fat or thin, husband or wife, boss or employee. Waking-state awareness is primarily physical-body consciousness. Even the subtle-body activities of the mind and emotions are primarily those that are related to the physical realm and what is happening there. Sadly, for most of us this comprises all of what we will give our attention to for our entire lives. But there's infinitely more to who we are and what we have available to experience and learn from.

The subtle body is another realm entirely.[2] We experience the subtle body most exclusively when we are in the dream state of consciousness and in some meditative states. In the dream state, the experience of the subtle body that people are most familiar with, we are out of the physical realm. The laws of physics no longer apply—we leave behind the constraints of ordinary time and space. We experience consciousness relatively free of the fetters of the physical body, but consciousness is still bound in certain ways. We're still identified with a limited sense of self, with the thoughts, feelings, and reflections of our body identity. At the same time we can move about through time and space in ways the physical body never can. In our dreams we fly, move back to the past, ahead to the future, or to some alternate present. Because we are so identified with the body and waking-state consciousness, the subtle body and the subtle realms of dreams, thoughts, feelings, imagination, and intuition are often disorienting. These realms may seem alien, unknown, perhaps even incomprehensible to our waking-state sense of self. Usually our waking-state "I" dismisses or devalues our dreams and other unusual subtle body experiences. Through meditation we can enter and explore the subtle realms quite consciously. The great yogic sages have done this and reported on the physiology of the subtle body.

Just as our physical body has conduits for vital fluids and nerve impulses, the subtle body has conduits for the energy of consciousness. They are called *nadis*, and they carry the living conscious energy called *prana*. In meditation the nadis may appear like the filaments of light in fiber optics or a laser light show. Where several nadis join together, the conduit is larger, like a bigger fiber-optic cable. In our physical body, the main nerve conduit running from the brain down to the base of the spine is the spinal cord, a great bundle of nerve fibers that connects the highest centers in the brain to the entire body. In roughly the same location in the subtle body there is the main conduit of pranic energy, called the sushumna nadi, running from the head down to the base of the spine.

The sushumna nadi is not only the major channel for the creative energy of Consciousness to flow through as it manifests the universe of personal experience; it is also the repository for all the past impressions left by our actions, both mental and physical. The sushumna contains the impressions, called *samskaras*, of all our many lifetimes. In this way it is the storehouse of all our *karmas*, all the consequences of our past actions that we have yet to experience. Most people are familiar with music CDs or the CD-ROM in their computers. On a CD, millions of subtle impressions are stored. When the laser light of the CD player mechanism passes over the CD it picks up those impressions and converts them into music, pictures, video or whatever it was that was stored on it. In a similar way, the sushumna nadi stores in an energy field the countless impressions of all our various actions. When the light of our individual consciousness passes through them it picks up those patterns and manifests them. In this way, patterns of thinking, feeling, acting, relating, and creating are built up over lifetimes and reproduced again and again. It is these samskaras, the patterns and consequences of our own past actions, that bind consciousness to the forms of identity that we normally experience as ourselves each day.

To become liberated or enlightened requires becoming free of those samskaras. This is the work of the awakened Kundalini. She does this in two ways. First, the Kundalini moves through the sushumna nadi "erasing," if you will, the impressions stored there and releasing the energy bound up in those impressions. This extraordinary purification process then releases us from the patterns in our lives created by those impressions. Secondly, she opens up states of consciousness that give us access to unbounded awareness, awareness of the transcendent Self, what some call God-consciousness. These are the altered states of consciousness, the experiences of mystical union and profound meditation that allow us to perceive, perhaps for the first time, that we are much more than we think we are. They lead to the proclamation of the ancient Vedas of "I am Brahman," "I am the Absolute," or in the words of the Christian mystic, St. Catherine of Genoa, "My Me is God, nor do I recognize any other Me except my God himself."[3] In order for that state of unity consciousness to become stable and fully manifest in the mind, body, and actions of the individual, the sushumna nadi and all the lesser nadis must be purified, cleansed of impressions and blocks that contract or restrict consciousness to the confines of ordinary human experience.

Along the sushumna nadi there are energy centers where numerous lesser nadis intersect the sushumna, similar to the nerve centers along the spinal cord (Figure 1). These energy centers along the sushumna are called *chakras* in Sanskrit, meaning "circle or wheel." They may appear to the inner eye during meditation as wheels of energy or light. Chakras are also described as lotus flowers with various numbers of petals. The energy channels intersecting at a chakra form what appear to be the petals of a flower. The highest center, technically not a chakra though it is commonly referred to as one, is the thousand-petaled lotus of the sahasrara. Because the energy in the subtle body is conscious energy, these energy centers are actually operating centers of consciousness.

The descent of Consciousness from the energy center at the top of the sushumna, the sahasrara, to the energy center at the base, called the muladhara, marks the process of Consciousness going from the highest transcendent Unity Consciousness to the limitations of embodied consciousness that you and I normally experience as we live out our existence on earth. The muladhara chakra represents the element of earth and is the final destination of Divine Consciousness, the Kundalini Shakti, through the process of descent and manifestation of the world. It is within this chakra that the Kundalini lies dormant after creating the world and embodied existence. It is here that She awaits the Great Awakening that will reverse this process, removing the limitations Consciousness has taken on, and allowing us to once again be aware of our transcendent, unbounded, divine nature; as the wave merges back into the sea.

The process of involution is that of Consciousness descending from the formless transcendent Godhead, condensing to the earthly realm of human existence, "involving" itself in all of creation in the process. Evolution reverses this, with Consciousness ascending back up through the chakras, becoming ever freer of limitations, restrictions, and the illusion of being bound and separate from it's source—God/dess. Between the sahasrara and the muladhara, between Divine Consciousness and earth-bound awareness, there are five major energy centers or chakras, representing the intermediate stages of Consciousness in the processes of involution and evolution.

In descending order (see Figure 1) the energy centers are: the sahasrara at the crown of the head, the ajna chakra between the eyes, the vishuddha chakra in the throat, the anahata chakra near the heart, the manipura chakra at about the level of the solar plexus, the svadhishthana chakra at the root of the sexual organs and the muladhara chakra at the base of the pelvis. The involution of Consciousness from the transcendent realm of the sahasrara on down to the muladhara is in part symbolized in the progressive order of the elements that each chakra represents. Involution is a process of Consciousness coalescing, becoming grosser, denser, and more limited.

Just below the sahasrara is the ajna chakra, the "third eye" between and above our physical eyes, and this is the realm of pure individualized mind. Consciousness at this level has lost its formless, all-encompassing universality but hasn't yet coalesced into the physical realm. Here Consciousness may be experienced simply as a limited sense of "I-ness" that doesn't yet have all the qualities we normally experience as ourselves, like our gender, body shape, and role.

The subsequent five chakras represent the manifestation of the five elements comprising the physical realm. In descending order there is a progression from the subtlest to the grossest of the elements. The next chakra the vishuddha, at the level of the throat, represents the element of ether or space, the subtlest of the physical elements. After this we descend to the anahata chakra, the heart chakra, and the element of air, symbolizing Consciousness becoming a bit denser and grosser than it was at the level symbolized by space. Next is the manipura chakra with the element of fire. Fire is still subtle, but it has more definition and is grosser than air. Then comes the svadhishthana chakra, which represents the element water. Water is denser and more substantial than fire but not as gross and dense as earth, the last element, which is associated with the muladhara chakra at the base of the sushumna nadi. At this level we've come to the densest, grossest, most limited and bound form of Consciousness, the earthly physical realm.

Thus everything from the most subtle sense of "I" awareness to the physical domain of earthly matter is made of Consciousness in varying levels of contraction. Even within the most bound forms of the physical realm the full power and presence of God, of Divine Consciousness, are present. The release of that bound energy is like the release of the potential energy bound in matter

The Principle Chakras of the Subtle Body

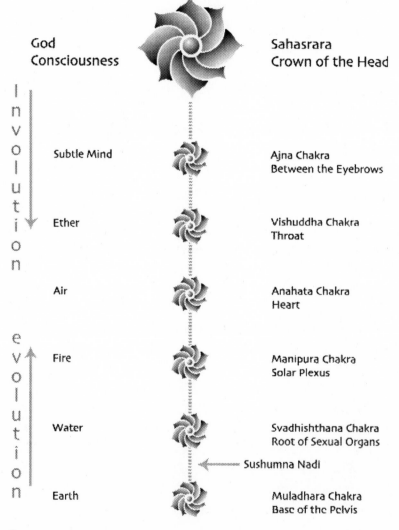

God
Consciousness

Sahasrara
Crown of the Head

I
n
v
o
l
u
t
i
o
n

Subtle Mind

Ajna Chakra
Between the Eyebrows

Ether

Vishuddha Chakra
Throat

Air

Anahata Chakra
Heart

e
v
o
l
u
t
i
o
n

Fire

Manipura Chakra
Solar Plexus

Water

Svadhishthana Chakra
Root of Sexual Organs

Sushumna Nadi

Earth

Muladhara Chakra
Base of the Pelvis

Figure 1

that suddenly results in the extraordinary power and light of nuclear reactions. The awakening of the Kundalini is the release of the bound Power and Light of God present within the human form.

When the Kundalini awakens—in other words, when our ability to move our awareness beyond the limitations of body and mind comes to life—then the energy of Consciousness, also called Shakti, moves up the sushumna nadi and pierces the chakras in ascending order. Consciousness moves from the constrictions of the earth realm, ever expanding, shedding limitations along the way until it finally reaches the unbounded realm of the sahasrara once again. The wave once again knows its union with the ocean, and we experience re-union with God, the Self of All.

Now this is the briefest possible look at the chakras and what they represent. There's much, much more to them and what they symbolize. Each is a level of consciousness, and the yogic sages have explored and given detailed accounts of them. Each chakra has associated with it certain powers and characteristic feelings that affect how we create our individual reality—our relationships, our world-view, our sense of self and our ways of interacting with the world—when we are acting from the level of that chakra. If you read Sir John Woodroffe's *Serpent Power*, which includes translations of the yogic texts dealing with all the chakras and the Kundalini, you'll be awed by the rich symbolism and the extraordinary map of Consciousness they provide. For those who would like a general understanding of the yogic paradigm and how it compares with the traditional Western psychological paradigm there is a discussion of this in the Appendix.

When I went to write about the Kundalini this was roughly how much I knew on an intellectual level. But I didn't feel I had the necessary deeper, personal understanding of the ascending journey through those centers of Consciousness that is the spiritual quest. My understanding felt so shallow and inadequate that I couldn't write anything about the Kundalini.

I knew I needed to turn directly to the Kundalini for the understanding I longed for. I began to contemplate how best to approach her. How could

I open myself to receiving whatever wisdom She might share with me? I knew She was a part of me, but how to invoke that part, how to relate to Her, how to connect with Her, were mysteries. I proceeded by going into meditation and contemplating these questions, trusting that She would bring to consciousness what I needed to know in order to move ahead. Two events that made it clear how I should approach the Goddess Kundalini immediately came to mind from years earlier.

First was a story I had heard in 1981 about the time a renowned author, who had written about the Kundalini, went to meet a world-famous yogi (Baba), known in part for his exalted visions of the Kundalini and his devotion to her. The author too had visions of the Kundalini, but to him she appeared quite unimpressive, looking like an ordinary woman, not like a Goddess at all. As he waited outside the room where Baba was receiving visitors, he was totally astonished to have a vision of the Goddess Kundalini entering the room where Baba was. Only this time she appeared in her most regal and resplendent form, magnificent and awe inspiring. The author was shocked. When he finally went in to speak with Baba, he asked why it was that she appeared so ordinary to him, while for Baba she came as the Goddess of the Universe. Baba replied simply, "Because I worship her."

After I first heard that story I began contemplating what it means for an accomplished yogi to worship the Kundalini. I kept wondering how a yogic master worshipped the Kundalini and why? After a year, my mind finally gave up its vain attempts at piercing the mystery on its own and I prayed to the inner guru, the Shakti, for an answer. In a profound series of meditations, the Kundalini, this great power of revelation, showed me how worship, i.e. actively honoring and revering the divine power of grace, is the key to receiving all the wisdom She wishes to impart. This is the path of *bhakti yoga*, the yoga of devotion, where the worshipper and the worshipped merge, where duality surrenders with love to nonduality. On this path the seeker and the Sought, lover and Divine Beloved delight in the play of shifting back and forth between the sublime joy of dualistic worship and the ecstatic consummation of the worship in union.

The meditation experiences occurred in 1982, while I was attending a special two-day meditation retreat at Baba's ashram in upstate New York. Before going into the first meditation of the retreat, I inwardly bowed to the Shakti and asked to be shown how to perform the highest worship of the Kundalini. Nothing could have prepared me for what was to happen.

I knew something unusual was going on even before the meditation began because I could feel the Kundalini Shakti vibrating throughout my body, and, though I never sit on the floor, I felt compelled to do so. I've had surgery on both knees, and sitting on the floor for more than a few minutes is extremely painful. However, this time the inner sense of having to assume a yogic, cross-legged posture on the floor was so great that I had to set aside my certainty that I couldn't do it.

In the first meditation I went into a profoundly deep and still state of consciousness. I had no awareness of my body, or of the meditation hall, or the several hundred other meditators there with me. Suddenly, a Goddess appeared in front of me, within this place of inner stillness. She looked like the classic paintings and statues I had seen of the various forms of the Goddess in India. She was exquisitely beautiful with jewels in her hair and gold ornaments around her neck, arms, wrists, and ankles. An ambrosial scent filled the air around her. Her only other adornment was a short skirt of pleated silk covering her hips. She held her hands up in a mudra, a special position that confers blessings. Her entire form gave off light illuminating the dark space of awareness I was in with her. I was staring at her, awestruck, when I noticed that I had the body of a yogi wearing only a loincloth. In my hands I found a gold tray on which were arranged the classic elements for doing puja, a form of worship, to a deity. It was an arati tray for doing arati (an ancient ritual of worship) to the Goddess before me. Trembling, I began waving the tray, with its lighted flame, in the traditional way.

The Goddess was looking directly into my eyes with unimaginable love. I kept doing puja to her, feeling enormous love and devotion welling up inside me as tears ran down my cheeks. Then she began to approach me. The tray disappeared from my hands and she embraced me. Her embrace can't be likened to anything we know in this world. Her embrace transcended the body, giving me the feeling that she had embraced me in my entirety, fully encompassing my heart, my soul, and my deepest, most inaccessible self in pure love. We began to merge. I was seated in a cross-legged posture while she continued enfolding me in her arms. I could feel myself losing any sense of a boundary between us. I was losing my awareness of where I ended and where she began. She lowered herself into my lap, embracing me and we exploded into Divine Light. I merged into the Light. I was Light, all was Divine Light. The Light had the quality of all-embracing love. I had no awareness of anything other than Light, no time, no space, no "I."

After an unknown period of time I began to be aware of having a body again, but it was radically different. My body felt like it had expanded, as though all the love and Light had filled not only my heart but my body too, blowing it up like a balloon. I felt extraordinarily expansive. I gradually regained awareness of myself sitting in the meditation hall with everybody. I began to wonder what on earth had happened to me? I had no time to contemplate the experience, because I was again pulled into that profoundly deep state of awareness from which the whole experience had begun.

The entire sequence repeated itself but with a different Goddess, equally resplendent, regal in baring and richly adorned. Over the course of the next four sessions of meditation, an hour or more for each meditation, the same thing occurred again and again with a different form of the Goddess each time. During the breaks in the meditation retreat I wandered around with part of my consciousness still in meditation. I could hardly speak to anyone. I ate very little. I continued to be amazed that I was able to sit on the floor for hours and still walk, a feat I've never been able to repeat. My body felt bloated even in ordinary waking state awareness. By the second day of the meditation retreat part of me was a little worried. I felt like I was going to explode, I just couldn't take in any more love, Light, or ecstasy without physically exploding! This is exactly what the Shakti wanted to do, to explode my limitations. I knew I had to just abandon myself to the Divine and trust in her.

On the second day of the retreat, after the sixth episode of a Goddess appearing in meditation, my worshipping her and our merger into Divine Light, I was sure it had to be over. I could take no more without my sense of "I" exploding or dissolving. Then the grand finale occurred in the final meditation of the retreat. Suddenly the Goddess standing before me in meditation was very different from the others.

Her skin was blacker than black, like deep black velvet in a darkened room. Yet in some miraculous way her form was radiant, revealing her own richly magnificent blackness. I began doing puja to her, shaking with a mixture of fear, awe, and love. I thought, "My God, this is Kali! She's the Great Mother, Goddess of the Universe, creator and destroyer of all that is." The sacred ritual repeated itself; only this time as the Goddess embraced me everything slowed down. I could feel myself slowly merging into her and I could hear her laughing the most ecstatic laugh. My awareness shifted and I could see the whole solar system, with all the planets and then stars and galaxies being withdrawn into her. The entire universe was merging into her, and all the while it was merging, the cosmos reverberated with her ecstatic laughter. Finally, I disappeared into her as I dissolved into Light and then into a nothingness beyond even the Light.

The next thing I was aware of was the Light and her laughter once again. Her magnificent black form reappeared and I began seeing galaxies, stars, and planets re-emerging from her womb. I too began to emerge and take on a subtle form of I-ness, still without a body. I felt sad and pained taking on form and was startled to hear her laughter continuing unabated. She then reversed the process and everything, myself included, began dissolving back into her. I was ecstatic once again, feeling her laughter as a part of me. She continued reversing back and forth between creation and dissolution. Each time it was the same for me, ecstasy on the dissolution and pain during the taking on of form. Clearly for her both were equally ecstatic. I tried to get hold of the ecstasy of taking on form and limitation and just couldn't do it. Finally she let me take on my complete set of limitations and form for this life.

I returned to my awareness of being seated on the floor in the meditation hall, my body trembling. She also returned my clarity of mind. The experience ended, and feeling profoundly grateful, I bowed to my inner guru, my Goddess. This had all unfolded from my initial prayer to know the highest form of worship of the Kundalini. True worship is to merge with the one you worship. Through worship and prayer the Goddess reveals the mysteries of the universe to the seeker.

I was stunned by the experience and didn't realize until I was telling someone about it after the weekend was over that there were six Goddesses that appeared before Kali. I wondered if these were the Goddesses of each of the six chakras that the Kundalini manifests and moves through before returning to her primal form as the Maha Shakti, the great power, that takes the form of Ma Kali. It is this highest power that dissolves the universe as she merges into the sahasrar and creates it once again as she descends from that transcendent realm.

Just as the aspects of Divine Consciousness were being presented to my awareness symbolically in the forms of the Goddesses, in the same way the union with those forms of Consciousness was symbolized by sexual union. Readers familiar with the experiences of mystics of many spiritual traditions will recognize that this is a common way for union with the Divine to express itself. Very often in the Indian traditions dealing with Shakti and the Kundalini depict union this way. This sexual symbolism and the experience of that form of symbolic merger in meditation are often confusing for people, especially westerners, who take it literally. That type of misinterpretation has led people to conclude that the Kundalini is just a form of psychosexual energy. Nothing could be further from the truth.

The mysteriously radiant blackness of Kali arrests my mind every time I recall her divine form. I've often wondered if this was some peculiar way my mind perceived her, or worse, some way that I distorted Kali's appearance. I was delighted to learn more of the significance of her exquisite blackness when a friend gave me an extraordinary book, *Mother of the Universe*, by Dr. Lex Hixon. He presents the ecstatic hymns to Ma Kali by the eighteenth century Bengali saint, Ramprasad Sen. In his introduction Dr. Hixon writes:

> The mystery of Kali, impenetrable to conventional, dualistic thinking, is her blackness, her beautiful midnight blackness. The Goddess tradition, along with many other authentic spiritual transmissions during planetary history, fundamentally emphasizes divine inconceivability, the indefinability of Reality. The rich darkness within what Christian mystics call the Cloud of Unknowing is the radiant blackness of Mother's womb. Ramprasad is a consummate poet of this dazzling divine darkness:

> *Why is Mother Kali so radiantly black?*
> *Because she is so powerful,*
> *that even mentioning her name destroys delusion.*
> *Because she is so beautiful,*
> *Lord Shiva, Conqueror of Death,*
> *lies blissfully vanquished*
>   *beneath her red-soled feet.*
> *There are subtle hues of blackness,*
> *but her bright complexion*
>   *is the mystery that is utterly black,*
> *overwhelmingly black, wonderfully black.*
> *When she awakens in the lotus shrine*

within the heart's secret cave,
her blackness becomes the mystic illumination
that causes the twelve-petal blossom there
to glow more intensely than golden ember.
Whoever gazes upon this radiant blackness
falls eternally in love.

This black light expresses the highest teaching of the Goddess. It is the radiance beyond whatever we know as light, yet at the same time it constitutes all physical, intellectual, and spiritual light.[4]

As I read that, I gained an even more profound understanding of the vision the Goddess Kundalini had given me in that meditation twelve years earlier. I've heard so many stories of visions and other experiences people have had after sincerely praying to the Goddess that I am sure She is as available to seekers today as ever.

The Goddess gave me all the insight and knowledge I needed in order to proceed. If I hoped to have her reveal to me something of the divine mystery behind Kundalini awakening and the movement of Shakti up through the chakras, it would be through worship of Her. I made a vow to myself that I wouldn't do any more work on my dissertation until I had received some deeper understanding from the Goddess Kundalini herself. I stopped all work on my thesis in order to devote my entire attention to the Kundalini. Each morning before meditation I worshipped her by chanting the Kundalini Stavaha (a beautiful, ancient Sanskrit hymn of praise) and doing arati (a traditional Eastern form of worship) to the Kundalini. I spent the remainder of the day meditating on Her and contemplating Her nature.

One morning, after two weeks of these practices, I did my usual worship and went into meditation with a prayer to the Kundalini that she give me a deeper understanding of the transformation She bestows upon the seeker after Her awakening. What followed was an extraordinary vision.

The vision unfolded before my inner eye during the initial two and a half hours of meditation, though the vision itself spanned years, much as a movie might tell a story that takes place over a lengthy course of time. When the vision ended I started to drift up out of deep meditation, but suddenly the Shakti Kundalini began speaking to me from within, giving me instructions. I knew she was really a part of myself, but for her invoked presence to take on such an independent form shocked me and filled me with gratitude. I was grateful that the Goddess would bestow such grace upon me. She didn't have an actual shape or form, simply a strong presence that pervaded my consciousness as she spoke. The beauty of her voice still haunts me.

The Goddess Shakti said the experience was a gift, but not meant for me alone. The Shakti directed me to write down all that I had experienced and see to it that it was published, making it available to anyone. Having the Shakti speak to me from within and give specific directions was not my usual experience! I was hesitant to believe what was happening and even more reluctant to do it, but the Divine Mother was insistent. She said it was very important for the knowledge of the spiritual journey and the nature of the Kundalini to become more widely known in the West. She also said that there was a great deal of confusion and misunderstanding about the Kundalini that needs to be corrected. She went on to say that Christians could come to appreciate and understand the Kundalini Shakti by recognizing that the Holy Spirit and the Kundalini Shakti are one and the same.

For some people the idea of the Holy Spirit, God or Goddess speaking or revealing visions and truths to someone other than the Pope, a saint or some religious authority is nearly sacrilegious, but the Holy Spirit in all Her forms belongs to everyone. The materialism of our age has so divorced us from the mystical and the divine which are the birthright of each one of us that many have given up even looking for access to God. And we're highly suspect of anyone who claims to have received any kind of communication from the Divine. We certainly don't expect to be the recipient of one ourselves. I surely didn't. As we proceed on our spiritual journey we reclaim our God given right to commune with the Divine, to know the Holy Spirit, the Shakti or whatever you prefer to call the One within us. In so doing this power of Divine revelation does indeed impart profound and humbling truths to us. Dr. Joan Borysenko in her book *Fire in the Soul* quotes comedian Lilly Tomlin's quip that when you talk to God it's prayer but when God talks back you're labeled a schizophrenic. Joan notes that 35% of Americans report having had visions but most won't talk about them for fear of ridicule. That's ninety million people from every spiritual tradition who have directly experienced the Divine for themselves in this country alone. You may be one of them and know what it is to converse with the Holy Spirit or the Divine Mother or God. Certainly it's time to discard the myth of it being a rare experience to be in touch with a Higher Power!

While I was writing down the details of the visionary experience, the Shakti or Holy Spirit repeatedly pulled me back into meditation, showing me the images, enabling me to more accurately describe them. At other times while I was writing, the Shakti (I generally use the name "Shakti" for referring to this divine power; whenever you see it you can substitute any term or name of the Divine that feels right for you) would give a commentary on the meaning of some portion of the experience or emphasize a lesson to be learned from it. This usually wasn't in a linear, verbal form, but rather the whole meaning-gestalt of a scene from the journey would present itself at once in my mind. The process of drifting in and out of meditation and writing descriptions of what I saw or heard went on for 9 hours nearly without break. Only once during that time was I able to get up briefly. I immediately returned to our meditation room where for several more hours I continued writing about what the Shakti was showing me. Afterward I was quite energized, but also physically exhausted. I felt spacey, as if I wasn't fully dialed into physical reality. I wasn't! When my wife came home that night from her post-doctoral research work at Yale University and saw me she said, "What happened to you? You look completely dazed!" I could hardly speak. I told her the story and then fell into a deep sleep until the next morning.

The experience was too profound, too unintegrated, and too far outside the bounds of academia for me to include it in my doctoral dissertation. Even though I felt it was the most valuable finding of that research project, I carefully and reverently put the experience aside and went on with my life and meditation practices. From time to time I would take the experience out of the hidden recesses of my mind to contemplate it and try to fathom it. It was as if I kept it in a special container on my altar and I would allow myself to take it out only when I was prepared to gaze at its sacred light. I was a little afraid of the experience at first, because I would get lost in it. The experience would so absorb my attention that I would struggle to pull my awareness away in order to have energy for other dimensions of my life.

When I did contemplate the experience I felt as though I were descending into the most exquisite depths of my being, to a mysterious realm of unimaginable beauty and wonder. Returning to the surface level of existence, I felt disoriented, as if a part of me were refusing to leave that mysterious realm. Because it was so difficult to come back to ordinary awareness, I went there less frequently and prayed that the processing and integration of the experience would be carried out by the Shakti in the depths of my being and not demand much direct attention.

Two years passed during which I did little conscious work on the experience, when one day in meditation I suddenly heard Her voice once again. She asked, "Why haven't you written the experience for publication? It is meant to be shared." I offered no excuses to Her. I vowed to see to it that it was published. A few months later a very abbreviated version of the experience came out as an article. Much to my amazement, after I wrote that piece the Shakti gave me several more visionary meditation experiences that are, in a sense, additional chapters to what She wants communicated. All I've had to do is surrender to Her and try to remain conscious.

The account of what the Kundalini showed me in meditation that first time is titled "Ascent to Union." It's divided into two sections. First is the journey as it appeared in meditation. The second part is the commentary and meaning primarily given by the Shakti after the initial experience.

I've recorded all that I experienced to the best of my ability, but the reader should remember that the limitations of my mind and understanding surely have tainted what the Divine Kundalini wants to communicate through this story. Any faults or shortcomings in what you read should be attributed to my mind and not to the One who at times moved it. This applies to much of this book. As a general principle, I believe that whatever images, insights, thoughts or other expressions of the truth that come into my mind, heart, or body belong only to the Divine and not to the "me" or the "mind/body" with which I am ordinarily identified. To that limited self belongs only the distortions. In yoga the ego is referred to as the power of self-appropriation, and it appropriates or steals all that it likes. I can see the part of me that wants to say these are "my visions," but the truth is they aren't. They belong to the power of Consciousness in all of us—they happened to have occurred in me. In a sense I view the mind/body like a TV set. If it's dialed into a divine channel then the images, sounds, music, and dialogue originate from that source and not from the TV. The television is only a receiver, and if it's not working properly the show won't be clearly visible. I can only pray that what I share with you is clear enough for you to see both the picture and the receiver, but not confuse the two.

Part One: The Journey

As I sank into meditation I found myself descending through space and time, as if from high above the earth, to an island nation of old in a northern sea. I was present there not as a person but rather as a formless witness-consciousness viewing the scenes and often aware of what people were thinking, feeling, or experiencing as I watched them. A fiery, independent young Queen ruled this country. She was loved and respected, as well as somewhat feared by her people. But, the Queen had grown bored with rulership.

"I've done all, conquered all, and experienced all. What am I to do now?" she asked her advisors. They had no answers. She paced around the royal castle and roamed the shores of her great nation, unable to spend the restlessness that agitated her. She finally took refuge in her private chapel, praying in earnest for guidance. In a moment of inspiration, the Queen saw what she must do next. Gathering her ministers and advisors together, she told them, "I'm going in search of the mysterious lands beyond the vast oceans far to the south. We've always heard rumors of a wondrous rich land beyond turmoil, beyond time. I'm going to find that place." The ministers were stunned by her announcement but knew that once her mind was set there was no altering it.

She called upon a brave, commanding sea captain to outfit a sailing vessel and prepare for a lengthy voyage across the great oceans into the unknown. The captain, hailed by most simply as Captain or Cap, had a trusted first mate, Will, with whom he always sailed. Together they gathered a crew and provisions. The crew was typical of the day—a band of drunkards, thieves, and low-lifes pressed into service. Cap and Willy would whip them into shape so they could man the Queen's ship on her quest.

Captain procured various charts and maps indicating unexplored lands far to the south. Only a handful of people had ever attempted the journey and none returned to tell of it. The maps were certain to be inaccurate, but they were the only ones available. The Queen prayed to God for guidance and protection on their journey. She had trusted in the unseen hand of grace before and had never been let down. They set sail, driven by the Queen's restless spirit, directed by Cap's scant knowledge, and unaware of the true power drawing them toward their destination.

Month after month they followed the charts, until at last they sailed beyond even those unreliable guides. High atop the main mast the lookout searched in vain for landfall. They were grateful merely to find an occasional tiny island with fresh drinking water. The crew began complaining about their miserable conditions and sparks of anger threatened to ignite a mutiny. By now they were drifting, becalmed, lost on a limitless expanse of sea. Provisions were running out and drinking water was nearly gone. The minute rations didn't meet the body's need for food or drink. All were racked by hunger and thirst. The Queen's indomitable spirit barely kept them afloat.

At last, on the horizon the lookout spotted something—not land, but storm clouds! They rejoiced as the breeze picked up and rain began falling on their parched lips. For the first time in weeks the ship's sails billowed in the wind. Finally, they were moving ahead once again. Hope renewed their spirits!

The rain and wind steadily increased. The storm worsened as thundering black clouds turned day into night. Powerful gales churned the seas into towering waves. The tempest blew the ship according to its whim. Hope fled as fear, spurred by thunder and lightning, took the crew's hearts. Men hurled overboard by wind and waves drowned in the boiling ocean. The fury of the storm built until a brilliant bolt of lightning struck the main mast, blowing the vessel to bits!

As the Queen regained consciousness, she could smell the rich scent of fertile earth. She was lying face down on grassy soil. The sun shone in a blue sky dappled with fair-weather clouds. Unconscious, Cap and Will lay sprawled on the ground not far from the Queen. Her eyes scanned the surrounds. No other survivors were visible. A short distance from them stretched a white sandy beach washed by ocean waves.

The Queen arose, stretching. She helped Cap and Willy to awaken. The two men were disoriented and slow to come around. They couldn't believe they had survived that enormous bolt of lightning. The trio searched for survivors but none were found. Not so much as a splinter of the ship remained. The storm had consumed everything.

Cap and Willy were despondent, mourning all those who had been lost. They felt stranded, everything familiar was gone. Their whole way of life, even the hope of returning home—disappeared with the ship and crew. "What will become of us?" they anxiously wondered.

In contrast, the Queen felt renewed determination. She knew she had to move on—to explore the place where fate had deposited her. She offered a prayer of thanks to God for sparing their lives and asked for strength, guidance, and protection on the journey ahead.

While the two men sank into despair the Queen investigated the area. When she returned, she reported to them that simple farmers inhabited the land. They worked the soil, tended their animals, and were content to maintain their existence. This sounded most appealing to Willy. He wished to remain right there, safe and secure. The local people knew little of the territories beyond their own small township, and at this point Willy didn't care. Cap thought it would be a good place to rest and take time to figure out how to get back to sea.

During her searches, the Queen had found a road originating in the area and leading inland to some distant city. She sensed that something tremendous awaited her on that road. She told Cap and Willy "You must continue on. There's no sense pining over what is lost or indulging such sentiments. Great discoveries lie ahead for us, greater than you can ever imagine." The Queen persuaded them, as her subjects and fellow explorers, to leave with her for the unknown city.

Taking action and moving on lightened their spirits. After a few days travel the city appeared in the distance. In a strange way, it seemed to be floating. Indeed, as they approached it, they found it to be built on water. This city, the City of Water, had a surreal quality. A festive mood of celebration pervaded the city. The trio found the citizens feasting, drinking, and openly playing around sexually. The Queen and Cap realized that the festival was a fertility rite. Willy didn't care what it was, he just ran after every alluring woman who beckoned him!

This watery town and its beautiful women fascinated the Captain. He thought, "I bet I could fulfill every desire or fantasy I've ever had!" He looked forward to remaining there for some time. Willy shared the captain's desire to stay, but the Queen felt no attraction for this city. Exploring the City of Water, she discovered that the road that had brought them here continued straight through and into the wilderness beyond. She felt an urge to continue their journey, to follow the road onward. She prodded Captain and Will to forego their pleasures and accompany her. They had already found there was a dark side to this place of passions and weren't entirely resistant to moving on. Jealousy, greed, and rage showed themselves in back-alley fights they had narrowly escaped.

The Queen had learned there was another city farther ahead. The main road went directly there, while smaller roads and footpaths branched off into the countryside. Willy and Cap, like children, always wanted to explore some byway. The Queen, determined not to lose any time in side adventures, kept them to the main road. After several days of travel, as night fell, a red glow on the horizon marked their next destination: the City of Fire.

The City of Fire was just that—fiery. Glowing molten lava pits, steamy hot springs, and flaming volcanoes marked the landscape around it. The people of this city were very different from those of the City of Water. These people were strong-willed, disciplined, and proud of their accomplishments. They had conquered the flaming countryside and expected to further increase their domain.

Willy liked these people. He joined them for the pleasure of their company. He felt invigorated from the hard work that they did with such enthusiasm and determination. Captain was also very impressed by the people of this fiery land. He saw in their desires for expansion a place for himself. A great army could be assembled from a body of self-disciplined, mighty people—and who better to lead that army than himself! He envisioned commanding them in conquest of greater and greater lands.

The Queen met with the rulers of the City of Fire. They brought her up to the top of a high ridge that encircled the city. The leaders explained how they had conquered the land and put the element of fire to their use. From their high lookout they pointed to all the city boasted of: a populace of industrious and determined people; great trades built on fire—blast furnaces, steel and iron works, and much more. The city fathers were very proud of their citizens and all they had accomplished.

The Queen commended them on their achievements as she surveyed the surrounds. Suddenly, something outside the city piqued her curiosity. While on the ridge she noticed what appeared to be a speck of light on the horizon. It seemed to change colors as she gazed at it. The Queen asked the men what it was. Immediately they warned her not to stare at it.

"The light has an alluring quality," said one of the rulers. "Those who stare at it become irresistibly drawn to it. Its source is rumored to be in a distant city, but people who go there almost never returned; those who have made it back never fully regain their minds!"

From their high vantage point the Queen could see that the road by which they had entered the City of Fire continued straight through and headed directly towards the curious light. She knew she must go there at once. She had a growing sense that a final destination lay before her, a place where her restlessness would cease. Could the next city be that place?

The Queen sought out Captain and Will. She prevailed upon them to give up their ideas of remaining in the City of Fire and accompany her. Thus the trio set off for the unknown city ahead.

The road traversed a broad plain that rose in the distance. Winds swept down the plain from the direction of the light. The nearer they came to the city the more distinct the light became. It constantly changed color in a slowly shifting manner. The effect of the light grew stronger as they traveled toward it. First the Queen, then Captain and Will, noticed that their moods and feelings altered with changes in the light's hue. By the time they reached the city, a steady wind was blowing, accentuating the fleeting quality of the moment and of one's moods.

Once inside the windy city, located upon a high plateau, the effect of the light was dramatic. People in the city were totally enthralled by it. Cap and Willy immediately succumbed to it. Rather than accompanying the Queen, they sat on a bench in a plaza, content to experience the play of thoughts, feelings, and moods that danced to the changing light. The constant flow of their minds matched the ceaseless winds.

The Queen searched for the source of this bewitching light. Her determination to find it and the strength of her mind empowered her to be detached from its effects. She watched the light, refusing to allow herself to be swept away by it. After some time she noticed that occasionally it would flash brilliantly and clearly. Everything would be illumined as it truly was, undistorted by the mysterious colors. In those flashes of clarity the source of the light stood revealed. Oddly enough, the Queen was the only one in the city interested in going to the source. Everyone else was so lost in the play of colors and moods that the moments of clarity were mistaken for just another projection of their minds and not recognized as revealing anything more.

The Queen saw the light radiating from atop a stone pinnacle in the heart of the city. She wound her way through the streets to the base of the towering rock. There was no way to ascend it except by scaling its nearly vertical side. The wind swept around her as she clung to the stone and inched her way up. The top of the pinnacle was flattened and invisible to her while climbing. With tremendous effort she reached her goal.

The Queen drew herself onto the top and was stunned to see a small, brilliant, blue-white orb of light present as if suspended just above the pinnacle. It's transcendent beauty dazzled her while its utter stillness brought all her agitation to a halt. The light radiated an aura of pure divinity, enveloping her, embracing her with love. Falling to her knees in reverence before the light, tears of joy streamed down her face. As she gazed at it, the boundary between herself and the light began to dissolve. The light was pure, effulgent, Divine Consciousness, absorbing and stilling her mind. The most profound peace settled over her. She floated in quiet ecstasy, totally unaware of her surroundings, absorbed in the pure Light of Consciousness.

After a while, the thought arose in her mind, "Ah, finally I've reached my destination."

From within her mind the Divine Light's greater consciousness answered, "No." She again became aware of her separate identity, sitting atop the pinnacle, staring at the exquisite light. She looked around and saw crystal-like filaments of various colors dangling in mid-air around the light. It was these wondrous crystals that colored the light and changed the effect the pure light had on the mind. Her attention returned to the unwavering effulgent orb. She felt so content gazing upon it, she thought, "How could this not be my destination?" From within her the Divine Light answered, "Your road continues on, your destination lies ahead." Her attention was directed towards the city and plain far below. She could see that the road that brought her to this city continued on toward the towering mountains in the distance. What the Light had revealed was undeniably true. The Queen longed passionately to reach the end of her journey, all the more so now that she had tasted what was to come. She bowed reverently to the Light and began her descent from the pinnacle. The tireless wind whipped around her. Once on the ground she searched for Captain and Will.

The Queen found them still sitting enthralled in the plaza. She had to force them to pay attention to her as she explained how the lights deluded the mind. The two began to watch the shifting lights without being totally swept away by them. The Queen finally enabled Willy and Cap to act independently of the play of lights, though Willy moved more out of obedience to her than from any understanding or freedom of his own. The Queen told them their destination still lay ahead. The road was clear and off they went.

Willy and Cap again found many side-paths leading away from the road but the Queen had no patience for diversions! With mounting anticipation she sought her destination.

The road climbing into the mountains became more arduous with each mile. The three explorers had become leaner and stronger from persevering through the physical and emotional demands of the journey. As their path rose higher it tested the men's endurance. The Queen's energy seemed boundless and she inspired Willy and Cap upward.

Finally they caught their first glimpse of the next city in the distance. It was nestled in a high, snowy, mountain pass. Gleaming white peaks towered above it. The city shone blue-white and ethereal in the sunlight, as if it were made of crystal or ice. While on the outskirts of the Ethereal City the trio began meeting its citizens. Many different languages were spoken there, yet in some strange way, even if you didn't speak an other person's language, you could understand and be understood. How this occurred was a mystery to Cap and Willy, though the Queen intuited what powers were at work here. They also noticed that the closer they came to the city, the more distinctly they could hear what sounded like chants or mantras rising from within it.

Entering this blue-white glittering city they found great halls with high, vaulted ceilings. Some halls were used for chanting mantras that transported one to sublime states of meditation. In other halls people could be found gathered listening to a storyteller spinning tales of incredible intricacy. The stories became real to anyone present, allowing the listener to feel as though s/he were fully participating in the tale. Such story halls were so alluring, so captivating for some people, that they spent all their time in them, preferring those dramas and illusions to reality. Cap and Willy lingered in one of the story halls while the Queen sought the leaders of this mysterious Ethereal City.

She was told that there were three masters of the city whom she could trust completely, for they spoke only the truth. The Queen sought them out with only one purpose in mind—to find out if this was her final destination or if indeed it still lay ahead as her heart told her. Finding the masters she gained an audience with them. They recognized her noble nature and treated her with great honor and respect. She immediately asked, "This isn't my destination, is it?"

"No," they replied, "your goal remains ahead in the distance. To reach it you must continue on a narrow path high into the mountains." She was glad to have them confirm what she already knew. The Queen had intuited the nature of the power underlying the chants, mantras, and stories coming from the Ethereal City. As she discussed the creative power of sound and words with the masters, the clarity and depth of her understanding amazed them. The Queen bid them farewell and returned for her traveling companions.

Captain and Will would have been content to stay, but the Queen's determination burned fiercely, ready to consume all obstacles and distance between her and their journey's end. She had to drag Cap and Willy from their fantasy world and lead them out of the Ethereal City. The Queen tried in vain to tell her companions about the power of Consciousness to effect the mind and body through words and sounds. Willy couldn't understand any of it, and Captain grasped only a small portion of her explanation. The complex science of the power of vibration was beyond them.

The path, barely wide enough for one person, took them straight up into the highest mountains. Making progress became more and more difficult. Often the path wasn't even visible to the two men. Though Will and Captain had been toughened by the journey, the rigorous climbing overwhelmed their strength and perseverance. On several occasions Captain tried to convince the Queen to stop, to be satisfied with the heights they had achieved thus far. He told her to look back and see for herself that all the lands and cities lay far below them. What city could possibly lie ahead, what little territory could be gained by struggling on, he asked. Captain argued with the Queen, but she would neither look back nor stop, except to allow them to regain their strength for continuing onward.

Many days of enormously difficult climbing beyond the Ethereal City brought them to the highest peak of the world. At last the nearly invisible path led them toward the summit. The Queen was making the ascent easily, but Willy and Cap struggled and could not continue without her. They marveled at her strength. She infused them with all the energy they needed. As dusk fell they approached the broadened summit covered with snow and ice.

Astonishingly, atop the summit in the distance they could make out a small cottage! On either side of the door, square windows, each with four square panes, poured warm candlelight onto the snow, while smoke curled from the chimney. An old man sat outside the open door, apparently waiting for them! The Queen again wondered if this were her destination.

The trio reached the cottage and the old man invited them inside. As they entered the cozy warm home they found a table set for three and a meal prepared. The old man refused to answer any questions until they had eaten and rested. That suited Cap and Willy just fine! They ate ravenously and afterward lay down to sleep. The two were out in no time.

The Queen, however, neither ate nor slept. She couldn't take her eyes off the old man. He emanated profound stillness. How had he known they were coming? Why did she feel as if he knew her completely—perhaps even better than she knew herself? Was he her destination; would her restlessness cease in him? Thus her mind went on as she sat drinking in the old man with her eyes. Fine streams of subtle blue light radiated from his eyes. The Queen's gaze became fixed on his eyes, absorbed, lost in their light.

After some hours, Cap and Willy awoke. They had slept much of the night away, awakening in the pre-dawn darkness. The Queen was eager to pose her question. In the candlelight, the old man sat ready to answer her. She asked if this were her destination. He simply said, "No."

"Where then?"

"Ahead, still farther."

Captain and Will started arguing. How could that be? They were on the summit. Did they have to backtrack? Did more mountains lie ahead? Why should they bother? And on and on. The old man sat back quietly watching them. The Queen paid little attention to her companions' objections.

Finally the old man said quietly, "Only she can continue. You two must remain here and await her return."

Will and Captain were startled and angered by his pronouncement. They objected further. Who was this old man to tell them what to do? They had made it this far without his help. Why should they pay any attention to him? Cap told the Queen they should leave immediately.

The Queen sat still during their dispute, absorbed in gazing at the old man. She knew he spoke the truth, no arguments could alter that. The Queen turned to Captain and Will, telling them quietly, yet forcefully, that they must remain here while she continued her journey. "You have faithfully obeyed my commands all the way to this point, and you must do so again. I promise I'll return," she said.

The old man beckoned her to follow him through the door into the night. Leading her along a path visible only to them, he held her hand. The night sky glittered with stars. As they walked she saw in the distance, high above them, an orb of light like the moon. They continued along, seemingly drawn by the light. Her gaze was held fixed on it. The light reminded her of that exquisite orb of divine effulgence that she had encountered atop the pinnacle in the Windy City. They continued toward the light.

For a moment she glanced down and realized they were off the ground, ascending straight up! She caught sight of her own body, which no longer had form, but appeared to be glowing light. Astonished, she turned to the old man, but he too was radiant light! She looked up at the rapidly expanding orb of light, as all three merged. "I AM LIGHT! I AM LIGHT! All is Light, Divine Conscious Light, exquisite, blissful, Light!" The universe was the Light of Consciousness, she was that Light of Consciousness. All distinctions, all separations, all boundaries dissolved. There was no time, no Queen, no journey, and no destination. Simultaneously she transcended everything and yet encompassed all of creation within her being. Words cannot describe or even approach that state of Consciousness. Absorbed in perfect unity awareness an eternity passed....

Or was it a moment?

It seemed that after some time her form re-emerged from the Light, forever transfigured, in essence forever one with the Infinite Effulgence. She descended to the summit, where her faithful companions, Captain and Will, awaited her. As she approached, they stared in wonder. Her stunning radiance and profound serenity overwhelmed them. They fell to their knees in reverence. With great love she raised them up, seeing them as rays of her own Self. She dwelt with them until the end of their days.

Wherever she went she was honored and revered. Her blessings flowed to anyone who saw her or made even the smallest offering of love or devotion. Captain and Will served her with loving abandon and total surrender. Though they traveled the world, wherever she went all she encountered was the one Self, the one Light, revealing its inexhaustible power to take on infinite forms. With great delight and love she embraced all forms of her Self. In time Captain and Will began to shine as if from the reflected brilliance of their Queen. At their death, in a flash of light, the three finally merged into the Infinite Effulgence.

Part Two: The Meaning of the Ascent to Union

After this extraordinary vision of the entire spiritual journey unfolded before my inner eye, I slowly began to drift up out of that profoundly deep state. Before I came back to ordinary consciousness I heard a beautiful, strong feminine voice speak to me from within; it was the voice of the Kundalini. She said that the vision was a gift, not meant for me alone, but for all who would read it. She instructed me to write it down and have it published. I was stunned by the vision, but now to hear the Divine Kundalini Shakti Herself speaking to me, directing me to write— this was overwhelming. Although I knew She was really a part of my Self, it was clear She was much greater than the "I" I'm usually identified with was. I'm sure I would have been totally overcome if She hadn't also given me the strength of mind to withstand Her radiant presence. I couldn't conceive of remembering all I had been shown, and I began to feel as if I would fail to fulfill Her command. The Divine Kundalini took care of that too. She proceeded to take me back to the beginning of the vision and show me the events again, so that I could write them down. As She did this, She also showed me more about the meaning of various portions of the vision. Occasionally She would also speak, telling me what the symbolism meant, though for the most part the thoughts concerning the meaning of each scene would simply appear in my mind as my awareness revisited it. The following explication is what I received from the Shakti Kundalini concerning the Queen's journey.

The Ascent to Union is a journey symbolizing the spiritual quest and transformation of consciousness from ordinary worldly existence to transcendence and union with God. The Queen represents our inner power of consciousness, the Goddess Kundalini. She is the Divine Light of Consciousness, the indwelling Holy Spirit. The Kundalini made it clear that it is very important for us to understand that She is not something foreign or alien to us, even if the words or concepts used to describe Her are. She is as much a part of you and me as our flesh and blood, our thoughts and feelings. The Kundalini is even more basic to us than those things; She is the dynamic power of our true eternal Self.

Captain symbolizes our ego/mind, our limited sense of self and ordinary waking-state intellect. Captain has Will as his faithful servant, companion, and first mate. Will symbolizes our body, with its more instinctive quality of awareness. Willy and Cap remain close to each other throughout the journey, just as the mind and body are intertwined in human existence. The Queen rules both and is independent of them, just as the supremely free inner spirit, the divine Kundalini, rules the mind and body, directing them from within.

At the beginning of the journey the Queen is restless and bored with her worldly life. She longs to go beyond the confines of her island nation. This symbolizes where we are at the start of our quest. Each of us is an island nation ruled by the spirit, by the Kundalini. A time comes in our evolution when we've accomplished all we need to accomplish and experienced all we need to experience in ordinary life. It may be a time when we're simply weary of the drama of our lives. We want to go beyond ourselves and beyond all that is known to us. The Queen's advisors can't counsel her, for they know nothing of the inner realm from which her restlessness arises. They only know the outer world dynamics of social, political, and commercial relations. They know nothing of the inner world or the needs of the spirit.

At this point in our journey the people to whom we usually turn for directions—friends, relatives, career counselors, perhaps even a psychotherapist—may offer their best advice, but it belongs to the wrong domain. Our spirit, our inner Queen knows it, and finds no comfort in their words. The Queen doesn't merely want to explore some other nation or even conquer other lands. She wants to go beyond all charted territories. At some point the restlessness of our spirit demands that we look beyond others, beyond relationships, beyond worldly possessions, beyond mastery of worldly things, beyond all that is familiar and seek the Great Unknown. This is divine discontent, one of the first manifestations of the power of Consciousness letting us know it's time to return home to our Source. Discontent makes a seeker. Discontent, coupled with the right understanding, makes a spiritual seeker.

At first the Queen doesn't know how to deal with the restlessness she feels. The words of her most trusted advisors are of no help. Roaming the countryside and shores of her nation fails to bring her any closer to the knowledge of what to do next in her life. The energy of divine discontent will not allow itself to be dissipated through the ordinary ways of discharging energy that people develop, like doing things, accomplishing things, or dreaming of new things to do or accomplish. It's not until she retires to the sacred place of her private chapel and gives herself over to meditation and prayer that she receives the inspiration, the influx of grace, that allows her to see clearly where she must go next. Sitting still is often the last thing we think of doing when that inner restlessness is demanding movement. When all outer movement fails to calm the agitation, then we may stumble onto the solution—to be still and allow for the necessary inner movement to occur. That's the movement the energy of Consciousness is trying to create. We are so used to translating inner movements of energy into action aimed at objects of desire that we may misinterpret the initial stirring of Consciousness beginning to lead us on our quest. What is required then is a shift in consciousness, a movement of awareness away from the external world. This brings about the necessary opening for grace, for inspiration, to arise from within and guide us onward.

While praying in her chapel, in her sacred space, internally and externally, the Queen receives her new direction. She doesn't think of the new direction, she doesn't reason it through to that conclusion, she receives it as anyone receives an inspiration or intuition. Such things come from beyond the realm of ego control and can only be received. To receive such gifts from our inner guide, our inner guru, we have to create an open, receptive awareness. The Shakti said, "You must develop a regular practice of meditation to access your inner wisdom."

The Queen's inspiration is charged with energy and the total certainty of its being absolutely the right thing to do next. Without any doubt distracting her or fragmenting her efforts, all her energy immediately focuses on moving ahead. As you develop proficiency in quieting the mind and accessing your inner source of wisdom and inspiration, then you will be able to move forward with the same Godspeed.

In the beginning of her quest the Queen uses whatever means and knowledge she has at hand to take her to the limits of the known world.

She relies on Captain and Will to take her through the initial stage of her journey. In the same way we begin our searching by first defining things in terms of what we know, until we exhaust them all or receive by grace an experience of what is beyond. We make use of our mind and body to begin our journey. Many of the initial practices done by aspirants of Western and Eastern spiritual traditions focus on the disciplined use of the mind and body, training them to gather the energy of attention and gaining control of that energy for new uses.

Captain gathers all the charts and maps he can find to guide them. Together with Will he organizes a crew and outfits a vessel to begin the journey. The crew and the ship represent the strengths, limitations, and negativities of our lower nature. We marshal them as best we can to begin our journey. Every true spiritual path has codes of conduct, values, and attitudes to be practiced, along with physical and mental disciplines that serve the purpose of marshaling and focusing our energies. At the outset of our journey we may gather books and read of the spiritual journeys of others in hopes of being guided ourselves. We may look to various spiritual or religious traditions for maps of what lies beyond the boundaries of the world we are accustomed to. The seeker needs to be aware that even the best and most detailed map is radically different from the reality that the map is trying to collapse and condense into the limited dimensions of the map.

At the outset the Queen prays for grace to guide and protect them on their journey. She has trusted and relied upon God's grace in the past and invokes the Lord with complete faith that God will answer her call. We need divine intervention right from the beginning in order to succeed on our quest. Remember, it is the Lord's power of concealment, Maya Shakti, that prevents us from experiencing the divine nature of our Self and the world around us. Nothing less than the Lord's power of revelation, the bestowal of grace, will illumine what is concealed by the cloaks of individuality. The Queen retired to a sacred place, her chapel, where she previously had received the inspiration to go on her journey. She returns to that sacred place to begin her journey with prayer and humility, asking for help and being open to receive it. The practices of prayer and meditation give access to grace. Humility and open receptivity are the right attitudes for the seeker to practice and eventually to embody without effort. The power of grace was with the Queen from the very beginning of her journey, guiding her from within in the forms of discontent, inspiration, and intuition.

Later in her quest grace manifests in another traditional symbolic form. The old man whom the Queen meets only at the final stage of her journey is the master teacher, the guru, who in the yogic tradition is known as "the grace bestowing power of God." A power of God, not a mere individual, even though that power may be more apparent to our limited vision when it seems localized in an individual through whom it flows and who becomes revered as a guru.

When you are thirsty, do you drink the water vapor from the air or try to quench your thirst with a draft of water from a nearby gutter? No, of course not, you go to your bottled spring water or the tap, knowing it comes from a reliable, pure source, available at any time. That's the guru, no more, no less. The most sublime and rare gurus are ones who over lifetimes of spiritual practices, have had the power of grace flow through them, purifying them, cleansing them of selfishness and egohood, leaving them hollowed out and able to serve humanity as a conduit for grace. "Examine them closely," the Shakti said, "some are more hollowed than others!" We have to use our discrimination.

The power of the guru is a universal power of God. It is the power of divine revelation. One who functions as a guru is a channel for that power, and there are no perfect channels. A seeker must develop the discrimination to differentiate between the two, the power itself and the conduit. A seeker also must be able to evaluate how pure or how tainted the knowledge and experience the teacher they are looking toward for guidance is transmitting to them. It is the seeker's responsibility to become familiar with the scriptures, the writings of other enlightened beings, and with the voice of their own inner source of wisdom. These three sources of knowledge provide a way of checking the validity of the teacher. If the teacher's words aren't in accord with the seeker's inner experience, the scriptures, and the words of other enlightened beings then doubt arises. If the seeker's experience isn't in accord with the scriptures, the words of enlightened beings and the teacher, then self-doubt arises. In either case one must proceed with caution, resolve the doubt, and abandon the teacher or abandon delusion.

The Captain and his crew weren't aware of the grace in their lives as they sailed beyond the best of their maps, struggling against starvation and thirst, lost, becalmed at sea and lucky to find small islands with fresh water. Our journey is full of tests and obstacles. During those hardships they could have turned back, and many times the crew pressed them to return. So it is on our spiritual journey. We feel lost at times, fortunate to be refreshed upon occasion, gleaning hope from the experiences of others and happy to have some small experience of our own that we can call "spiritual" or meaningful. These are the small islands that appear in the sea of confusion upon which we may feel adrift in the early stages of our quest.

Feeling lost is exactly what is supposed to happen. Even when the soul loses sight of the Lord, the Lord never loses sight of His child. Being lost humbles the Captain and his first mate. It confronts our mind and body with their powerlessness and the limitations of well-reasoned plans. The mind gets intoxicated by its own theories and constructs about the nature of consciousness, God, and the Universe. The mind may be deluded and act as if the quest is to find a truly all-encompassing theory of reality. So it envisions ever-grander models and spectrums of awareness, dragging the seeker's attention into new forms of maya, illusion, and distracting the soul from its real purpose. Map-making is fine, but it is no substitute for walking the trail, and it can't protect the limited self, the ego-mind, from feeling lost or out of control. Within its world it is lost and out of control. Within God's world no one is lost or out of reach of the Divine.

Our longing and spiritual thirst during this period can also be a danger. Someone lost and becalmed at sea, dying of thirst, may imagine an island oasis in the distance, a mirage, and expend precious energy trying to get there. In a similar way we may distort or twist ordinary experiences into "divine" ones, deluding ourselves in the process. If we're fortunate enough to have a true spiritual master in our life, then we may be spared some of this pain and aimless searching. People suffer this most intensely before finding either a reliable and trustworthy mystic guide or a consistent means for accessing their inner source of wisdom.

When the ship ran into trouble the crew desperately wanted to return home and end the journey. Similarly, our lower nature or past tendencies, represented by the crew and the limitations of their sailing vessel, demand that we go back to the ways of the world, based on sense pleasure and ego gratification. All of us confront such a battle within ourselves at some point during our evolution. The battle tests our resolution and our commitment to the spiritual journey. It can't be won without grace.

The trio were dying of thirst and lost beyond the limits of their knowledge. As spiritual seekers we reach the limits of where our mind and body can lead us, where we're thirsting for spiritual knowledge but receive little or none. Our longing intensifies. Though we're on a sea of water our thirst cannot be quenched. Like the salty brine, all the things of the world that surround us cannot slake our spiritual thirst. Only the water that falls from above, only grace, can save us. At the height of their despair the storm came upon the Queen, Captain, Will, and the crew. But what was at first welcomed, later seemed bent on their destruction.

The descent of grace into our lives may seem like a storm of turmoil or it may seem to come at a time when we are most despairing, most fearful, and yet most longing. Grace may come into our lives and disrupt or destroy much of that with which we're familiar and comfortable. Of course these aren't the only ways in which grace flows into people's lives. Grace may pour into us sweetly and freely, but those aren't the occasions that cause doubt or fear. It's during those times, when we feel as if we're without grace or when some force seems to be turning everything in our lives upside down and inside out, that we become frightened. Every genuine quest, every spiritual journey of significance has this period of turmoil, the "dark night of the soul" or the "night sea journey," as radical transformation of our sense of self and the re-creation of reality occur. When this happens seekers needs to know that they are fine, though in pain and turmoil, and they need the company and support of others who know this.

The storm culminates in a brilliant bolt of lightning that destroys the ship and all the crew, leaving the Queen, Captain and Will, safely on the shore of a strange land. This is Shaktipat, the descent of Grace, the true awakening of the Kundalini, the true awakening of the Queen. The bolt of lightning was the mighty impulse of grace. In an instant all the negativities and limitations of worldly existence, symbolized by the ship and its crew, were destroyed. In the same instant the Queen, Cap, and Willy were safely delivered from the perils of being lost at sea and deposited on firm ground with their road clearly before them. This is precisely what happens when one receives Shaktipat, the descent of grace that awakens the Kundalini. One goes from being awash in the world and trying to find one's spiritual path to having the road clearly opened and many of our negativities and binding habits destroyed. The path onward is immediately apparent to the Queen, to our Kundalini, our power of Self-revelation. It isn't so obvious or alluring to Cap and Willy. Our mind and body, our normal sense of "I," may be disoriented by the reshaping of their reality and resistant to moving further into the unknown.

With Shaktipat the Kundalini awakens and takes over leadership of our spiritual development. The Queen awoke first and commands Captain and Will from then on. At sea she was subject to the winds, the currents, and the advice of the Captain as to what course they should follow. Before Shaktipat we follow our mind, our body, directions from the winds of culture—materialism, music or film stars, new age paths, or whatever. With Shaktipat our spirit is fully awakened within, the whole landscape of our existence changes and our own inner power of Self-revelation, of divine recognition, guides us. The center of gravity for our self-definition begins shifting from mind/body to spirit and beyond. With the great awakening, the Queen takes over and never again relinquishes control. Throughout the remainder of the journey she is in charge. Because she is the embodiment of the highest power of Consciousness, she is able to lead in a way that the Captain never could.

There are parallels between all the cities and corresponding chakras from the system of Kundalini yoga. The cities/chakras represent realms of consciousness from which we normally operate at various times in our ordinary daily life. The direct road that the Queen follows from the earthly realm of awakening to the mountain peak with the wise old man is analogous to the sushumna nadi, the energy channel that forms the path of the awakened Kundalini and connects all the chakras from the muladhara to the ajna chakra, the seat of the master, the abode of the wise old man, and beyond to the transcendent realm of Unity Consciousness in the sahasrara.

The Queen awakens on the ground with the smell of fecund earth present, symbolizing the awakening of the Kundalini in the muladhara chakra with its earth element. Here the body and mind, Will and Captain, have to confront and move beyond their attachments to pre-shaktipat ways of living and to the security of simple, basic, earthly living. Issues of survival and existence predominate, survival of body and the mental construct of self, of who I am. Willy is concerned about how they would obtain food and shelter, while Cap is despondent over the loss of his ship and crew. He is a sea captain; he doesn't know who he is without a ship and crew to command. He symbolizes our mental/egoic levels of attachment and identification.

The security and simplicity are very alluring to Willy. Our body seeks physical comfort, security, predictable patterns of eating and sleeping. When our consciousness is identified with the body we feel attached to those things. Willy and Cap aren't able to free themselves from their attachments. It's their nature to be attached to these things, but Consciousness, the Shakti-Queen, doesn't have to be restricted or governed by their attachments and what they identify with. The Queen is now the one who carries them through; it's the power of her command that repeatedly moves them on. This is the power of grace moving us ahead. We must remember the Queen, as the Kundalini, is the embodiment of grace. Obedience and surrender are all that are demanded of Willy and Cap, body and mind.

One of the Queen's first tasks is to move Willy and Cap through the despair they feel from having lost their ship and crew. The Shakti literally spoke about this to me in meditation, strongly emphasizing this point.

She said, "People who receive Shaktipat often get stuck mourning the loss of old ways of living, old negativities, old habits, and limitations that are at root destroyed with the descent of grace. People waste their time and energy trying to breathe life into their old patterns, clinging to them, holding onto the illusion of their continued existence. Shaktipat destroys much of these and people could be free of them *at once* if they would just let them go. Anything which is destroyed with the descent of grace or falls away during the course of the journey is limiting or binding. Nothing is gained by sustaining them or mourning their loss."

Cap and Willy retain such attachments, but not the Queen. The mind and body, not the supremely free Kundalini, are subject to attachments and conditioning. Our inner spirit delights in moving on, leaving behind bondage and seeking its goal—complete freedom in union with God. At the same time, our mind and body may go through periods of grieving and feeling the loss of what they were familiar with and attached to. We must be compassionate with them.

The Kundalini is the power of grace moving and directing the seeker from within. The Kundalini is actually more than just attuned to the will of God, it is one with the will of God. When our spirit signals to God its readiness to move beyond the ordinary pursuits of the world, God responds. It is God's will that we experience our union with the Divine.

The Kundalini and her actions are the unfolding of God's will. It is the will of the Divine that all the mysteries of creation be revealed to us from within. Our mind and body need only surrender to that power and obey it as best they can for our journey to proceed.

The command of our inner spirit is not usually as obvious to us as the command of the Queen is to Cap and Willy. They are accustomed to carefully and attentively following the Queen. Our mind and body usually need to develop such qualities over a lengthy period of time in order to be capable of knowing and carrying out the subtleties of the Kundalini's commands.

To attain that subtle awareness, the sadhana, the set of spiritual practices, prescribed by one's mystic guide is indispensable. Very few people can initially connect to the Queen, the Spirit of God within themselves, and know with confidence Her divine will. By being with a mystic guide, doing the required spiritual practices, and developing inner discipline, we refine our consciousness, with the result that the stirrings of the Kundalini begin to stand out more clearly from the clamorings of the mind and senses. Through dedicated spiritual practice we also build the strength necessary to carry out the commands of our inner Queen, the Shakti. These are no small tasks. They are the heart of sadhana, of spiritual life, and may take all of one's time on earth.

The Captain and first mate are able to know the Queen, obey her, and carry out her commands right from the beginning. They embody good discipleship. The reward of their obedience is that they are taken swiftly and directly to the heights of spiritual attainment, and in the end they are absorbed into the Divine. Once we are able to know the promptings of the Divine Will and obey them, the completion of our journey is ensured. The outer relationship of the mystic guide and disciple helps to form the inner relationship of God to self, teaching the self to be surrendered and obedient to God. The true mystic guide connects one to Divine Consciousness, not merely to himself or herself.

The full flowering of Captain's and Will's obedience are also a reflection of the Queen's grace. They, like us, are not left to their own devices. The Queen keeps them from meandering and getting lost. She also prevents them from getting stuck in any city, due to attachments and desires that are stirred in them by the powers in each city. The storm, the awakened Queen, and later the wise old man are manifestations of divine intervention, the power of grace that repeatedly saves Cap and Willy, mind and body, from unconscious identification and binding involvement with the things of their world. The Kundalini, God's grace, and the spiritual master prod us along our journey. The Queen commands Cap and Willy to accompany her as she leaves the site of her awakening, the earthy realm of the muladhara chakra, and heads for the watery city in the distance.

The City of Water represents the svadhishthana chakra. This is a realm of passions and illusion. It had a drifting, floating quality. It is a realm of human existence related to primal feelings and sexuality. Willy and Cap, body and mind, fall right in with what was going on. Willy responds physically to what was alluring, while Captain is intoxicated by his fantasies. The body and mind respond according to their natures. At first the pleasures of this realm are most apparent to them. Later, with increased consciousness, the dark side of this realm becomes visible, and Captain and Willy are ready to leave. The dark side includes the greed, attachment, jealousy, fear, pain, and anger that go with the pleasures and passions of this realm.

Not surprisingly throughout the journey, mind and body, Cap and Willy, repeatedly act according to their nature, a nature conditioned by likes and dislikes, attachments, and fears. By accompanying the Queen they become purified and strengthened, but certain aspects of their basic nature don't change. Instead, they manifest more and more the nature of their Queen by obediently following her commands. Body and mind, Willy and Cap, are always susceptible to influence by the cities, always ready to wander off the path. Their discipline primarily consists of their unwavering obedience to the Queen. They are not inherently detached or ready to ignore the alluring aspects of each city. The cities embody root qualities of mind and body. That's why Cap and Willy so easily identify with and join the inhabitants of each realm. Remember that each city, each chakra, is a center of mind/body consciousness. The Kundalini as the Queen is the power that moves them beyond each realm of attachment and desire. She moves the totality of our awareness beyond the limitations of being identified with any realm.

Cap and Willy, loyal to their Queen's wishes, leave the City of Water and head for the City of Fire. They have to curb their wandering natures in order to keep up with the Queen as she goes directly for the next city. The Kundalini, one-pointed on her goal, contains the wandering of the mind and body.

The City of Fire symbolizes the manipura chakra, the center of consciousness represented by the element fire and located near our navel. Our will power and power of aggression are centered here. The City of Fire brings out other characteristics of the mind and body through the actions of Cap and Willy than those seen in the previous two realms.

Willy takes pleasure in joining the people as they work with determination and enthusiasm. He enjoys being part of such an energetic group. There's a visceral, physical pleasure that we experience while being part of an energetic hard-working group. The body feels exhilarated having that kind of energy running through it. Willy goes for it, just as he went for the physical pleasures of the Watery City. His actions lack any discrimination or self-reflection; what feels good is the main criteria. The more one is solely identified with the body, the more one's actions will resemble Willy's actions. He doesn't think about what the people of the City of Fire are working toward, whether the group's aims are lofty, healthy, or righteous. Willy portrays an unconscious seeker of pleasure, be it sense pleasure or the pleasure of being an unconscious part of a group. It's a trap that can get us into trouble on the spiritual path as well as in worldly pursuits. We must never surrender our discrimination. The Queen fulfills that function for Willy and moves him on toward a higher goal. The Kundalini and a true spiritual master guide one in that way, but there are untrue gurus and inner impulses that don't arise from the Kundalini that one must be wary of. Seekers must be vigilant and make every effort to sharpen their discrimination.

Captain's thoughts reveal another set of desires and attachments that entrap us in this realm. He is drawn by his desire for power and the fantasy of being a mighty leader, acquiring fame, new territories, and more power. He exemplifies the willful, acquisitive, self-aggrandizing nature of our ego-mind. He revels in his own nature and fantasy. If left to himself he would pursue it wholeheartedly. A commanding Queen and his devotion to her save him from becoming stuck in the City of Fire. Without the awakened Kundalini, we too follow the ways of Willy and Cap. (Even with the aid of an awakened Kundalini most people are liable to follow their old ways. Throughout the journey I was struck by how rapidly Cap and Willy moved along the path due to their surrender and obedience to the Queen. It's such a contrast to the familiar scenario within me, of mind and body resisting, arguing, or ignoring the promptings of the Kundalini or the wisdom of the guide and the scriptures.)

The Queen is entertained by the leaders of the City of Fire and is recognized by them as a great ruler. They take her to a place high above the city, from which to view it. The Queen surveys the surrounds and appreciates it for what it is, and for what it is not. It certainly is not her destination. Clearly, there's great power here. These people manifest the ability to access their willpower and focus it with sustained determined self-effort. Great things are accomplished by humanity in this way. The elements can be conquered, industries built. But this isn't the end point. Without a higher knowledge guiding the use of the people's energy it serves only the power drives of the leaders.

The Queen sees that the road continues. The lords of the city may rule it but they are also bound by it. They cannot look beyond it. They fear what is beyond their realm, and they fear the mysteriously changing light beckoning in the distance. But the Queen transcends the environs and is thus free to go beyond the City of Fire. Even if we gain power and mastery over a realm, unless we can be detached and transcend it we'll be bound by it. Our spirit has the necessary wisdom and mastery. If we dare to break with the herd then we can follow her. The Queen's vision leads her onward. She gathers her two companions and heads for the mysterious light.

They find the Windy City bewitched by the ever-changing light that colors and controls one's moods, thoughts and feelings. Cap, Willy and all the inhabitants of the city are entranced by the light's power, but the Queen pierces its mystery. Just as the City of Fire represents certain characteristics of the manipura chakra, the Windy City symbolizes the anahata, or heart chakra, with its correspondent element air. The heart chakra, according to yogic seers, contains a lingam, a phallic symbol of God, with a steady flame of Light, the pure Light of Consciousness. Similarly, atop the pinnacle in this city, the Queen encounters the Divine Presence as an orb of Light radiating love. So exquisite is the Divine Light that the Queen becomes completely still and absorbed in it, enveloped in love. The peace and contentment she experienced lead her to think that this must be her destination, but it's only a foretaste of what is to come.

The Light of individual consciousness is in essence one with Universal Consciousness, though it takes on a limited form. The Queen came to know the ecstasy of merger in that Divine Light, but the Light, speaking as her own Self, pointed the way onward, beyond all limitations.

The Divine, symbolized by the orb of light, is the power of Consciousness behind the mind. The light is colored and distorted by the crystal filaments around it, but the filaments have no power in and of themselves. The power emanates from the orb of Light. The actual contents of the mind—thoughts, feelings, and so on—are gross manifestations of the power of Consciousness. One's moods, thoughts, and feelings change with the play of lights as the pure power of Consciousness is colored. When I saw the filaments in the vision, they seemed to be some kind of projection from the Divine Light. Their existence depended on the power of the Light in some way that I didn't understand. As with many of the details of the cities, the Shakti didn't consider this one important enough at this point to go into. She was most concerned with imparting broad meanings and overall lessons about the journey.

The Queen, rather than being dazzled or enthralled by the colored lights, simply watches them, detached. This is the essence of many meditation techniques for dealing with the mind—witnessing it, not identifying with the play of thoughts, sensations and feelings that make up its content. By doing so, the Queen is able to see in moments of brilliant clarity the source of the deluding light. The source reveals the way to itself. She follows it. In meditation, by watching the mind, we come to see the source of Consciousness behind the mind. The clear Light of Consciousness illumines our way.

Merging in that Light brings such stillness, contentment, and love to the Queen that she thinks this must be her destination. There is bliss and contentment that comes from going beyond the mind in meditation, but it isn't the end of the journey. There is ecstasy and expansion that goes with dropping the limited identities that go with body and mind. With the first realization of "I am Consciousness" great peace washes over one's spirit. The agitation produced by the desires and fears of those limited identities ceases, just as the weighed down feeling of walking with a heavy overcoat on ends the moment you take it off. However, limitation of a subtler nature remains. This is the realization of "I am Consciousness," but not the realization of "I am Universal, All-encompassing Consciousness." The Queen longs for the highest, and the Light informs her that her path continues on to loftier places. It doesn't allow her to get stuck on this high, but not ultimate level of attainment. She sees and knows this to be true. Without hesitation she continues on her quest.

The Light of Consciousness in the heart is a living flame of love and illumination. It is a spark of the Universal Light of Consciousness. When the seeker opens the heart chakra and makes his or her way to the center where the Light abides in all its glory, then the seeker becomes flooded with love. By bringing one's consciousness into the presence of the Light in the heart, the clarity and love of that Divine Light will flow into the mind and body, purifying them of many old habits. In addition, the Light will spontaneously flow through the seeker to others nearby, healing and uplifting them.

The Shakti said, "The heart chakra is of great importance because it is a place where the Light of God flashes forth into the world with radiant love. Most people follow those shimmering rays of love outward until they bounce off something or some one and come back at them. Confusion sets in when the reflecting object is taken to be the source. The source is in your heart. Follow the shimmering rays of Divine Love emanating from the Light within your heart back to their true source, back to the Radiant One seated there. Rest for a while in the warm embracing presence of the Living Flame of Love shining in your heart. Return here as often as you like...."

After penetrating the mystery of the enthralling lights, the Queen is able to free Captain and Willy from their spell. The colored lights' grip on them is so strong that the Queen has to force the awareness of her presence upon them, commanding their attention and pushing them to understand what is happening to their minds. Cap is able to understand to some degree what the Queen reveals to him about the power of the Light. It helps to free him but he doesn't fully comprehend the Light's mysterious nature. Cap, the personification of limited mind and egohood, has little hope of comprehending the power that is really his root source. The part cannot encompass the whole.

In another way the Captain exemplifies the limitations of understanding through rational knowing. The Queen knows and understands through the direct experience of merger, of union with the power of Consciousness. Our spirit leaves the mind and body behind in meditation and makes its way to greater heights of consciousness. The mystery isn't explained to her but disappears from the vantage point of a higher level of knowledge. Only part of what our awakened spirit knows can be translated into terms that the mind will understand. The Captain, our mind, gains partial release through such limited knowledge, but still must rely on obedience to the Queen, to the Divine Will, to become free.

Willy understands even less than Cap, but his loyal devotion to the Queen enables him to follow her command. For the body, obedience alone is the key; however it must know to obey the Queen and not the Captain. During the journey the Captain is always submissive to the Queen and argues little, except near the end. On our own journeys the mind seems all too willing to lead the body off in contradiction to the way of God.

The threesome continued their way into the mountains, with the Queen checking the wanderings of Cap and Willy. The steep mountain road tested the fortitude of those two, while the Queen's energy was boundless. She inspired and drove them onward. The trials and challenges of the spiritual journey become greater as one progresses, and the power of grace, the Shakti, is ever present to support one. The path becomes more and more arduous for Cap and Willy, but the Queen continues on with greater energy and excitement at the anticipation of reaching her destination. Her true nature as pure Shakti, pure Divine Power, becomes increasingly evident as all obstacles fall before her. Obstacles that will stop the mind and body are nothing to the Kundalini. The Captain's and First Mate's dependence on her for continued progress becomes increasingly obvious. Efforts of the mind and body simply aren't enough to attain the heights of purity and transcendence. Without grace, without the divine Kundalini Shakti, progress would halt. She moves them through physical pleasures, traps of ego, willpower and pride, through emotions, fantasies and through the deluding power of the mind. The Queen is our own transcendent power of Consciousness that draws the mind and body as far up the path of evolution as they can go. The Queen leads Cap and Willy to the Ethereal City in a high mountain pass.

There they encounter the creative power of words and sounds. The realm reveals the power of words to manifest reality. The vishuddha chakra, symbolized by the Ethereal City, is the center that represents the level of consciousness where words and language form. Being at the source of language allowed the Queen, Cap, and Willy to understand all languages. The source of the power behind words lies deeper. This is just the point where that power begins to take the recognizable forms of language and thoughts, the substrate of spoken words. The reality they create unfolds due to the creative power of Universal Consciousness expressed through words and sound.

In the ordinary everyday world, too, people choose to experience collective fantasies while being part of an audience in a story hall, captivated by a storyteller. The storyteller may be a politician, a religious figure, a movie producer, or a reporter. The hall may be your living room, church, temple, school, office, or theater. We're all influenced by the power of words. The story halls capture one's consciousness and hold it in the gross world of actions, desires, pleasures, and pains. Some people choose to experience the energy and inspiration that the mantras and chants produce in the mantra halls. The chanting in the mantra halls transports one's consciousness to ecstatic realms of awareness beyond common thoughts. The story halls reflect the power of words to create grosser and denser levels of reality, ordinary reality for most of us, while the mantra halls reflect the power of words to take our consciousness higher. Yet, the same power underlies the experiences had by those in either hall, and ultimate freedom lies beyond them both. The halls and the city have to be left behind.

Cap and Willy choose to rest in a story hall while the Queen searches for the three truthsayers, the masters of this realm. Total mastery of this realm requires complete dedication to the truth, for to say anything else but the truth would create untold pain and chaos. The masters must be absolutely vigilant in upholding the truth, because even a casual slip or an unconsciously spoken word manifests some reality. Spiritual teachers of any school must be vigilant if they want to serve in God's work of bringing souls back to the recognition of their unity with the Divine. If you want to give directions about a path, then you better know that path. Otherwise you will bear the karmic burden of having misled others, a burden it could take you lifetimes to free yourself of.

The Queen sought the masters to question them about where her destination lies. The masters instantly recognized her nobility, her rulership. They welcomed her as an equal. She was honored and welcomed by the rulers of every city through which she passed. The sovereignty of the Queen was acknowledged in all realms. The Kundalini, our Divine Goddess of Light, reigns throughout the inner world. Her power and majesty become more and more visible to us as we progress on the spiritual journey. As the Queen entered each city, she went directly to the heights of it and from that vantage point saw its entirety. Our Kundalini, our inner divine power of Consciousness, enters into each domain of human existence, each city, and from the heights of detached pure awareness grasps the essence of that domain and moves on toward its destination. By passing through all the domains of human existence, all the cities, the Divine Consciousness absorbs into itself all the levels of individual existence, thereby transforming them. The process continues until all levels have been purified of attachment to them and transcended.

True to her nature as Kundalini, the very power of revelation and pure Consciousness, the Queen knows the mysterious power of words and sound to create reality; she also knows her destination still lies ahead. The masters of the realm confirm this all for her. As the Queen advances on her journey through the cities her true nature becomes more and more apparent. The upward movement of the Kundalini through the chakras is evolutionary. The shedding of limitations and expansion of consciousness mark this upward movement of the Kundalini just as the downward involutionary movement is characterized by taking on limitations and contraction of consciousness. In order to proceed beyond the Ethereal City, the Queen must gather her companions.

She has to pull Willy and Cap from their fantasy in a story hall and lead them higher into the mountains. It is by her will that they are moved beyond the realm of the Ethereal City. These higher realms of human existence, realms of consciousness, are extremely difficult for the body and mind to attain, much less surpass, on their own. The ability comes from the Divine Will alone. Passing through and beyond all the cities recapitulates the experiential realms of individual existence with the demand that we detach and move on from each one toward some higher goal. Cap and Willy were better able to walk away from the lures of the lower realms, the earthy, watery, and fiery domains. The experience of breaking free of the binding qualities of those cities for a higher goal is a more common human endeavor, and more accessible to the body and mind. People sacrifice passions, security, and power needs for loftier pursuits. But when it comes to the higher realms of consciousness, the heart chakra and the throat chakra, involving the actual power of Consciousness underlying the mind, the binding forces are greater. The Queen has to be much more forceful to move Cap and Willy onward. Our individual will must increasingly depend on the Divine Will, surrendering more and more to its impulse. What sweet ecstasy comes with that surrender! Cap and Willy, mind and body, are freed from the shackles of each city by the infusion of the Queen's will. They are inspired to move on. As the journey proceeds to the summit, they depend almost solely on the Queen's energy to keep them going.

The Queen tries to explain to Willy and Cap the nature of the Ethereal City they've just left, but with almost no success. Captain understands little of what she reveals about the power behind words and Will grasps none of it. Willy moves on at her bidding and is content with that. The body experiences the power of words through the effects words have on it but doesn't grasp how. One who is thoroughly identified with the body exhibits the limitations that Willy does, in this and other realms. Cap, the ego/mind, is able to understand some of what the Queen reveals about the power of words but is stuck on a conceptual level. The limited mind exists through the power of words; thus it cannot truly know how that power operates until it transcends it. The

Queen is that transcendent power of Consciousness that encompasses and reveals the true nature of every realm. In that sense, she is the unbound mind, the pure power of Consciousness.

The arduous climb to the top of the world brings out weakness and resistance in Cap and Will. For Will, the physical demands of the climb make him want to stop or turn back. Captain argues against continuing the journey because there's little more to be gained. He wants to convince the Queen to be satisfied with the heights they have already attained. Gaining the heights of spiritual attainment taxes the body and mind. There are times when the body feels like it just can't continue and weaknesses and latent illnesses may come out, but the Queen is there, grace is there to carry us onward.

Even in its fatigue, the body has a purity and simplicity that is met by the Queen's nurturing, mothering compassion. The body is given the strength to continue. In contrast, our ego/mind will congratulate itself for all it has attained, for how high up the mountain it has gone, as if it were above all others. Our mind may try to convince us there's nothing more to be attained, when in fact the true attainment still lies ahead. The ego/mind's limited vision and clinging possessiveness can make it complacent. It may get a fiery prod from the Queen. The Queen will not be turned back. She will envelop the body and mind with love and carry them to the summit. She may tarry awhile to infuse them with strength or embolden them against their fears, but she will never give up her goal.

Once on the summit, they see the mysterious old man waiting for them outside his cottage. He won't speak to them until they have eaten and rested. The Queen is burning to reach the end of her journey. Cap and Willy are all too eager to eat and sleep; for them the quest can wait. Though the climb was exhausting and it seems as if they have been traveling for lifetimes to get to this mountain peak, the Queen desires neither food nor rest. She wonders how the old man knew they were coming, why she feels as though he knows her fully, and what does he have to do with her final destination? She absorbs herself in contemplation of the old man, meditating on his form. Stillness radiates from him. At last she becomes absorbed in the divine sparkle of his eyes. The Shakti, the Divine Light of Consciousness, may stream from the eyes of a great master and fill one with grace. Our spirit becomes still; consciousness expands in profound meditation.

At this point in the symbolic journey through the chakras we've arrived at the ajna chakra. "Ajna" means command. It is at this level of conscious- ness that one must receive the command from the inner Guru, the grace- bestower, to rise to the exalted state of union with the Divine. Only those who have purified themselves of egocentricity and have their mind and senses in control can proceed. The Queen is in command of Willy and Captain. She has given herself totally to the quest. She is ready.

In time Cap and Willy rise from their slumber. The old man agrees to answer the Queen's questions. The omniscient old man is the inner Guru, the grace-bestower, the vehicle to union with God. In him and through him the Queen's destination lies, but first she is tested once again. She has passed many tests since leaving her island nation—storms at sea, hardships of the journey, splendid attractions in each city, great powers—all failed to sway her from her course. Upon reaching the limits of the world, the very highest peak, the wise old man offers her and her companions food and rest before answering her questions. That is her test, or if not a test, then another situation in which she demonstrates her true nature. Will her hunger be satisfied with food, will her thirst be quenched with water, will her restlessness find quiet in the unconsciousness of sleep? Cap and Willy, the mind and body, were attracted to the gross substance of food and com- forted by the shallow repose of sleep, but not the Queen. She passed the test, she was true to her nature as spirit, as Consciousness, as the sublime Goddess Kundalini. She feasted on the wise old man, she absorbed herself in him, she drank him in with her eyes, her attention rested on him alone. The light from his eyes, pure Shakti, Divine Light, poured into her. She neither ate nor slept but was nourished by the sweet nectar of God's grace flowing through the form of the spiritual master. The Kundalini delights in the pure Consciousness radiating from a saint, one's mystic guide, or the numinous inner form of the Guru.

The old man and the Queen speak for the benefit of Captain and Will. She is already prepared to follow the master's subtlest command. The drama is played out for the benefit of the body and mind—including yours and mine. Cap argued most against what the old man had to say. He refused to believe there could be any destination beyond where they were, and if there was, why bother with the old man—hadn't they gotten this far without him, and why should they believe him when the old man said Cap and Willy would have to remain behind. Cap continues to be true to his nature as ego/mind. The ego/mind, the consciousness of limited individuality, doesn't recognize the true nature of the Guru, the wise old man symbolic of the Self, and doesn't see how the guiding hand of the grace-bestower was directing them throughout their journey. The ego tries to appropriate to itself, to take credit for the progress that is made on the spiritual path. It mistakes the true spiritual master or mystic guide for just another individual like itself. The vision of the ego/mind is bound to the world, the realms of individuality; it cannot see what is beyond. Because this is as high as it can go, the ego assumes this is as high as anyone can go.

Our minds may try to deceive us in this way, but this is the end of the line for individuality; universality lies ahead. To go further one must transcend the limited forms of mind and body. The Queen knows. It was presaged in the Windy City where she left Cap and Willy behind in her ascent to the top of the pinnacle and merged with the Jivatma, the Light of Individual Consciousness. As long as their forms exist, the mind and body are earth-bound. The Kundalini alone can shed her form and transcend worldly existence. Our unleashed inner power of Consciousness, the awakened Kundalini, knows the true nature of the inner guide and follows his or her command without hesitation. She directs Cap and Willy to wait for her there as she goes ahead. Our unbounded spirit, our Queen, leaves behind the bound forms of body and mind to follow the power of grace, the power of Self-revelation. She promises to return. There's nothing for the body and mind to do but be still and wait. Their surrender is total and final.

Meditation involves a similar process. We put the body and mind to rest while our consciousness transcends them and merges with God. Of course the mind and body don't always surrender without a struggle! They may act more like cranky, overtired children refusing to go to bed than obedient servants waiting quietly and patiently for the return of their master or mistress. In the end they have to obey the Divine Mother, though the end may seem to be a long time in coming.

The Queen and the wise old man leave the cottage and go out into the night. Side by side they walk, drawn toward an orb of exquisite scintillating blue-white light high in the night sky. There's an equality in their side-by-side step, the two are one and the same; two sides of the same coin. The awakened Kundalini is the Guru, the grace-bestowing power of God. Leaving behind the abode of individuality, they rise above the world. The Queen suddenly sees herself as formless Light, she sees the old man as formless Light, and realizes they are the same Divine Light of Consciousness. As all differences between the old master and the Queen dissolve, we can see that in essence our Kundalini is the same divine Power of Consciousness as the ideal Guru. The Queen returns her gaze to the orb of Light above her and they all merge into one ecstatic Divine Light, the entire universe dissolves into shimmering Consciousness, dancing Blue Light. This is the point in the evolution of consciousness where the last remaining form and contraction of Consciousness are shed, revealing the underlying truth of unity, of identity between the individual, localized form of consciousness created by the Kundalini, and the Universal, All-encompassing Consciousness of the Divine. Because our mind works in a linear way it is hard for it to grasp that the unfolded, expanded, formless Consciousness exists at all times and places along with the individualized contracted form of that same consciousness. It appears that this evolutionary expansion occurs resulting in the boundless, formless Divine Consciousness. Thus the all-knowing power of Consciousness referred to as the inner Guru is the same power of Consciousness known as Kundalini.

The Queen pulled my awareness into hers, showing me that at this point our awareness expands to include everything. "I AM CONSCIOUSNESS, I AM THE LIGHT, THE UNIVERSE IS CONSCIOUSNESS, THE UNIVERSE IS LIGHT, I AM THAT." Shapes and forms exist and don't exist, boundaries melt, no longer is there a self and non-self, no longer an experiencer and an experience, no beginning and no end, just all-encompassing Consciousness. The transcendent orb of pure Light is God, the pure illuminating source of all that is. Merger with the Divine brings total illumination, total enlightenment. This ineffable union was the goal, though in that moment all notions of a journey and a destination disappeared. Time itself dissolves into eternity beyond duration.

Considerable time passed for Cap and Willy before the Queen returned. Her form re-emerged from the Light, forever transfigured, for-ever one with the Infinite Effulgence. She descended to the summit where her faithful companions awaited her. They stared in wonder as the Queen, truly the Goddess of Light, approached. Her stunning radiance and pro-found serenity moved them to fall to their knees in reverence. With great love she raised them up and dwelt with them there until the end of their days. The Queen knows them to be a part of her, like rays of Divine Consciousness. In time Cap and Willy began to shine as if from the reflected brilliance of the Queen. In a flash of light at their death Cap and Willy merged into their beloved Queen and into the Infinite. The forms of the body and mind may be more rigid and limited than that of the Kundalini, but their essential nature is the same as that of the Queen. In the end they too dissolve into Consciousness.

The Queen has infinite love and compassion for Cap and Willy. She never abandons them; she's committed to leading them from beginning to end. The Queen didn't denigrate the two of them for repeatedly identifying with the people of each city, nor did she revile the cities for their limitations. She simply accepted her two companion's propensity for getting stuck as part of their nature, just as she accepted the characteristics of each city as the nature of that realm. As a part of our journey we experience all the realms of human existence, recognize their limitations, and move on. The difference between the "old realms" of experience and the characteristics of the "new realm" cities, or life before and after shaktipat, is the presence of that dynamic consciousness, the awakened Kundalini, who recognizes the limitations of each realm, each domain of experience, and who one-pointedly heads for the final destination.

In essence, the Divine Mother was saying that the earthly realm of basic existence, survival, and security is part of the larger domain of human existence but it isn't the destination. Don't identify with it and get stuck there. The watery realm of passions, sense pleasures, and procreation is part of the domain of human existence, but it isn't the destination; don't get stuck there. The fiery realm of willpower, pride, determination, and dominance is part of the domain of human existence, but it isn't the destination. The windy shifty realm of moods, thoughts, and feelings, illumined by a spark of Universal Consciousness, isn't the destination either. Nor is the ethereal realm, with its tremendous power of words and sound, the destination, though it is a part of the human domain. Even the seldom attained and rarefied realm of the wise old man on the summit of the world, the Guru's abode—whether it's an ashram, a monastery, zendo, or retreat center—is part of the domain of human existence and it isn't the destination. There is only one ultimate destination for the evolution of our spirit: union with the Divine, merger into the all-encompassing Light of Consciousness, the dissolution of all forms, the simultaneous existence and nonexistence of all boundaries, pure transcendence and transfigured re-emergence. This alone is the final resting-place for our Kundalini, our power of Self-revelation.

The attainment of the state of union isn't intended to leave one in a disembodied state of transcendence. Instead, this state divinizes worldly existence. The Queen re-emerges transfigured, shining with the Light of Divine Consciousness, and brings that Light down to earth, down to the summit where Captain and Will await, down to the realm of the body and mind.

The final scene of the transfigured Queen returning to the mountain-top reveals something of the nature of an enlightened person. Captain and Will are in a way still bound—the mind and body remain limited structures until their forms completely dissolve—but Consciousness, as embodied by the Queen, is no longer bound to the world nor tied to the limiting structures of the mind and body. Captain and Willy, mind and body, have become totally surrendered to the will of the Divine Consciousness, the Queen. Their actions reflect only her presence; they reflect the light of her consciousness alone. Divine Consciousness "enlightens" the mind and body of saints in this state. They glow with this illumination.

The transfigured Queen continues her descent back into the world accompanied by her devoted companions, though for her there is no descent at all. She moves entirely within the Self, all she perceives is God manifesting God. Because she embodies God so fully, she serves as a perfect channel for God's grace. Blessings flow to those who simply see her and to those who make an offering of love to her.

Just seeing a great saint allows the soul a refreshing draft of grace. This is true regardless of whether they are seen in a dream, in meditation, or in the waking state of consciousness. Many, if they had an opportunity to be near a saint, might think it is important to be seen, to be noticed, to have the saint acknowledge or recognize their presence in some way. However, it's not important to be seen but to see, to truly See, to apprehend the reflection of your Self. The Shakti said, "Be the seer not the seen." Whether you are aware of it or not, the Light and Grace that emanate from a saint will enter you through your eyes as you behold such a holy being. The eyes, as well as the other senses, are always searching for the reflected light of one's own projected love, one's own projected Self. When these gateways to the soul focus on the blazing form of a God-realized being, they are flooded with Light (even in dreams and visions). In that moment the soul receives an enormous influx of grace. If the person is new to the experience of being in the presence of a bearer of Light, he or she may be confused, bedazzled, and miss what has happened. Instead of knowing what truly happened, the individual may remember and even imitate something unimportant about the holy one—his or her speech, dress, physical looks, surroundings, or some other irrelevancy, positive or negative. It doesn't matter if their conscious mind keys in on the wrong element, the soul knows the truth and takes in the blessing. Even if the person is unconscious of it, the effects of seeing such a holy being are always beneficial.

The other senses can also be portals through which the grace of an enlightened one will enter the heart. To hear the spoken words of a saint, to receive the gracious touch of a saint, to taste the food blessed by a saint, to inhale the divine fragrance of a saint, these are rare gifts of God. Again, this is true if it occurs in dreams or meditations, as well as in the waking state of ordinary reality.

As the radiant Queen traveled the world, blessings also flowed to those who made an offering of love to her, regardless of whether they were able to see her or be near her. People are in danger of forgetting the profound importance of making an offering, a sacrifice, to the Divine. When you make an offering, when you sacrifice something of lesser value for some-thing of greater value, you create a space within your spirit for grace, an opening for God to more fully manifest the Divine Presence within you. The most valuable offering you can make is your conscious attention.

The more you invest your consciousness in something, the more valu-able it becomes. Consciousness is the most precious commodity in the world, surpassing even precious metals and jewels. The value of anything is really a symbol of the consciousness, the attention, invested in that thing. Companies are willing to pay four million dollars per minute for advertising time during the Superbowl because of all the attention, all the consciousness they hope to attract to their product. Your attention is the most valuable asset you own. Look at how you manage it; look at whether or not you are in control of it. You can tell what is truly valuable to a person by looking at what they give their attention to. If you were to make a record of what you thought about, what your consciousness dwelled upon during the course of a day, you would become shockingly aware of what that says about your values. Not what you profess to value, or would like to think you value, but what you actually value enough to give it your attention.

The Shakti said, "Wake up! It's your consciousness and you can change what you are investing it in. Make your conscious attention an offering to God. Continually offer your consciousness to God through prayer, meditation and service. In time you will see God as everyone, everything, everywhere."

The Queen sacrifices everything, even putting her life in jeopardy, to pursue the highest. Before her true awakening she didn't know she was seeking union with God. She knew that all the worldly attainments she had didn't satisfy the longing and restlessness of her spirit. She trusted the discontent she felt. She trusted her own inspiration and intuition. She trusted in God to guide her and protect her on her journey. Her discontent, her inspiration and her trust in God were the greater treasures to which she sacrificed the lesser—the rulership of her nation, the advice of her ministers, and the needs and desires of others for her to stay.

After her awakening she continues to be guided by her restlessness, her intuition and her faith in God. She sacrifices the despair and attachment to what was familiar and lost at sea in order to follow the path given to her. The Queen sacrifices all that could be had in each city in order follow her heart, her longing for the highest, which compels her onward. Through

Divine Grace and trust in her own discontent and intuition she attains the highest. Her attainment then allows her to be of the greatest possible benefit to people everywhere. By seeking the ultimate personal good, realizing one's union with the Divine, the ultimate public good, bringing God's grace into the world, is also achieved.

The Captain and Will sacrifice everything to their loyalty and love for their Queen. Their total obedience and surrender to her command purifies and polishes them to the point where they mirror her Light. If you want to progress most rapidly on the journey led by the Kundalini, then purify your awareness in the crucible of meditation, attune your inner senses to the commands of the Kundalini, and joyfully allow your mind and body to accompany her on this miraculous quest.

You'll need guides on this journey, ones with great wisdom and experience. Take care in choosing them. Some guides can lead you out of your homeport and into the sea, but no farther. Others can take you as far as the first cities and then they become lost. When you see that your guide has reached the limits of his or her knowledge, don't hesitate to leave and search for a more competent one. If you find a guide whose knowledge and experience encompass the entire journey through the inner realms, then know you are enormously blessed.

With that last gift of advice on choosing a spiritual guide, the Shakti's commentary ended. I've been contemplating the experience of the Kundalini's journey ever since the day it occurred, discovering new meanings and symbols that weren't apparent to me before. Sharing it with others has also been beneficial to me, as they invariably have their own insights and ways of relating it to their own journey. In that way other people teach me more about my own experience.

In the Indian tradition the Shakti is seen as ever playful. Part of her play with this experience has been the ongoing delight of discovery, finding truths she enfolded in it and watching others discover truths in it relevant to their own paths. I invite you to contemplate this gift of the Divine Mother, the Kundalini Shakti, and play with it in ways that will allow you to gain whatever is meaningful and valuable in it for you on your quest.

Chapter 3

Gifts from the Goddess

O desperately seeking mind,
      invoke the primal resonance *Kali, Kali, Kali*
      and plunge into the ocean of her reality.
Do not imagine this transparent sea to be empty
      if you fail to discover living gems
      during the first few dives.
Sink deep with a single breath,
      awakening her energy that abides secretly
      within his precious human body.
The priceless pearl of love is manifest
      only at the uttermost depth
Of Mother's wisdom ocean....

Treasures of revelation
      emerge from the Mother ocean,
      from unthinkable profundity.
This courageous poet confirms:
Dive with abandon into her mystery.
You will discover a new gem every moment.

Ramprasad[1]

Earlier I mentioned that after an abbreviated account of the Queen's journey was published, additional visionary experiences occurred that are further reflections of the soul's journey and the workings of the Kundalini Shakti. New lessons and insights were presented in these visions along with ones that reiterated teachings from the Ascent to Union.

The following vision unfolded on a January afternoon in 1990, while I was driving along the parkway on my way home from my office. Suddenly I heard the Shakti's voice in my mind saying, "Tell me the story of the rabbit and the hare." I hadn't heard her voice so clearly in years. I felt I immediately had to set aside my shock at hearing that exquisite sound in order to attempt to fulfill her demand for that story. I was trying to put into practice one of the lessons from the earlier vision: simply obey the Goddess. The problem was that I didn't know any such story. I thought She had confused it with the well-known story of the tortoise and the hare. No sooner did I have that thought when She said in a very definite way, "No. The rabbit and the hare." I assumed if that's what the Shakti wants it must exist, though I had no idea how to access it. In that open state of mind there was a moment of utter stillness, and the following tale came up on its own. I watched it on the inner screen of consciousness. Fortunately the Shakti also gave me an adequate awareness of the road so I could drive home safely. The experience ended just before I pulled off the parkway. When I arrived at my house I offered a prayer of gratitude to the Shakti for another of Her gifts.

The Rabbit and The Hare

In a beautiful lush meadow dwelt a big bushy rabbit. He lived well in the midst of plenty. As a result he had luxurious fluffy fur and a pleasingly plump body. Luscious berries and tender grasses grew all around his burrow. He never had to go more than a few hops to get all he needed to eat. One day he was thinking of his cousin the desert hare and decided to invite him for a visit. Each had heard of the other though they had never met.

The desert hare always wanted to meet his rich cousin but the opportunity never presented itself before. With great delight he accepted the invitation and set out for the rabbit's home, leaving the desert behind. When he reached the verdant meadow he was amazed to see how comfortably his cousin lived. He was equally amazed by how good his wealthy cousin looked. What rich fur! Such a large full body!

On the other hand, the rabbit looked at his desert hare cousin and was shocked by what stood before him. The hare was thin and sinewy with only the barest coat of scraggly fur. But, despite his appearance, the hare was so light and cheerful that the rabbit welcomed him heartily. Rabbit said to himself, "I'll certainly have to fatten up cousin hare before he leaves!"

The next day was chilly and raining. They stayed in the rabbit's home. He told the hare all about his life in the meadow. Cousin hare envied rabbit's lifestyle. Rabbit said it had its hardships though, and described winter storms, cold rainy days, and freezing weather that went on for months. Cousin hare figured that must be the reason why cousin rabbit was so somber and cynical. "Still, he looks very good," thought cousin hare.

A new day dawned sunny and pleasantly mild. Rabbit decided to take his cousin to his favorite strawberry patch and off they went down the trail. Just as they reached the area near the edge of the meadow where the strawberries grew best, they heard a snapping sound. The ground suddenly gave out beneath them and they fell smack into a pit! They jumped and leaped but couldn't reach the top. Cousin hare kept trying, but rabbit collapsed in despair. Rabbit said, "Oh cousin hare, you're so lean and strong. You'll jump out, but I'll never get free." Before the hare could leap to safety, a trapper arrived to survey his catch.

First he picked up the desert hare by the scruff of the neck. He looked at the scrawny creature with disgust, saying, "Look at you! Your fur is worthless and you don't even have enough meat on you to make a cup of soup." With that he threw the hare aside and reached down to pick up the rabbit. The hare dashed away, diving under a giant sticker bush for protection. From there he peered out at the trapper.

He had the rabbit by the neck and was very pleased, "Now you're just what I'm looking for! Your fur is so beautiful and you're so plump, you'll make a delicious stew!" He killed the rabbit on the spot.

The hare ran scared all the way back to the safety of the desert. He told the whole story to some friends. They trembled at the thought of the trapper. The hare finished his story saying, "Never again will I wish I had what someone else has. Who knows what fate goes with it!"

It's interesting that this vision came a few days after I had a conversation with someone about the earlier experience of the Queen's journey. I was dismayed that it had stirred envy in him; he really wanted such an experience for himself. For some people the Kundalini provides visions, for others divine sounds, or an inner refuge of peacefulness, while others receive profound wisdom and insight. We don't awaken the Kundalini or meditate in order to have any experience other than that of union. Along the way the Kundalini gives the seeker what he or she most needs, not necessarily what is wanted. Her devotees receive total transformation in due time. What they will experience during their journey will depend on the samskaras, the past karmic impressions, that must be released.

When I asked myself what forms envy takes in my mind, the first response from a part of me was to deny that it was at all present! I laughed as I ignored that part and continued looking. I could see the subtler, more acceptable form envy disguised itself as. Envy no longer boldly stood up and proclaimed itself in the obvious ways it used to. Now when it rises it tries to hide itself in the background of my awareness by causing my attention to linger on something or by very quietly saying something like "Wouldn't it be nice if I had...." and thereby insinuating itself into my consciousness. With that thought can begin the initial stirring of wants, needs, and desires. Any form of envy cuts us off from the unbreakable wholeness of the Self; it denies the Self by saying we lack something. We then project a piece of the Self outward and feel if we just had that thing we would be whole once again. In the ensuing state of deficiency, a state of depletion that focuses on the external thing we feel the envy and desire for, we embark on a process of groping after the thing, perhaps never realizing that whatever it is, it will never have the power to restore the wholeness of our Self. A wholeness that hasn't actually been altered, but a wholeness from which we are now alienated. Envy destroys the awareness our true nature, thus agitating the mind and creating the illusion that the agitation will cease with the possession of the thing.

Fortunately the remedy is simple (though it usually needs repeated application!)—return our attention to the Self, our true wholeness. For me that may take the form of saying to myself, "No, I don't need that. I have everything," or repeating a mantra (mantra means "that which protects", it protects us from the habits of the mind by bringing us back to the Self), or shifting my awareness directly to Witness Consciousness.

The inner Witness, the awareness that simply watches and is conscious of what is passing through the mind without reacting to it or judging it, is Self-awareness. Joining one's awareness with that pure Witness Consciousness gives one the perceptual standpoint of the Self. The Self surveys the entire universe, the inner worlds and the outer worlds, with total equanimity. When you repeatedly merge your awareness in that of the Witness then in time your consciousness expands to embrace everything, agitation ceases, and a sublime stillness settles over your entire being. The more you practice shifting your consciousness to the Self, to the Witness, whether in meditation or during any other time, the more accessible that expanded awareness becomes to you. At first Witness Consciousness may seem quite restricted, as though it were witnessing only the thing you were focusing on. As you further explore Witness Consciousness you discover it has no boundaries, your experience of it expands and expands until you see that it includes everything. From that place of abundance and all-inclusiveness you can serenely watch the passing streams of needs and desires, thoughts and emotions, and all the other mind-stuff that floats through your awareness. The forms and experiences of self, positive and negative, take shape and dissolves in awareness. Even concepts and images of your Divine Self and the Witness take on form only to dissolve in spaciousness. Within that limitless ocean of awareness, myths, visions, and scriptures also coalesce.

Contemplating the rabbit and hare story brought to mind the differences in the two types of lifestyle, the ascetic life of the desert hare and the more opulent, indulgent life of the rabbit. I wondered if the Shakti was also saying something to make me more conscious of where different elements of my lifestyle take me. The rabbit, for all his good looks, is somber, weak, fat and feels superior to his cousin. The hare is good-natured, lean, strong, and humble. When confronted with one of life's traps, the rabbit has little strength and quickly collapses into despair. His lifestyle hasn't prepared him to deal with adversity. The hare has the agility and endurance to get free, though he's caught before he has a chance. His life in the desert has equipped him with the emotional and physical strength required. Even when the hare is caught, the trapper, one who desires the sensory pleasures of soft, plush fur and good food, rejects him; he's saved by what he doesn't embody. It's ironic that the rabbit, liking plenty of good food and proud of his hefty body and rich fur, falls victim to one who shares those same pleasures. It's the hare who lives to grow wiser from the experience.

The differences between where the rabbit and the hare lived make another symbolic statement. The rabbit lives in a world that is much more diverse and filled with a variety of things to consume. The climate varies more, seasonal changes and rainy weather bring periods of diminished sunlight and cold temperatures. The hare thinks the rabbit is somber and cynical because he's cut off from the sun so often where he lives. The seasonal changes and the weather produce a great deal of vegetation, but what grows from that? What happens if we take in too much of what the world produces? What happens if we're cut off for long periods from the sun, symbolic of the light of the Self? We may look good to one who appreciates things of the world, but our spirit could be malnourished. The hare lives where the sun shines most of the time and food is adequate but limited. What virtues and strengths grew for him on a steady diet of light and simple pleasures? He grew strong, agile, and high-spirited.

This is not a story about moving to Arizona; it's not about where we should live geographically. Instead, the story raises the question: what kind of inner climate do we seek to maintain? Do you like it hot and humid, with a dense rain forest of emotions, sensations, and moods? Do you prefer a temperate climate with a mix of cold and hot, wet and dry? With all the things that grow in your climate, what do you eat and what do you reject, what do you cultivate and what are the weeds to be composted? The point is to be conscious of the climate we create, be conscious of the kinds of mind-stuff which we are cultivating in that climate and be conscious of whether or not it is supporting the growth of our spirit.

Through our spiritual practices and conscious intention we're trying to effect a shift in consciousness from earthbound awareness to sun-centered awareness, and finally to both and neither. The "both and neither" are particularly confusing for our poor minds. Sun-centered consciousness is the Witness Consciousness that gives you the experience of being detached from all that is happening on the surface of your earthly existence, while at the same time illuminating it with the consciousness that allows you to be fully aware of what is occurring. As you explore the vast expanses of Witness Consciousness, you begin to discover that the same Consciousness emanating from the Self, the Eternal Witness, takes the form of all the contents of the mind, including all sensory perceptions of the world. Thus all experience is created from Consciousness. In this way, you discover that you are both the sun-centered awareness and the earthbound awareness. You are the knower who knows all and you are the known—all the objects of knowledge. You are the creator and the created. Expanding your awareness beyond the sun and the earth, you discover there is an infinitude of being that is neither, that is the indescribable, transcendent Absolute. "Thou art That," proclaim the Vedas. It exists eternally untouched by the cycles of the mind and the cycles of creation and dissolution. You are that, too. In all you'll discover that the real you, the Self, the Witness, is both and neither, both the limited individual on earth and the blazing Consciousness of the Self supporting and illuminating all existence; and you are neither. You are the transcendent, ineffable Beyond, the Void, neither the creator nor the created, neither the thinker nor the thought. The Witness watches all thoughts, as well as the illusion of a thinker, come and go with unperturbed equanimity.

> In the cloud raindrops swirl,
> In the mind thoughts stream,
> There is no rainmaker.
> > by Lawrence Edwards

The discovery of one's total Consciousness as 'both and neither' may seem to happen linearly; sadhana seems to progress along a line. However, that total Consciousness is fully present right now. The fragment of Consciousness that we call our mind has, as part of its reality, limitations that create the illusion of time and linear progression. The experiences and ideas that you are reading in this book are unfolding in your awareness over time as you read, yet the whole book already exists fully and totally in the present. Only your ability to perceive the words is bound to a linear time-line. Similarly, the totality of Consciousness, our full enlightenment, is completely present all the time, yet from the perceptual standpoint of being bound to limited individuality, we go through sadhana, the process of rediscovering our Unity Consciousness.

To support the process of expanding consciousness we need to be conscious of the effects that our lifestyle, our emotional climate, and what we consume mentally and physically have on our consciousness. Before you consume a book, a movie, an idea, food, or whatever else you might take into yourself, ask yourself, does this lead to expansion or contraction of consciousness, does this support the health of my body, mind, and spirit? And remember that play and delight are also expressions of the Goddess to be enjoyed!

With increasing frequency during sadhana the voice of the Eternal breaks through into the consciousness of our limited mind and reveals something of our true nature. It's the voice of our own enlightenment. The Shakti and the visions are some of the forms that the energy of the Divine assume for me, forms that my limited I-sense, my ego, can deal with and not be so overwhelmed or shattered as to lose my ability to function. The Divine assumes these and many other forms for revealing the Eternal to people. It takes an inner discipline to remain conscious and listen to the Inner Voice without being swept away into a rapturous state, missing what the Voice is revealing or asking of us. Fortunately the Divine is very patient and allows us to be swept away many times while our steadiness is strengthened.

Even as we seek to have an experience of the Divine Presence or move toward opening ourselves to the experience of union with God, we have to simultaneously heal the fractures of our individual identity. Otherwise we face the risk of falling apart, disintegrating from the force of the impact that the Divine has on our mind and body. In the eleventh chapter of the *Bhagavad Gita*[2], Arjuna asks the Lord to reveal his Divine Form. The Lord graces him with the vision to perceive the Divine in many of its forms. In no time Arjuna is begging the Lord to stop; it's too terrible and frightening for him to see God. Arjuna pleads with the Lord to take the familiar, limited form of his friend Krishna once again so that he may be spared the onslaught of the divine revelation. If one as noble, virtuous, disciplined and righteous as Arjuna had difficulty withstanding the Power and Glory of God, how do you assess your own strength and readiness? What are you doing to prepare yourself to be a vessel for the Divine? What holes and cracks need to be mended so that the power of Self-revelation doesn't run out more quickly than it runs in? What golden virtues, what inlays of self-discipline and what jewels of dharma must you possess and craft together to form the Holy Grail, the cup of your soul meant to hold a draft of the Divine?

One way that Consciousness helps me contain the currents of Shakti that move through me, is by maintaining the seeming dissociation between the Goddess and myself. This leaves my identity as Lawrence Edwards relatively intact and functional. It allows Lawrence to strengthen that identity by doing what he can to be a better servant and student of the Divine. At the same time, I experience the Shakti gradually shifting my sense of self away from just the mind and body of Lawrence Edwards and into the Divine. This doesn't negate my limited identity as this partic-ular man, but adds to it such an extraordinary vastness of Being that the previous sense of self seems like a droplet of water blown off the crest of a wave, and having enjoyed coursing through the air, it now looks with great joy at the infinite expanse of ocean into which it is about to fall.

As she does for countless seekers, the Shakti pulls my awareness and sense of identity into Consciousness for periods of time and allows me to experience the infinite love and compassion that the Creator has for Her servants. Everything and everyone serves Her, while some are trying to do so consciously. She allows me to see how She witnesses my struggles to place in Her service my voice, my thinking, my relating, typing, cooking, husbanding, fathering, and all the rest of my life. Her Witnessing isn't some bland All-seeing Consciousness, it is filled with All-embracing Love. To experience even a tiny drop of Her Love floods the eyes with tears of ecstasy. Waves of rapture sway the body, the humbled mind retreats into joyous silence, and the heart feels like the cup reveling at being thrown into the ocean. We have much to look forward to! Her gifts are infinite.

After the vision-story of the rabbit and the hare was given, the Shakti provided this next experience and its additional commentary on the spiritual quest.

For many years one of my morning practices was to chant a 181 verse Sanskrit chant while I played the harmonium. What was unusual on this particular morning was that I went into a meditative state in which I could see a story unfolding as an inner vision, while another part of me continued playing the harmonium and chanting the Sanskrit verses. It's a vision-story that speaks through symbols about sadhana, our spiritual life and practices.

The Golden Spoon

Once there was a community of people who lived in a very hard and barren land. The entire town was built on an arid rocky plateau. As far as the eye could see not a blade of grass grew anywhere. The monotony of gray stone assaulted the eye in every direction. People lived on small plots of land with high stone walls enclosing their little dustbowl yards. The walls rose nearly as high as the stone houses imprisoned within. None of these homes had basements—the ground was too difficult to excavate. Life here was as hard as the land. People owned very little, and in their effort to survive they clung to every bit of it—whether it was food, valuables, or beliefs.

One night a young man with a wife and two children had a strange dream. In his dream a luminous old man dressed in royal robes, resplendent with gold and gems, told him to begin digging in his backyard. He awoke with a start, looked around in the dark, and seeing nothing, dismissed it. "What a ridiculous idea—digging in this rocky country," he thought before going back to sleep.

The richly dressed old man appeared again in his dream. "Dig in your backyard, dig until you find the great treasure. You and your family will never want for anything again," the old man told him.

Jolted awake, he carefully got out of bed, leaving his wife undisturbed. He looked in on his son and daughter where they were lying peacefully asleep. On his way downstairs he thought to himself, "This is more than ridiculous, it's impossible. Nobody has any kind of tool that can dig into this ground. What am I doing up at this hour?" Back to bed he went.

Sleep overcame him, and for a third time that night the old man appeared in his dreams. He handed the family man a gleaming, golden spoon and instructed him to use it for penetrating the rocky ground. This time he slept on, and when he awoke in the morning he found his hand clutching the golden spoon.

He got up and ran outside; the golden spoon shone in the morning sunlight. Somehow it seemed to glisten with more than just the reflected light of the sun's rays. Could such a little thing actually break through the granite-like earth beneath his feet? He went to the far corner of his yard hoping no one would see him attempting what everybody knew was impossible. He was embarrassed just thinking of using a spoon to dig into bedrock! He knelt below the high stone wall, took out the golden spoon, and struck the ground with it. He fully expected it to bend as soon as it hit, but to his amazement the golden spoon slid into the stone and dislodged a piece of rock as he pulled it out! "It's a MIRACLE!" he thought, as his mind raced forward. Did this mean that the words of the old man in his dream were true! Would he find great wealth for his family?

The man kept digging enthusiastically with his magic golden spoon. All day he toiled. Bit by bit the hole grew bigger. The golden tool never dulled or showed so much as a scratch from the hard use. Before retiring to bed he told his family of all that had happened. They were incredulous.

"After all", said the wife, "for all your work today what do you have? No jewels, no treasure, only fatigue and a small empty hole in the back yard."

He wouldn't be discouraged though. He kept remembering the dream from the night before and the old man's words. Exhausted, he fell asleep.

Each day the man went out to his backyard and dug deeper. The hole grew slowly. Weeks passed by in this way. The initial amazement of neighbors and friends wore off, becoming skepticism and scorn as the months went by. The man's enthusiasm faded along with the dreams of the old man. Finally, one night as he was getting ready to sleep, he told his wife he thought he would quit digging and take the spoon to the city, where it could be melted down and sold for its precious metal. She was delighted.

The man slept fitfully that night, and just before dawn he found himself in a dream. The old man appeared once again and told him not to give up, his toil was not in vain. Placing his hand on the family man's head, the old man seemed to draw out all his weariness and infuse him with renewed vigor. The dream ended. As the sun rose the man awoke determined to continue until the promised wealth was his.

Every day he worked in his backyard with the magic spoon. The hole continued to expand. After some years it was larger than his house, taking over the rest of his property. His son and daughter were nearly adults by now. The father rarely thought about the riches anymore. He simply went out each day and did the work the old man in the dream had told him to do.

One afternoon at sunset, just as the father was finishing his labors, something glowed from the depths of the excavation. He scampered down the sloping sides of the pit and there in the rock was a jewel filled with a faint light. Taking out his magic spoon, he used it to free the gem from the stone. It was perfectly exquisite. The gem rested in the palm of his hand, giving off a pale emerald light. " It must be priceless!" he thought.

His family was delighted over the newfound wealth, and the next day the father kept working. He sent his son to the city to sell the jewel. The son got a very good price but squandered some of the money on the way home. His father forgave him and continued digging with the magic spoon. Over time, more and more jewels appeared, but he and his family continued to live modestly while they saved up a cache of gems.

The old man appeared in a dream again and gave him several of the magic gold spoons. He instructed the father to tell everyone in the town that the same wealth could be theirs if they just used the magic spoon. He was to give one to anybody interested. The next day he offered them to people, but to his astonishment almost nobody took one! They either didn't believe him, or they wanted a guarantee of when jewels would start appearing for them. Week after week he tried to give away the magic spoons, but no takers came forward. He hoped that one day the villagers would finally discover the truth for themselves as he had. Occasionally a person would take a magic spoon and go home to begin the work, but invariably they would quit, complaining to the father that it demanded too much effort. Once a wanderer appeared, took the offering and disappeared. He was never seen again. The spoons mysteriously disappeared shortly thereafter.

The father had grown old and was near death. One evening he called his children to him and instructed them to continue using the magic spoon for the work of uncovering the treasures buried in the rock. He divided the store of jewels between them and told them to take good care of their mother for her few remaining years. Quite contented, he died.

Not long after his death the jewels ceased to appear. The family had more than enough stored up to allow them to live very comfortably for all their lives. The son wasn't the least bit interested in continuing to mine for the jewels. Instead, he satisfied himself traveling the world spending and investing his wealth in global trade. The sister carried on the work of digging alone. She enjoyed the solitude in the mine.

One day the brother returned after months of being away and learned that his mother had died. His sister continued to work the mine in their backyard. He tried to convince her that she should give up her futile endeavors. She had yet to find a single jewel, he argued, while his wealth was growing from all his business deals and trading. He left her to consider what he had said. She returned to her digging and thought about what she should do.

While working with the magic spoon in the depths of the mine, an old man dressed in fine robes studded with gems suddenly stood before her.

She remembered her father speaking of such an old man in his dreams. The old man told her to persevere, to keep digging, and more than mere treasure would be hers. As suddenly as he had appeared, he vanished. Later she told her brother of the apparition and his message. The brother said he had enough of old men in dreams and didn't want to deal with the mine anymore. The sister decided to trade her share of the remaining jewels from their father for the brother's share of the magic spoon and the mine. He took her up on the deal, forfeiting any claim to future finds in the mine. He was certain there wouldn't be any, and besides, with his growing financial empire, what did he care for a few jewels.

The young woman lived alone and continued her endeavors with the magic spoon. Her brother loved her and visited regularly to make sure she had all she needed to live. He couldn't understand how she could survive what appeared to him to be such an austere impoverished life. And what puzzled him even more was that she was so much happier and peaceful than he was.

"I have everything, I travel everywhere, and yet I'm still restless inside. How can this be?" he wondered to himself. He knew his sister no longer needed him, but he loved her company and came often to be with her. She found an occasional small jewel; this brought her enough to meet her simple needs and still be able to give some to those in need. Years went by in this way.

Early one evening the brother arrived home for one of his usual visits while his sister was still working alone deep in the mine. With a resounding crack, a fissure suddenly opened up in the rock-face deep within the mine and light streamed out! The sister wedged the magic spoon in the opening and the rock spread farther apart. The fissure expanded enough for her to climb through. A soft light emanated from within. At first she felt a bit afraid of going in there, until she remembered the old man saying to keep going, more than mere treasure would be hers. With great anticipation she stepped through the fissure into the heart of the earth.

In the soft light she could see a vast chamber of unimaginable proportions! Far off in what appeared to be the center of this immense cavern an exquisite orb of Light glowed, nearly too beautiful to behold! With its beams of Light it radiated love as the sun radiates warmth. She felt her own heart throbbing with love. Where she stood was dimly lit and shadowy, though she could see other people in the cavern. Those near her were dark and dense, while those closer to the Light were brighter. All were focused solely on the Light. Very slowly, imperceptibly, the Light drew them to itself. The ones who had moved nearer the Divine Effulgence were themselves lighter and clearer. The ones closest to the Light were nearly indistinguishable from the Light or each other; they sparkled like diamonds. Her gaze turned back to that magnificent Light. It stilled her mind, overwhelming it with divine beauty. Her consciousness became completely absorbed in the Light; she was no longer even aware of having a body.

Her brother heard the loud crack from the stone splitting open and ran to the mine. He called to his sister, and receiving no reply, he ventured down into the mine for the first time in his life. Fear threatened to overwhelm him as he made his way into the hidden depths of this dark unknown mine shaft. Only his love for his sister enabled him to overcome the fear.

At the very end of the tunnel he saw the fissure with the magic spoon wedged in it. A soft light streamed out through the crack. He yelled his sister's name once again, but still there was no response. The brother rushed toward the opening and caught a glimpse of his sister just before the fissure crashed shut. Only a portion of the spoon protruding from the rock marked where the opening had been just a moment before. He frantically tried opening the fissure, hurling himself at the sheer rock-face, but to no avail. He couldn't budge the spoon; it remained locked in the stone. His beloved sister was gone forever. Beating on the rock in anguish he cried aloud until, exhausted, he collapsed at the base of the tunnel.

"If only I had stayed with her, worked alongside of her, I could have prevented this terrible fate," he lamented. The earth swallowed her and answered neither his cries nor his regrets.

In desperation, the brother offered a huge reward to anyone who would open the rock and free his sister. Hundreds tried and all failed. Each year he increased the reward. Finally, on the seventh anniversary of her disappearance he let it be known that his entire fortune would go to the one who freed his beloved sister. Men using picks, drills and explosives assailed the stone with all their might, but the stone remained unscathed. Even witches and sorcerers tried casting their spells, only to find themselves cast out. No one could penetrate the rock.

As if out of nowhere an old man arrived in tattered robes walking with the support of a staff. People laughed as he slowly shuffled down into the mine. He never faltered as he descended. In the darkness a soft light could be seen surrounding him. The handle of the magic spoon stuck straight out of the rock at the end of the tunnel. It glimmered as his hand reached for it. Grasping hold of the golden handle he effortlessly turned it and the fissure reappeared, opening before him. Everyone gasped and stepped back. Before the brother could get there the old man stepped through the opening and the rock slammed shut behind him. Once again the entryway was barred to the brother.

Inside, the old man found the young lady. After seven years the Light had transfigured her. She was as clear as crystal, with Light radiating from her entire body. Love poured from her heart as she saw the old man, whom she recognized as the one from her earlier vision. To her he appeared in royal raiment of Light. He took her by the hand and led her back out. The stone split open and they passed out of the cavern. The brother and the whole crowd were awestruck by the sight of these two effulgent beings emerging from the fissure. They lit up the depths of the mine as if it were day The people fell to their knees in reverence before the holy ones.

They raised the people up and the brother rushed forward to embrace his beloved sister. Then he bowed to her with deep respect. Her love enveloped him as it did all who were near her. He called her the Holy Queen of Darkness and Light, for she reigned over both. People began shouting praises to the Holy Queen.

The old man now looked majestic, like a mighty and venerable king in his glowing robes. He told the people that all those who wished to know the Light must serve the Holy Queen with devotion and follow her commands with unflinching obedience. The brother asked how they could possibly continue as before, since the magic spoon had disappeared into the stone when it closed for the last time. The old man replied, "She will show you the way." Suddenly there was a blinding flash of light and he was gone! Only the Holy Queen knew what had become of him.

As they left the depths of the mine it began filling with water, wonderfully clear, life-giving water. In time that water softened the earth throughout the country, and flowers, trees, gardens, and waterfalls transformed the barren landscape. With the lush vegetation came all kinds of wildlife, and people here prospered as never before.

The Holy Queen blessed all who came to her. She instructed her brother and other seekers in the mysteries of Light. Those who were sincere took on a faint glow when the Holy Queen touched them. To invoke the Light and directly experience its transforming rays, she initiated them in the use of the Unspeakable Word, the Name of the Un-nameable, a practice done in silence that she had brought back from her journey into the depths beyond time and reason. Those who became adept at the practice were able to move about continuously bathed in light. To those with the vision to see, it looked as if a beautiful light was shining down upon them from just above their heads.

The vision ended a few minutes before I completed my morning chant. Playing the harmonium and chanting kept me focused and grounded in my body, even while part of my consciousness was completely immersed in the vision. As I continued chanting, my full awareness returned to my body. Chanting made the transition back to waking-state consciousness smoother than it had been when I tried coming directly out of a meditation vision. For several days afterward my meditations were filled with images from the vision, and in a way similar to what occurred with the Queen's journey, the meaning and importance of segments from it would present themselves in my mind. You might add these interpretations and insights to the one's you discover for yourself.

The barren landscape with the houses imprisoned behind rock walls represents the condition of an individual's ego-directed existence in a shallow, dry materialistic world. The individual in this cultural setting is little concerned with spiritual life, he dwells in a place lacking depth, and his pursuits are predominantly survival-related. Surviva' here means more than just biological survival, it includes the ego's constant efforts to sustain itself and its world view. Our western culture marks success in material dimensions and often gives only lip service to recognizing the existence of spiritual depths worth exploring and developing. One who pursues a path of the spirit is often misunderstood, and in the worst cases, is ridiculed or even persecuted. The ego, whether it is our own or someone else's, loathes admitting the existence of the Self or the Divine within that is so overwhelmingly greater than it is. It can tolerate the existence of the Absolute if such a thing is kept a safe distance away, in heaven or in the form of a dead saint. And it can tolerate one's spirituality as long as it is safely contained, limited to a Saturday or Sunday morning. But the ego rebels when it comes to recognizing the Divine inhabiting the same body that it does, and when the needs of the spirit take precedence over its desires. Divine intervention, the direct impact of the transcendent Self on the individual, is required to uplift a person's path through life and free one from the ego's perspective.

The family man symbolizes, in part, the individual living an ordinary life bound by limitations both self-imposed and culturally determined. In this way he represents ordinary waking-state ego consciousness. The richly dressed old man in his dreams symbolizes the Self, our inner guide, the transcendent function present in everyone. He directs the man through a dream, a time when the ego's grip over consciousness is weaker than usual. Each time he awakens, the ego mode of consciousness reasserts itself, denying what was given to it in the dream state. We frequently do this to ourselves by denying or devaluing knowledge and wisdom made accessible to us in our dreams, meditation or in spontaneous altered states of consciousness we might enter, such as the insights and intuitions we receive when we're in reverie states. Each time the father awakens, he goes through the doubting and denying of his dream experience and then returns to sleep. Once asleep, out of the grips of ego-consciousness, the old man prods him further along, overcoming his denial, until the final segment of the dream, in which he is actually given a means to break out of his barren shallow existence. He doesn't wake up, some level of ego-resistance has been overcome, allowing him to receive the gift and remain asleep. When he awakens naturally, not by the prompting of the ego needing to escape into waking consciousness, he finds the golden spoon in his hand. He has grasped the means to set himself free while in a state of consciousness that gave him access to wisdom and resources not available to his waking-state mind. In that deeper state he was promised great treasure if he were willing to go beyond the surface, to dig into the earth, the symbol of the ground of all existence. Entering altered states of consciousness through meditation, prayer, chanting, movement, or some other effective means is necessary to free consciousness from the binding limitations of ordinary waking state consciousness.

The golden spoon seems so small, almost insignificant; yet it's gold, it's invaluable, it has the power to cut through the rock-hard layers of concepts, karmas, and ignorance that cut us off from the Light in our heart, the Light of the Self at the core of our being. The gold spoon may be the potent mantra that seems so small, only a few syllables, or the deceptively simple meditation practice, or the prayer that a genuine master gives the seeker. Yet, it has the full power to take you into the depths.

The earth of the backyard that is to be entered through the mine symbolizes the divine Mother who gives birth to everything, who contains within her all that is or ever will be. In this form she symbolizes the totality our unconscious which contains within it the Light of the Self. Until we're aware of the Self, it's Light is buried in our unconscious. The Self takes on the figure of the old man, manifesting the power of grace, the power of Self-revelation, and compels the father to begin opening up a way into these greater depths. This is exactly what a true spiritual guide does. For some rare individuals it may be that they encounter their spiritual master only in dreams or visions. For the person confronting the dry existence of a life without depth, a life without spirit, the action demanded of them is to begin digging in their own backyard. They don't have to run away somewhere or try to be someone else.

The Shakti said, "Just dig. Start going deeper right where you are. You'll need a wise person to guide you and give you a golden tool to penetrate the hard ground of your existence. Once you have the golden means, the command to go deeper, and the knowledge of the great attainment to be had, your longing will keep pressing you onward."

At this point in the story the father, symbolizing our ego, hasn't entirely embraced the notion of breaking through the familiar boundaries of his existence. The ego-self continues to demean the gift of the Self and ridicules the notion that one can go beyond the ego's realm, that of the barren landscape. But the gifts of grace, the golden spoon, and dream visions of the old man, are so real, so compelling that the father puts aside his concerns of embarrassment, the ego's concerns, and puts the tool to use. As promised, it works. This scenario captures the ego's dilemma of having to act on the intuitions or inspirations that come from our depths. By doing so the ego is admitting there's something else within us with greater wisdom, greater resources, greater power than the ego itself. In the face of such an influx of grace or inspiration, the ego will do all it can to dismiss the inspiration as meaningless, just a dream, or indigestion from the meal eaten the night before. Often the ego will do almost anything to deny the reality of the transcendent experience in order to preserve itself. Another of the ego's strategies for preservation, not depicted here, is to take over the experience, to identify itself with the source of the wisdom and power, inflating itself in the process. The man in this myth demonstrates what happens when the experience of grace is so strong that it can't be denied and the ego has to serve the transcendent Self by acting in accord with what has been given to it.

At such a point the ego's resistance may go underground. We know what to do in order to act in accord with our higher Self, yet we find ourselves not doing it. (There are psychological difficulties other than the ego that can thwart one's progress on the quest. These may have to be resolved through psychotherapy.) We may have an experience in meditation that shows us the extraordinary value of meditation for bringing the Self into our day-to-day life, but then we're too tired to get up in the morning to meditate, or we forgot, or whatever the excuse may be. Much of spiritual practice and discipline involves retraining the ego to serve the Self, the true master, instead of itself. In fact, the word discipline comes from the Latin meaning "to accept, to learn," and a disciple is one who does so willingly. Through the master-disciple relationship the ego learns how to willingly accept the commands of the Self, of God. The outer relationship is a model for developing the inner relationship of surrender and obedience to the Divine. The self becomes the disciple of the Self.

The father, compelled by the kingly old man in his dreams and the golden spoon he has in hand, surrenders his judgment that it's impossible to penetrate the rock and attempts it. The spoon glides into the rock, chipping a piece free. The golden means, be it a mantra, breath meditation, or prayer, received from a true person of wisdom, can cut through the hardened barriers separating us from the Light. The golden spoon is a vehicle of grace. By experiencing the potency of grace the man is opened further to the possibility that the rest of what was revealed to him may be true, that great treasures could lay beneath the ground. This is the way faith develops, faith based on our own experience. For this reason yoga, like many spiritual disciplines, emphasizes direct personal experience. At first we may consider the possibility of something being true based on another person's experience; that may be what opens the door of disbelief far enough for us to try a spiritual practice or meet a teacher, but eventually we have to experience the truth for ourselves.

After discovering for ourselves that the practices given by the master work and after the rock imprisoning the heart is penetrated, we then encounter our next set of expectations. Does the practice result in the gains we thought should take place? Does it produce what we want as quickly as we want it? Do love and bliss suddenly fill our every moment? No. Like the father we may find our initial enthusiasm and belief in the miraculous nature of the mantra or the meditation practice eroded by the cynicism and disbelief of others or by our unrealistic expectations going unfulfilled. To dig as deeply as one needs to requires a sustained effort over a long period of time, even with the awakened Kundalini wielding a shovel!

After months of digging, the man falls into a state of disillusionment and begins to view the golden spoon for only its material worth. His wife agrees wholeheartedly that he should sell the magic spoon for its gold. Family and friends welcome his giving up what they consider to be a crazy endeavor. As long as he continues it he is challenging their worldview. As it is, they have left him alone in his pursuit rather than confront the shallowness of their own lives and their inability to penetrate the ground of their existence. People engaged in their spiritual quest are sometimes puzzled by the lack of support and outright negativity that some friends, family members, or co-workers exhibit. Someone implicitly disputing their fundamental values and beliefs may unconsciously threaten these people. Seeking something more from life calls into question the conventional or materialistic values of many people.

The wife in part symbolizes a form of the inner feminine principle in men that C. G. Jung called the anima. In this case she is represented as one who is conventional, who can't relate to the spiritual because she has already been trained by the culture in what to want, what to value, what to consider worthy of putting one's efforts toward. Maybe there's a part of you that can't relate to being directed from within, directed by dreams and a figure of the inner Self. You might have to recognize that he or she represents an attitude that is a part of yourself and not think it is someone in your outer life who is keeping you from pursuing your quest. Spouses often receive such projections and are then viewed as the obstacle to the other person's spiritual development. If we have her (or a similar "him") within ourselves, then we need to be compassionate with her, embracing her as part of our psyche, without being ruled by her. We can care for her and help her to understand the great value of our spiritual endeavor. We can work with that part of ourselves so she can see how she's imprisoned by the values and beliefs she uses to judge our longing to go deeper. Perhaps we'll even be able to share with her the joy and expansiveness that comes from going beyond the familial and cultural walls that imprison us. Or, we may just detach from her and let her come to her natural end, as happens later on with the mother in relation to the daughter. The daughter comes to symbolize the positive feminine principle that can lead one into the depths, to the Light at one's core.

Just as the family man is about to abandon his digging and sell the spoon, the bestower of grace in the form of the royally dressed old man once again appears to him in a dream, outside the bounds of ego-dominated consciousness. The old man, symbol of the Self, reaffirms the truth that the father's efforts are not in vain and bestows grace through the divine touch. He lays his hand on the father's head and infuses him with vitality and strength of will. From that point on the father is no longer influenced by the lack of support from those around him and his determination never fails him again.

When we are touched by the Self it radically transforms our life, our actions, our relationships, everything. The man comes to this point after having prepared the ground; he has steadily dug deeper and deeper for months on end, keeping in constant contact with the vehicle of grace, the golden spoon. This is very similar to using the mantra regularly, or doing the profoundly simple breath awareness practice given by a teacher. It takes you deeper and deeper, purifying you and opening you up as you continue to use it. But the ego's efforts have a limit, and that kind of self-effort alone will not take us all the way. Grace is essential.

Self-effort, while necessary, can also breed pride. The poison of pride calls upon itself a fall that is a grace-filled remedy if it is swallowed with a draft of remorse. A Christian mystic, one of the early desert fathers, said, "If you see a young monk by his own will climbing into heaven, take him by the foot and throw him to the ground, because what he is doing is not good for him."[3]

The man then comes to a point of despair, feeling he has to give up his fruitless endeavor. He sleeps restlessly in conflict over it. The ego has to give up, to realize that it can't take over the spiritual practices, and it can't make it on its own. It has been given free reign to go as far as it could, but it can't carry consciousness into the depths. Having the experience of reaching the limits of one's own ego-commanded willpower is part of preparing the ground, part of opening our consciousness up so that we can receive more fully the grace of the Divine. This is part of the ego's training to become a good servant: first it has to be humbled. Our ego wants to believe it is the master, so it has to be shown its own folly, usually many, many times! To the extent that we are identified with the ego/mind we will suffer its humiliations right along with it. A wise friend once told me, "If the mind goes crazy, don't go with it." There are other options. We can step back from the ego/mind and support it learning its lessons without being caught up in its drama. As you can imagine, this takes considerable practice, dispassion, and detachment!

As long as you are identified solely with ego-consciousness, you live in a state of total confusion. You think you *are* what you're *not* and you think you're *not* what you *are*. Confusing enough? You think you are the bound and limited mental and physical instruments that you inhabit. We live in the delusion of taking the mind and body as our essential being. We think we are not divine, we're not God, we're not the Self. People consider the Divine Self to be either nonexistent or separated from them by some great distance. The truth is that you are the Self and the mind/body is your creation. The mind/body is your instrument created by you for manifesting your divinity on this level of existence. The instrument exists to serve its master—God, your true Self.

An influx of divine energy from the old man's touch is required to pull the man out of his despair. After receiving this in a dream he acts almost solely out of obedience to the divine will, the command to keep digging. He doesn't concern himself with material rewards or other ego desires. He simply goes out each day to fulfill his duty, his dharma, with little interest in what will come of it. Almost as if to prove his detachment and perseverance, he continues to dig for years without any outward signs of reward. He's being transformed on the inside. He rarely even thinks of the riches anymore. It's at this point, when he is completely detached from the results of his actions, that the jewels begin to appear. Doing one's daily work and spiritual practices in a selfless way, free of desires and free of expectations, creates a delightful spaciousness in one's spirit, a spaciousness that the Divine finds very inviting. The man receives the precious gifts, the jewels that are luminous, otherworldly. This symbolizes the time in sadhana when meditation and the practices have created the openness to receive the gifts from the Goddess that infuse life with new richness and meaning. These inner riches, mined from the depths of one's own being, become one's primary support.

But all is not well in this story. The jewels are sold and hoarded. They're used for their material benefits alone. The father doesn't look beyond the physical, he doesn't contemplate his experiences by asking himself how could this spoon have such a mysterious power, what is the source of its power, where do the jewels come from, are they the "great treasure" the old man spoke of, what lies deeper within the earth, what other treasures or secrets does she hold, who is the old man and where does he come from? These and many other questions fail to ever occur to the man. His vision of the world is so materially based that his mind can't even think of looking beyond the physical universe. He remains separate from the Self, from the source of grace, though he lives totally supported by it. In obedience to the command of the Self to dig into the depths of the earth, he penetrates the hard surface and enters a deeper level of existence, but his understanding remains superficial.

He's content with the material rewards he receives for his efforts and doesn't transcend them. This may be the reason he is unable to inspire anyone to take the golden spoons and begin the practice of digging. Since he's never experienced or understood the source of the spoon's power he can't communicate its true potency. I've met teachers like that who have experienced gains from some practice and sincerely want to pass it on to others, but they are not able to give more than the form of their practice. The power is missing. Unfortunately, people receiving instruction in a practice from an unqualified teacher are too often soured on the spiritual pursuit because of their ensuing lack of success.

Beyond the spoon and a hoard of jewels, the father is not able to pass anything on to his family, either. He dies content, but in this instance contentment is an enemy. It prevented him from looking beyond the obvious, beyond the material rewards of his practice. He had obedience and surrender, he had what the Shakti mentioned earlier, the golden means and the command to dig, but he had no longing, no seeking, no inquisitiveness that would have saved him from his passivity and unquestioned materialism. Being a seeker or a disciple doesn't mean being passive in relation to the Divine or in relation to the teacher.

The fifteenth century poet-saint Kabir wrote:[4]

Friend, hope for the Guest while you are alive.
Jump into experience while you are alive!
Think…and think…while you are alive.
What you call 'salvation' belongs to the time before death.

If you don't break your ropes while you're alive,
do you think
ghosts will do it after?

The idea that the soul will join with the ecstatic
just because the body is rotten—
that is all fantasy.
What is found now is found then.
If you find nothing now,
you will simply end up with an apartment in the
     City of Death.
If you make love with the divine now, in the next life
     you will have the face of satisfied desire.

So plunge into the truth, find out who the Teacher is,
     Believe in the Great Sound!
Kabir says this: When the Guest is being searched for,
     it is the intensity of the longing for the Guest that
     does all the work.
Look at me, and you will see a slave of that intensity.

The father's type of shallow contentment is really complacency, and it can arise in sadhana when grace is supporting our lives and a certain level of ease is established. The ego may seem more subtle or surrendered here. It's willing to do the practices because it finds the emotional and material stability they provide comforting. Like the father, our limited sense of self may have its cache of gems, meditation experiences, visions, or spiritual teachings that it holds onto and drags out during dry spells, not quite trusting the ever-present, abundant nature of the Self. It avoids questioning the value of its gems, it wants to cling to what it already has. It withholds from giving with true selflessness and loving abandon. Times like these require the compassionate prodding of the mystic guide or the relentless push of the inner guru, the awakened Kundalini.

The father dies and the son and daughter carry on the dual nature of his endeavors, material and spiritual. The son symbolizes the material path and its outcomes while the daughter embodies the spiritual path. The father's death symbolizes the necessary death of an old set of attitudes, a part of one's personality, or an old approach to the spiritual quest. Since the father embodied an attitude that was superficial and content with achieving material comfort, his death signifies the end of that. He served as a starting point for the process and he was able to make it to a certain depth, but he couldn't take consciousness any deeper. On the spiritual journey we may feel like a part of us is dying, we may even feel like we're dying if we're really identified with the part that has to go. Any materialism we have has to die, along with whatever else we're carrying that is an obstacle. This doesn't mean we can't enjoy material goods, it means not being stuck on that level of reality.

Death symbolizes the dissolution of a bound form. As some parts of our self die, the energy that is freed from those forms is made available to other parts of our self, which carry on in new ways. These little deaths may be followed by a dry spell, when nothing appears to be happening; the jewels we were accustomed to aren't appearing.

The father and mother had offspring who can continue the quest. The daughter embodies a new attitude and approach, she becomes the heroine, the redeemer. In contrast, the brother abandons the mine and the practice of digging, preferring to pursue the form of wealth he's most attracted to.

He pours his energy and attention into the material world and, like his father, gets stuck there.

The sister continued obeying the father's wish, and in that way the command of the Self or the master, by digging deeper and deeper in the mine. It wasn't enough for the father and what he symbolized to have come to an end; the mother and brother had to go also. It wasn't until after the death of the mother and the buy-out of the brother's share of the mine that the young woman's efforts began to show results. The mother symbolized a conventional viewpoint that didn't recognize the value of pursuing what is unknown or unheard of. She discouraged her husband's initial efforts and wanted him to sell the spoon for its gold. She had no feeling for his endeavor until it yielded money, material results. It took her death and the symbolic removal of the brother for the daughter's new way of engaging in the quest to develop and yield its fruit.

The brother returned after the mother died and tried to dissuade his sister from her efforts. This symbolizes the return of the worldly, materialistic attitude trying to influence her and test her resolve. He's like his father but with the look of a new generation. He seems more expanded than the father, he's richer and travels the globe, but essentially he's superficial and materialistic. In response to him she retreats into the depths of the mine and her practice of digging to consider what he's said. It's there that the Self makes itself known to her in the form of the wise old man and promises her more than mere wealth if she perseveres. She's free enough of ego to receive the divine presence not in a dream but right before her in the mine. She chooses the depths and her practice of digging as the sacred place to take refuge in while contemplating what her brother had said to her. She doesn't avoid confronting the arguable stance of her brother, but instead takes it to a place of depth and opens herself to grace. That allows for the possibility of an inconceivable outcome, a resolution that could never be brought about by the ego/mind. Only the transcendent Self, the grace-bestower, can intervene in such a way and promise more than material wealth. We can take our dilemmas and struggles into the sacred space of our practices—offer them up in prayer, contemplate, do self-inquiry, and seek the counsel of those whose wisdom we respect. This allows for unimaginable developments to occur. Additionally, the ego avoids getting caught in "I'm doing it all by myself," the pride of doership and surrenders to a higher power, making room for grace to transform the situation or transform how we perceive and deal with the situation.

Inspired by the old man she dedicates herself to mining the depths with the magic spoon. Unlike her father, though, she has an idea of rewards beyond wealth and treasures. She doesn't know what they are but trusts her intuition and her sense that the wise old man spoke the truth. She commits herself to going deeper and acts on that commitment by giving up what wealth she has in order to purchase her brother's share of the spoon and the mine. She is willing to sacrifice all that she has to take full possession of her pursuit. At this point her digging is no longer contaminated by her father, mother, or brother and what they symbolized. The woman, symbolizing our soul, needs to have her spiritual practice freed from the influences of past generations, freed from conventional materialistic attitudes and any other cultural and familial contaminants.

Prayer is a good example of a practice needing to be purified of contamination. Many people are struggling to discover the real power of prayer, but too often prayer is taught as a way to get something—get rich, win the lotto, get healthy, gain victory, get forgiveness, etc. Rarely is it a purely spiritual practice; instead it's taught as a way of approaching God like a beggar, and often a greedy beggar at that. How often is the sublime practice of prayer done solely to commune with God? Not that we shouldn't pray for help, abundance, or blessings, but why not *also* draw near to God as a friend or a lover, asking for nothing more than His company? When Jesus said the Kingdom of God lies within, where did you think the King dwelt? When the King is inviting you to dine with Him in His palace, why go to the scullery door and beg for scraps?

The sister frees herself of the last remnants of the contamination by putting all she has on the line to buy out her brother. Almost immediately her efforts and sacrifice yield unasked for treasures. When we act on our commitment to our quest and take full ownership of it, the universe responds, and we receive the gifts of grace. Self-effort draws grace.

The brother symbolizes the impoverished state of one cut off from his or her depths. He depends on his sister for such nourishment. He comes to be with her and is amazed that in the midst of austere conditions she's happier than he is. Many men develop so one-sidedly that they are dependent on an external, usually feminine, source for contact with a deeper side of life. In an attempt to hide or deny their spiritual need they may try to maintain the image of seeking such contact because the woman needs them. Some men are not only in denial of their spiritual needs but threatened by them. They often attack or ridicule other's spiritual pursuits, especially the spiritual interests of women in their lives, in an attempt to keep their unfulfilled needs at bay in their unconscious. In this case the brother isn't in that bad of a state. His inner restlessness is the stirring of discontent that may lead him out of his lopsided development.

If we don't try to assuage discontent with a new form of diversion—a new movie, different restaurant, new spouse, or job change—then discontent can reveal its intelligence. To do this we have to be willing to sit with the discomfort, to open ourselves to the discontent and ask it to show us what needs to be changed inside as well as outside. That can be quite scary, but the clarity and revitalization that come from it are great treasures in themselves.

The brother's discontent and restlessness compel him to return to be with his sister. She is his spiritual center, and he comes back to her over and over again. His bond with her saves him from getting totally lost in the world. When he does visit her he doesn't join her in digging; he makes no effort to enter the depths himself. He just sponges off her energy. Wisely, she doesn't concern herself with him. She doesn't try to get him to dig, she doesn't lecture him about his lifestyle; she doesn't try to change him in any way. The sister is totally independent and fully engaged in treading her path. She's not distracted by the material value of the jewels and gives away everything beyond what her basic needs require. Her work is in the mine and her dedication to her task makes her life simple. Being focused on our spiritual pursuit allows all but a few essential needs to fall away. She invests her energy solely in her practice. The brother has amassed material wealth while she has amassed inner wealth, spiritual wealth. He's restless; she's at peace. He remains on the surface while she proceeds into the heart of the earth, the Great Mother, where at last the divine Self reveals itself as pure Light and Love. By fulfilling her quest she is ultimately empowered to really help him.

The sister labored with the support of grace to arrive at the sheer rock face at the base of the tunnel, not knowing it was the last barrier separating her from the very core of all existence. The Divine puts such a barrier in place. It symbolizes the barrier between the realm of unity, the abode of the Divine, and the illusory realm of separateness. The barrier is a manifestation of the Lord's power of concealment, Maya Shakti, the divine power that creates the drama of being cut off from the Divine Self and having to merge with it once again. Maya Shakti can only be overcome by the divine power of revelation, the power of grace that allows one to ultimately recognize one's unbroken union with the Light. In the *Bhagavad Gita* the Lord says:

> How hard to break through
> Is this, my Maya...
> But he who takes refuge
> Within me only
> Shall pass beyond Maya:
> He, and no other.[5]

She has to set aside her fear of entering the inner abode of the Light. We can encounter a little remnant of ego that fears being annihilated by the Divine Effulgence. The power of the master's words gets her past that obstacle and into the vast inner spaciousness. Strengthened by the old man's promise that more than mere wealth would be hers, she's ready to enter the inner sanctum, to take refuge in the dwelling place of the Lord. She goes through the fissure that was opened by the golden spoon. The seemingly insignificant practice is the key to opening the way to the Divine. This a point of no return, a point where she abandons the outer world completely and is swallowed up by the great Goddess, symbolized by the earth. It's the Divine Effulgence in the heart of the earth that draws her and holds her there. The Light symbolizes the Self, the Absolute, buried deep in the unconscious, beneath the surface appearances of the world. It's also a symbolic configuration that says the Absolute is literally "in the world" just as it is above and beyond the world, as depicted in the symbolic image from the Queen's journey where the Light is above the highest mountaintop. The Self is both above and beyond the world and at the very heart of the world. The symbol of the immensely spacious cavern with the Divine Light at the center also speaks of the world having as its support, its foundation, the void; and at the center of the void, illuminating it, is the Light of Consciousness. By the power of Consciousness, the darkness of the void is known.

She discovers she's not alone there. Others have made it to this holy center before her and are being transformed by the Light. The Light draws all of humanity to it. In one way or another we are all seeking that Light. When we see it reflected in the things of the world we go after them, and eventually, in one life or another, we make it past these outer forms. We also have to make it past the inner reflections, more spectacular than the best of the outer world. Finally we make it to the realm of Light as the sister did. From then on the Light of the Self draws her ever nearer and effects the final transfiguration. Though many are there, each is totally alone, absorbed in the Light. The Light consumes everything. There's just you and the Light, then there's just Light.

Merging into the Light and abandoning the outer world is spoken of by mystics and saints of every tradition. When that Divine Light is seen it may totally captivate the seeker so that nothing else matters. Not that he or she literally won't do anything else; rather, all their dutiful actions will be bent to realization and service of God. All their feelings and motives will be related to the Absolute. Those who come to embody the Light illumine and enliven the earth in untold ways.

The sister experiences the divine love radiating from the Light and for the first time feels her own heart throbbing with love. In his great spiritual work, *The Adornment of the Spiritual Marriage*, the fourteenth century Catholic priest and Christian mystic, John van Ruysbroeck, writes of this encounter with the Divine:

> In this storm of love two spirits strive together: the spirit of God and our own spirit. God, through the Holy Ghost, inclines Himself towards us; and, thereby, we are touched in love. And our spirit, by God's working and by the power of love, presses and inclines itself into God and, thereby, God is touched. From these two contacts there arises the strife of love, at the very deeps of this meeting; and in that most inward and ardent encounter, each spirit is deeply wounded by love. These two spirits, that is, our own spirit and the Spirit of God, sparkle and shine one into the other, and each shows to the other its face. This makes each of the spirits yearn for the other in love. Each demands of the other all that is; and each offers to the other all that it is and invites it to all that it is. This makes the lovers melt into each other. God's touch and His gifts, our loving craving and our giving back, these fulfill love. This flux and reflux causes the fountain of love to brim over and thus the touch of God and our loving craving become one simple love. Here man is possessed by love, so that he must forget himself and God, and knows and can do nothing but love. Thereby the spirit is burned up in the fire of love, and enters so deeply into the touch of God, that it is overcome in all its cravings, and

turned to naught in all its works, empties itself; above all surrender becoming very love.[6]

In this Divine encounter the sister loses consciousness of her body. The physical universe ceases to exist for her in the presence of that Light. Many people experience the loss of body-consciousness in meditative states. Extended periods are harder to sustain for the obvious reason that waking-state reality demands action in the physical world. The needs of the body, family, and work call one back. In a society that values doing and accomplishing only in the physical realm, it is challenging to discover ways in which one can retreat for prolonged periods from the demand of having one's consciousness engrossed in the world of doing. Certainly being on retreat isn't the goal of spiritual practices any more than starting a fruit tree in a greenhouse means the seedling should forever remain in such a protected environment. When it is strong enough it is set out to harden off, mature, and develop its luscious fruit. In the daily practice of meditation and during retreats we greatly reduce the amount of ordinary waking-state demands that habitually hold our consciousness to waking-state reality. In that protected environment we nurture the growing awareness of the ever-present Absolute, the Divine Self. As our experience of it develops we are increasingly able to maintain access to it at all other times. The *Shiva Sutras* (I,7) state: "Even during the three different states of consciousness in waking, dreaming, and profound sleep, the rapturous experience of I-consciousness of the fourth, turiya, state abides."[7] That fourth state of turiya is the transcendental pure I-consciousness, the Divine Witness, to which the seeker abandons herself.

Our spirit needs time to separate itself from the world entirely in order to enter the realm of the Living Light. As one repeatedly enters the state of being in the presence of the Light, self-effort accounts for little more than raising one's sail to catch the winds of grace. The Light alone works to totally transform not only the sister's consciousness but her body as well. Seekers must have time to regularly bask in the transformative rays of the inner Light. In our daily routine we have time and activities dedicated to meeting our bodily needs for sustenance and rest, we invest time and energy in meeting our emotional needs and ego needs, and our home has space dedicated to these needs—kitchen, dining room, bathroom, bedroom and living room. Where's the chapel or the meditation room? How much time and attention do we give to our spiritual needs on a daily basis? What if every home had in it a sacred room or even just a sacred corner to which family members could retreat and gather wisdom and joy from deeper levels to share with each other? What about having such a place at work? Imagine how that would transform the ways we treat one another and our environment.

The brother tries to enter the realm of Light but the way is barred to him. He hasn't done any of the purifying spiritual work, the tapasya, required to enter that Divine Presence. He hasn't taken refuge in God. But his love for his sister keeps him totally focused on that realm without his really knowing it. For seven years he does his own kind of meditation on his sister. During this time his attachment to the world and his wealth grows weaker as his longing for his sister grows stronger. His focus on her is allowing him to receive grace, and he's being transformed. This is a classic technique that the sage Patanjali offers in *The Yoga Sutras* (I, 37), for purifying and stilling the mind "by meditating on the heart of an illumined soul that is free from passion."[8]

Through the brother it is shown that the object of meditation doesn't have to be the conventional image, word, or truth used to absorb one's attention. The brother's love for his sister naturally focused all his attention on her. The sister's purity and detachment made her a suitable object for meditation. The Shakti, the power of Grace, will use whatever works to uplift and transform the seeker. Once a man went to a meditation master and received instruction in the use of a mantra. He went home and tried to practice the way the teacher had told him to, but he got nowhere. After some frustrating months he returned to the master and told him of his failure. The master looked at him with great compassion and asked him what he loved. The man was a sheepherder and loved his sheep. He began telling the teacher about how he cared for them up in the hills all by himself. The teacher told him to meditate on his sheep and the love he feels for them. The herder was delighted; he knew he could do this. He returned to the mountains excited by his new meditation practice, and over time his love expanded to encompass the world. His attainment was complete.

At the brother's invitation people tried every means conceivable, physical and occult, to open the way to the Divine Light, though none succeed. No one can enter the domain of Light through gross, willful means. The barrier was created by the Divine and can only be opened by the Divine. Forceful breathing techniques, visualizations, and crystals alone will not open the way to union with the Goddess or make the Kundalini Shakti move according to one's desires. Some people think they can simply imagine what they think is the Kundalini moving up the sushumna through the chakras, like an elevator going up its shaft, and they will get off at the top floor, the sahasrar. The Shakti is the power of God, the power of Consciousness that creates the mind. She doesn't obey the will of the petty self or the imaginings of the mind. While the individual is busy fantasizing the movements of Kundalini through the subtle body and imagining directing the energy to go here and there, the Shakti is laughing in ecstasy at the play of Maya, illusion.

The Shakti reigns supreme, She alone commands and is never commanded. By nature She is loving and compassionate. She responds to heartfelt prayer. With love and humility you can pray to Her and ask Her to reveal Her presence in your life, ask Her to reveal Her presence in your body, and you can pray to Her asking Her to move through the subtle body, bringing the transformative power of Her great Light into all areas. And then wait with a quiet mind for Her gifts. When you receive Her gifts, in whatever form they may be, offer a prayer of gratitude. When you receive a gift of grace unfold it completely, appreciate it fully, take it into your heart. In this way you'll be transformed by it.

God's gifts can look so dazzling that people mistake the wrapping for the present. They may not open all the layers of the gift and thus miss what was hidden more deeply within.

The brother shows his readiness to receive when he finally offers everything he owns, just as his sister did. His sacrifice eventually gains him access to the Light through his sister. He will have to follow her command to attain the Light.

Only when the brother sacrifices everything does the humble old man, unrecognized by all, arrive and effortlessly open the way to the Light, though the brother is still barred. The old man symbolizes the grace-bestower, the spiritual master, and grace alone opens the way to the Divine. People laughed at the old man as he entered the mine. Those who think they can see power and mastery are blind on this level. They can't perceive the great force of the spiritual preceptor. The grace-bestower, the mystic guide, goes from one realm to another with ease and delight. He descends effortlessly into the depths of the mine. The old man takes hold of the golden spoon and opens the way into the expanses of the inner realm of Light. It remains barred to the brother. He has more sadhana, more spiritual practices, to do.

In the realm of Light the old man's true nature is revealed. Before the Light, everyone's true nature is exposed. He is the king in full splendor, both one with the Light and separate from it, roaming the world bestowing grace. The sister knows who he is and follows him as she has for many years. It was his command that brought her to the realm of Light. Now she radiates that very Light. He brought her back to the ordinary realm of humanity to bring the Light of grace into the lives of all who come to her. After that he merged back into Light, into the pure Consciousness from which he came, thus revealing his unity with that Light.

His presence was necessary to bring her back out of the Light into the world. She could have remained absorbed in the Light forever, but at the command of the master, at the command of the Light in that form, she returned to the world to serve the spark in every soul longing to return to the great fire of God. Not every soul that attains the Light will return to serve in this way. Many simply stay absorbed in the Light and through their physical body they serve as a channel for God's grace to pour into the realm of human existence. Others return to their ordinary daily lives, bringing the Light with them, illuminating the world around them through their compassion, their love, and their selflessness.

The sister was called upon to be a mystic guide, a spiritual master. Because she dispelled the darkness, bringing Light wherever she went, she was known as the Queen of Darkness and Light. Indeed her touch kindled the Light in those who sought her company with an open heart. Some people are wary of the touch of a great being. Perhaps they sense that once their spirit is inflamed, it will consume much that is familiar and safe.

The Shakti said, "How many are prepared to dance with fire? Will you embrace the living flame of divine love? Will you leap with ecstatic abandon into the fire of God's love? Will you allow all but your golden essence to be burned away?"

There are others who avoid the Light. They're not yet ready to look into their own darkness. They don't mind looking at other people's darkness, finding faults and making judgments. When it comes time to step into the Light, they either run away or hide behind an image of themselves. The Light is within them, so where can they hide? Have compassion for them as you would for a child who is afraid of the dark. Hold them by the hand and reassure them.

The radiant King announces to the people that the Queen will lead them into the Light. Together the King and Queen are the transcendent and immanent dimensions of God. He merges back into the transcendent Light. As the manifest power of God, she remains to guide people into transcendence. Because the sister entered the depths and gave herself to the Light she opened a way for the life-giving waters to well up, making a paradise for many where there had been only barren rock.

The mine created by her efforts filled with life-sustaining water that softened and enlivened the whole countryside. When we make an effort to open a way into the depths of our Self, then there wells up an enlivening flow of energy, of grace, that gives our life an extraordinarily vital quality. People often feel reborn when this occurs. When an individual makes it all the way to the source of Light and the life-giving water, then a great channel is opened that serves many people. The whole countryside is brought to life. The community that lived on that barren land was in desperate need of water. Our culture is in a similar condition. The Queen had spent years in solitary pursuit of her spiritual goal, nurtured by grace. Now her attainment is a boon to all. Everyone and everything around her prospers. Individually and collectively we need to recognize the enormous benefit that comes from going deep within oneself.

The sister becomes the spiritual master who can pass the Light to others. Like the Queen in the vision of the Kundalini's journey, in the end she represents the embodiment of the fully evolved Kundalini Shakti. She has the power to kindle the fire in others with her touch, and afterward they take on a faint glow. She becomes the means to their enlightenment, replacing the golden spoon. The people, her brother included, rejoice at having her with them. It's a great blessing to live in the company of a holy being and best to keep their company on the inside. How many people can make it to God without a spiritual teacher or mystic guide, relying only on a practice, a mantra, a truth, or the inspiration from a vision? With her they have a model, a guide, a person who can give instructions, corrections, and encouragement as needed.

She initiates people into a mystical practice, the Unspeakable Word, the Name of the Un-nameable. She doesn't merely instruct; any book or teacher can do that. A true master gives initiation. With initiation there is a transfer of power and knowledge to the initiate that gives her or him access to the impenetrable mystery that the uninitiated do not have. She initiates seekers into a practice to invoke the Light, to invoke God's power and presence.

The Unspeakable Word is the Name of the Un-nameable—the Godhead, God in full transcendent glory and power. It's not that the

Unspeakable Word can't be vocalized, it can. *Om*. Om is one form of the Unspeakable Word. It's not that the Un-nameable isn't named. Om. Om is a Name of the Un-nameable, along with Kali, Allah, God, Yahweh, Shakti, Shiva, and thousands of others, but the name and the vocalization themselves aren't the Godhead. However, with grace you may be able to use them to draw near the Divine.

The Shakti said:

> When you unfurl a sail to catch the wind, the sail is visible, the wind is not. You use the visible to catch the invisible. You use the perceptible to approach the imperceptible. At first you may sound aloud the word Om over and over again. Om...Om...Om...Om...Om...In time you stop sounding Om and continue repeating it silently within your mind, focusing your entire attention on it. Om...Om...Om...Om...Om....There's no audible sound, yet your consciousness reverberates with the unstruck sound of Om...Om...Om....The subtler vibrations of Consciousness have replaced sound vibrations. Keep repeating it silently and watch as the vibrations of Consciousness become finer and finer, more and more subtle, until they become Light, shimmering Blue Light, the Light of Consciousness, the Light of God. There you are in the presence of the Light. Be still, make no effort; your consciousness is being drawn nearer and nearer to God. Here you wait, in the Glory and Light of God, waiting for God to pull your consciousness into union with the Godhead. The Lord finally draws you in, and with that act of grace you move beyond all words and descriptions, beyond perceiver and perceived, beyond even love and ecstasy. Love and bliss are the last recallable impressions of the Light as it impacts consciousness before union and the first describable experience of consciousness taking form again within the field of Light.

Step into the Light as often as you can. Allow the Lord to draw you near and scoop you up in His arms. Your soul cries out for the loving embrace of the Lord! Don't deny yourself God's love any longer.

Those who go into the Light begin to shine as if a light were just above their heads, constantly illuminating them. The sahasrar chakra at the crown of the head radiates the Light of a thousand suns. Artists have long depicted holy beings with an aura of light or a halo around their heads. As you go to that divine realm more and more you become transparent to the Light of God. All the gross structures of your ego, personality, past-life impressions, and more are washed away. The Light illumines you and the world you perceive.

Others may or may not see the Light in you. There's an old saying that when a pickpocket sees a saint, all he sees are his pockets. What we're looking for determines most of what we see.

The Shakti said, "Look for God, look for your Self, look for the Divine all around you. You already know how to use your eyes for seeing differences. Now open your Divine Sight and see the One appearing as the many. It's the birthright of each and every human being. You're born with the ability; you just need the right conditions to unfold it. Seek to create the right conditions through prayer, meditation, good fellowship, the company of wise beings, and a disciplined life."

A few months after that vision another set of images concerning the soul's journey back to God was shown to me in meditation. It occurred in the summer of 1990 while I was at an ashram in upstate New York, along with hundreds of other people who had gathered for a holiday celebration that included an ecstatic chant of a powerful mantra. As I drove up to the ashram I was looking forward to immersing myself in the chant and feeling the renewal it brings. Arriving at the meditation hall and diving into the joyous energy of the chant, I had no inkling of what was to come.

The chant became more and more ecstatic with every round of the mantra. At one point my eyes were closed and I rolled my head back just to loosen my neck. Suddenly I shifted into deep meditation, totally unaware of the thousand or more people chanting around me. A vividly detailed scene appeared before my inner vision.

The Soul's Journey

I found myself looking at a lovely little country pond surrounded by trees and rocks. Up a steep embankment along one side of the pond ran a quiet lane with grass covering old wheel ruts. As the spring breeze blew through the trees, dappled sunshine danced on the water below. Near the edge of the pond, perched on a rock, sat a big old bullfrog and two of his younger buddies. I was present as a formless consciousness witnessing this scene. Two young female frogs swam by and immediately one of the younger bullfrogs jumped in after them, but the other one just sat on the rock looking troubled.

The old bullfrog turned to his young friend. "What's the matter with you? You look so glum. It's spring, go have some fun!" he said, trying to cheer him up.

"I'm just not interested," replied the young frog.

"What's wrong?" the old bullfrog asked.

Hesitantly he replied, "I, uh, I don't think you'd understand."

"Try me!" the bullfrog said, genuinely concerned for his young friend.

"Well, I mean, is this all there is? Is this all there is to life—just hanging out in a pond? Isn't there, I don't know, something more? It seems like, well, there should be something more. Otherwise, what's the purpose of living?"

The old frog was surprised by his questions, but he was sure he knew what to say. Full of conviction and enthusiasm he answered, "Life here is great!" Just then a juicy butterfly came too close to the old frog and he gobbled it up. "You see, everything is provided for us! We get to eat, bask in the sun, mate, and sleep through the nasty winters! What more could you want? Besides, you're a frog—what do you expect? Now, it's a fine spring day, go after your friends and have a good time. Just put your silly questions aside and have fun!"

As I watched I could feel the genuine yearning of the young frog to know the truth, to know the meaning of life. He hopped into the water swimming away from the old bullfrog, unconvinced by his answers. Suddenly there was a splashing commotion behind him. He turned to see that a big snapping turtle had lunged out of the water snatching, the big bullfrog in its jaws. His old friend was gone forever.

Stunned, the young frog swam for shore. "There's got to be more to life than eating and being eaten, there's just got to be. But who has the answer?" he wondered in despair. Remembering the road high atop the embankment, the young frog decided to look there for someone who could answer his question. The way up the embankment turned out to be rough going. Brambles, thick underbrush, rocks, and even snakes stood in his way.

At one point his friends called out to him saying, "Come on back, there's nothing up there, you'll die if you leave the pond." The young frog was determined to find an answer to the purpose of life and wouldn't be turned back.

Finally he made it to the dirt road and stopped. "Which way should I go?" he thought. Then in the distance he saw a man approaching. The little frog was delighted. "I'll ask him what the purpose of life is, maybe he'll know!" The man kept approaching. "But wait, how do I talk to a human being? What if he doesn't understand me, how can I ask him my question?" Thinking frantically, the little frog watched the man draw nearer. Just as he was about to pass, the young frog cried out with all his heart. Though it sounded like little more than a croak, the man stopped and looked down into the anguished eyes of the little frog.

It turned out that this was no ordinary man, but a great saint, a knower of God. Light shown from his eyes, raining down on the little frog. The little one's heart leaped with joy! He could see in this great being's eyes such compassion and wisdom. The frog thought excitedly, "He must know, he must know. I'll ask him my question!" But the saint simply turned and walked away.

Panic stricken, the young frog wailed, "Hey wait! How can I catch up with you, how can I talk to you, how can I find you?" But all that came out was a frog's croak. Gathering all his might, he was about to leap after the saint, when a hawk, streaking out of the sky, swooped down, picking up the young frog in its talons.

The hawk's claws pierced the young frog's body, crushing the life from him. But the light of that little one's soul was inextinguishable. A scintillating tiny star of light left the frog's body and ascended into a dark space high above the earth. In that space many other stars twinkled also. It remained there only briefly when it began to descend back to earth.

The hawk served only to free the soul from the form that housed it, from the form in which it was bound. As I watched this, it seemed in some amazing way as if the hawk had come straight from God, though outwardly it just looked like a hawk doing what it does naturally, hunting its food.

Next I saw a rural village of small simple houses. Inside one of them a young woman in labor lay on her bed attended by two midwives. Her husband waited anxiously outside their bedroom. The woman's bare belly, full of new life, heaved with each contraction. Just before she was about to give birth, that radiant point of light descended into the room and, passing through her swollen abdomen, came to rest in its new home. With that the baby boy was born, letting out a healthy cry, calling the overjoyed father into the room. The mother cradled her new infant at her breast as she murmured to him the unspeakable love that passes between mother and newborn. The young father embraced them both, his tears of love and joy mingled with those of his wife. He sobbed a prayer of gratitude to the

Lord for blessing them with this baby. They were a devout couple and had prayed for a long time to have a child. In their arms they held a miracle, the divine mix of their love and God's blessing that had formed the adorable little one.

As soon as the mother and infant were able to travel, the family made a pilgrimage to their spiritual teacher, their guru. They wanted to express their gratitude for the precious gift they had received and to have their newborn son blessed. Many devotees were with the teacher when they arrived. The couple brought their child up to their beloved teacher and laid the baby in his arms. As he looked into the infant's eyes a squeal of ecstasy erupted from that little one. The young soul once again recognized the saint's eyes—those eyes filled with wisdom, love and compassion—raining the light of grace, and that soul rejoiced aloud!

Everyone saw the baby wriggling happily, but only the saint knew the depth of the little one's joy. The infant's soul soared with delight at having been brought by grace back to the saint it had met on the road. Now with the great twin blessings of a human birth and a wise one's guidance, it would finally come to know the true purpose of life.

The vision ended just as suddenly as it had begun and I was again aware of sitting in the meditation hall chanting a divine mantra. I was stunned by what the Divine Mother had shown me. I bowed my head and offered a prayer of thanks to Her. My mind retreated into silence, quite literally awestruck. There it remained still for hours.

Later that night I began contemplating what the vision meant as I drove home from the ashram, with my way illuminated by the light from the full moon. The Shakti gave me a glimpse of the miraculous workings of grace as it operates behind the ordinary events of daily life. The frog symbolized all seekers who not only dare to ask the question,

What is the purpose of life? but who also have the courage not to accept the conventional answers that are given. The yearning to know the truth and the effort to find it draw grace as surely as a baby's crying brings the loving mother.

The frog's view of life in the pond made me think again about my life. The old bullfrog's assessment of life left out death stalking all those who live. Though there's no snapping turtle about to eat me, I have to look at how time is consuming my life with the passage of each second, tick by tick. In the end my body will be consumed by fire. Will I have fulfilled what I've realized are the two great purposes of life—to know God and to serve God? Will I have fulfilled the promise of the human birth I've been given, along with many great blessings from spiritual masters? How much more vigilant do I need to be in order to experience all that God offers? These questions brought me back to my sadhana, my practices, back to treading my path more consciously. I must never lose sight of the tremendous care I have to give my own sadhana.

The more I contemplated the vision, the more treasures it yielded and the more questions to contemplate. Whose voices have I heard, voices that are born of my mind as well as those from the outside, that are like the frogs in the pond saying don't leave our little domain or you'll die. How have I yielded to them and in what ways was I able to ignore them? What are the obstacles, the thorns and snakes, that have to be surmounted in order to take the high road? In what ways has the hawk of grace descended into my life, freeing me from bound forms, attitudes, or personality characteristics that restrict me or prevent me from following my path to God? There are so many questions to contemplate. You'll discover the ones that call to you for contemplation.

Consider, too, this poem by the Sufi saint, Rumi:

Each form you see has its unseen archetype,
if the form should pass, its essence is eternal.
If you have known beauty in a face or wisdom in a word,

let this counsel your heart: what perishes is not real.
Since the springhead is timeless, its branches refresh.
Since neither can cease, what is the cause of your sorrow?
Think of your soul as the source and created things as springs.
While the source exists, the springs continually flow.
Empty your head of grief and drink from the stream.
Don't think of it failing—this water is endless.
From the moment you came into this manifest world
a ladder was given that you might escape.
From mineral substance you were transformed to plant,
and later to animal. How could this be hidden?
Afterwards, as man, you developed knowledge, consciousness, faith.
See how this body has risen from the dust like a rose?
When you have walked on from man you will be an angel,
and done with this earth your place will be beyond.
Pass, then, from the angelic and enter the Sea.
Your drop will merge with a hundred Seas of Oman.
Leave him you called "Son," and say "One" with your life.
Although your body has aged, your soul has become young.[9]

Chapter 4

The Bird of a Thousand Lights

Remember God so much that you are forgotten,
until you are lost in the Call,
without distinction of caller and called.

Rumi[1]

On the afternoon of February 4, 1990, while I was in meditation, the last vision of this series began unfolding before my inner eye. Pieces of it would fall into place over the next several months. It was during this period that the visions of the Rabbit and the Hare, the Golden Spoon and the Soul's Journey also occurred. This vision, which I've called The Bird of a Thousand Lights, revealed itself while I was in altered states of consciousness during meditation, chanting, and at other times during the day when I would fall into a meditative state. The Shakti can bestow Her gifts at any time, in any place; the challenge is being ready to receive. Apparently much inner work needed to be done for me to receive the entire vision because it came in two stages with nearly five years between them. The first half of the vision completed itself in the spring of 1990 and the second half didn't begin revealing itself until December 1994, finishing in February of 1995. During the intervening years all I could do was continue with my daily practices and wait for the time when the Shakti would present the remaining portion of the story. I tried visualizing various ways for the mythic journey to unfold beyond what was initially given, but my mind would go blank. I couldn't produce a single image of what was to come next.

Life went on, our daughter Molly was born, and I took a couple of years off to take care of her while my wife returned to work. A wise meditation master told me Molly took birth to teach me. From her first breath she began doing just that. She's determined that I learn what boundless love and selfless service are on a very human level. All children have a great deal to teach their parents. If we adults can focus more on what we can learn from them and with them, instead of exclusively attending to the teachings and disciplines we want to impart, then our children will develop a solid sense of self-respect and a healthier way of relating to authority.

During these years of raising Molly, working part-time, and teaching meditation courses, I would occasionally wonder what was going to happen with the vision. Suddenly, during my morning meditation in December of 1994 it began completing itself. The final segments came during meditations in January and February of 1995.

The Bird of a Thousand Lights

A young man lived on the outskirts of a city near a great dense forest. The woods were dark and mysterious. Few people ever attempted to make their way through the thick undergrowth into the forest, but the young man began to regularly stroll along the edge of it. Growing up he had listened to stories of marvelous creatures dwelling in there and strange sounds from the wildlife could be heard even where he walked. Of course there were also tales of vicious beasts and people disappearing forever within the mysterious woods. These tales were enough to dissuade most people from even going near the shrouded forest.

What really intrigued the young man was the magical creature he had heard about. She was said to be more splendid than any other on earth.

Legend had it that she lived in the forest, and if one were very fortunate one might hear her hauntingly beautiful call. Our young friend longed to hear the sound of it. Years went by but his weekly visits to the forest yielded nothing.

One day on his walk he came across an old man sitting on a log with his eyes closed as if asleep. The young man approached him, and as he neared, the old man said quietly, without opening his eyes, "Shhhhh, be still. Listen." The young man stopped in his tracks, and turning his attention to the sounds of the forest, all he could hear was what he always heard—a distant cacophony of bird calls and animal chatter.

"Did you hear it?" asked the old man as he opened his eyes.

"Hear what?" the young man replied, a bit annoyed. There were so many sounds, who could ever sort them out!

"The Bird of a Thousand Lights, didn't you hear her?"

The young man's heart leaped! He cocked his head, straining to listen for what the old man spoke of, but it was no use. He had no idea what he was even listening for! In frustration he yelled at the old man, "No, I can't make out anything!" Then it hit him—the old man was the only person he had ever met who knew the call of that rare creature. He knelt down in front of where the old man sat and begged him to teach him how to hear the mystical song of the Bird of a Thousand Lights.

"Why do you so passionately want to hear the bird's call?" the old man asked.

"I don't really know why," replied the young man, "except that ever since I was a little boy and was first told the story of that bird I wanted to hear her divine song for myself and perhaps even see her one day in the forest. I've been coming to the forest edge regularly for years hoping to discover a way into the forest or to stumble across the bird and hear her call. The more I come to the forest, the more strongly it pulls me back."

"What do you know of the bird?" the old man asked.

"Only that her call is said to be so hauntingly divine that hearing it makes even the mountains weep with joy and that's the origin of the rivers and streams which flow from the forest to feed the city."

The old man explained. "The bird's name describes the myriad rays of light which emanate from her magnificent form. She has great powers. Only the most dedicated and purest of seekers ever makes it to where the Bird of a Thousand Lights dwells. Many difficulties, great hardships and the most severe tests await those who would try to find her. Are you sure you want to seek her?"

"Yes, yes! *Please* teach me to hear her call and tell me how to find her," implored the young man.

"We'll see, we'll see. Come back here tomorrow," said the old man before disappearing into the forest.

The next day the young man began his apprenticeship. He spent long hours practicing the sounds the old man was teaching him. Every day, month after month, he met the old man at the forest fence. The old master was strict and demanded a great deal of him, but he was also compassionate, encouraging him in the face of numerous failures. It seemed to him he would never learn the subtleties of that divine bird's call. He could barely discern it even when the old man made it right in his ear. Certainly he would never be able to make the call himself. The old master prodded him along, keeping him focused on listening, on being able to hear that exquisite sound.

The young man was astonished by his master's ability to make the ethereal call of the Bird of Light. What mystical art had he learned that empowered him to do that? Finally, one day he asked the old man.

The master told him a little about his life. "I too was like you at one time. I yearned to hear the mysterious call of the Bird of a Thousand Lights; I longed to see her with my own eyes. Eventually I found a master who could show me the way into the forest and teach me to recognize the bird's song. Once the call is heard, it draws one to her like a magnet. But the way isn't easy. You have to sacrifice yourself totally to what you're seeking or you'll never get there. Each seeker faces his or her own trials along the way, and what awaits you in the forest can't be foreseen. If you stay attuned to the call of the Bird of Light and your master's voice, all will go well." What the master encountered in the forest remained a mystery. He wouldn't reveal anything about it. The old man concluded by saying only that he felt extremely fortunate and blessed to have succeeded.

The young man was already feeling pressed by what the endeavor demanded of him. Family and friends ridiculed him for constantly going to the forest. "Stay in the city, earn a living, raise a family," they told him. How many times did his parents say to him, "When are you going to make something of yourself?" As much as he loved them all he simply wasn't interested in "making something of himself." Instead, he gave himself more and more to the practices the old man taught him, preparing for the day when he would enter the forest.

The old master pushed him harder and harder. The young man rarely went home any longer, preferring instead to sleep beneath the shrubs and refresh himself in the pure waters at the forest edge. He practiced constantly, listening for the call his master made, stalking him, following him. The master would disappear ahead of him and reappear behind him, evading him, losing him. He made the young man continue for days on end without sleep or food, heedless of weather or darkness—on and on the pursuit went. A couple of years passed by in this way.

One day just before dawn, as the full moon was setting and the sun was about to rise, the old man came out of the forest to find the young man lying beneath a holly tree. The young man heard him approach but didn't stir, hoping to fool him. The old man laughed; he knew he was awake. "Get up," he said, "today you enter the forest." The young man leaped up excitedly. After he bathed, his master showed him the way to the secret trail that led through the otherwise impenetrable undergrowth into the forest. Before sending him off, the old man fed him and gave him a gift. He told the young man that from that point on he would have to continue by himself, and if he listened along the way, his master would be there to guide him. The old man warned him to be vigilant in the face of danger. "Just follow the call and my voice," the old man said, "and everything will be fine."

The young man was eager to go. He had learned to hear the Bird of a Thousand Lights from the old man but he had yet to hear the true call in the forest from the Bird herself. He was afraid *and* determined to succeed.

The trail led through thickets of thorn bushes with vicious spikes that tore his clothes to shreds. Eventually he had to take out the gift from the old man. It was a beautiful shawl. Wrapping himself in it he pressed on. Much to his surprise it protected him. It was impervious to the sharp thorns sticking out from every branch. This dense brush seemed to go on forever as he fought his way through it. Days passed by. He was hungry, exhausted, and more than once he thought of turning back. The path behind him always looked like easier going than what lay ahead. Suddenly he broke out into a stand of ancient cathedral pines. The wind swished through the high canopy of branches that shaded the open forest floor. Soft pine needles carpeted the ground, filling the air with a rich scent. He sat down resting against a great towering tree.

"It's so serene in here," he thought. The city and all its concerns were less than a distant mirage. He turned his attention to listening. It was easier here. His eyes closed as his awareness expanded, filling the space in which sound vibrated. It was a practice his master tutored him in, testing him until he perfected it. All the voices of the forest creatures filled his mind, thousands of cries, calls, grunts, and even insect noises. Some were absolutely fascinating to hear.

Then cutting through it all he heard his master's voice, "Listen, do you hear her?"

His listening went deeper. Lost in the tumult of sounds was that hauntingly beautiful call. He strained to hear. Yes! There it was! So faint, lying hidden below the rubble of noise. Ahh, it's so indescribably exquisite. He let the divine call fill his awareness. A wave of quiet ecstasy washed through him. Nothing, nothing on earth could compare with what he was experiencing. He sat absorbed in the divine song of the Bird of a Thousand Lights.

He could only sustain the listening for a short time. When he came out of it he knew he could never return to the city. "I must find the Bird of a Thousand Lights; I vow to let nothing stop me," he said out loud.

The elusive bird's call drew him deeper and deeper into the forest. By nightfall he was hungry and exhausted, when he came upon a small opening in the forest with a little cottage nestled among the trees. Candlelight shown from the windows and delicious smells of cooking food mixed with the smoke curling from the chimney. An elderly woman appeared at the door beckoning him to come inside.

She spoke to him kindly, asking where he came from and where he was going. They talked over a tasty meal that she served him. The old woman appeared quite sweet and humble. She went about serving her young guest attentively and always kept her gaze lowered, never meeting his eyes. He was famished and ate heartily, enjoying her interest in his search for the divine bird. She offered him lodgings for the night, which he gratefully accepted. After eating dinner he went out to practice listening, attuning himself to the divine call. He had great difficulty and could barely even hear it, much less become absorbed in it. "I must be too exhausted," he thought, and returned to the old woman's cottage.

He joined her sitting on the hearth before the fire. She told him a strange tale of an evil king who had cast a spell on her, imprisoning her in this forest glade. She begged the young man to help her. All the while she spoke her head was bowed and her eyes lowered. To the young man she looked so helpless and beaten down. Taking pity on her, he said he would see what he could do in the morning. She thanked him profusely and promised a special gift for him the next day.

He awoke to the aroma of breakfast cooking and tea brewing. She had fixed him as fine a meal as she could. After eating his fill he went out to practice listening and for a moment caught a faint echo of what he strained to hear. It was gone in an instant. As he headed back to the cottage he realized with some dismay that he was powerless to do anything to set the old woman free. He told her so when he saw her.

"I really do wish you could stay, but perhaps you could just gather some wood for me. I'm too old now to chop down all the trees I'll need for heating and cooking through the winter, and if you could stay long enough to lay in a store of wood for me I'd be so grateful."

With her bowed head she looked so helpless. He thought, how can I say no to her? I can't leave her to freeze to death. It won't take too long and then I'll be on my way. He told her he would cut the wood for her.

With great delight she took out a pair of shoes she had stayed up through the night making for him. She said, "These are your gift, put them on. They'll protect your feet as you work in the woods for me." He tried them on. They were quite heavy and stiff, slowing him down as he walked. Not wanting to offend the poor old woman, he wore the shoes despite the fact they hindered him, and after a few days he didn't notice them anymore. What did trouble him was that listening seemed to be growing even more difficult. He could barely make out the call and often heard nothing at all. The young man figured it was just a passing problem and decided to really work on getting the woodpile done so he could move on. In this way he cut back on his listening practice, chopping wood instead. Weeks passed by.

Just as he finished stacking the last cord of wood for the old woman, he thought he heard his master's voice telling him, "Move on, move on." Then it was gone.

He went into the old woman's cottage. She had prepared a feast for him. He told her of his plan to leave in the morning. She was saddened. Dawn came and with it the old woman served the young man a sumptuous breakfast. He ate heartily, thinking of the journey ahead. With bowed head and lowered eyes the old woman asked if she could make one more request of him. She said since he had been with her all these weeks, she had fed him all her food for the next months. Couldn't he stay a little while longer and catch enough game for her to cure and keep. He felt awful. "How can I leave her here to starve? The least I can do is hunt some game for her," he thought. He agreed.

The old woman was delighted and presented him with a new jacket and pants, which she had spent all night making. They were rugged and stiff but she said they would protect him from the brush as he went out hunting. It was difficult for him to move in those clothes and they weighed him down, but not wanting to offend her he wore them. In no time he hardly noticed them.

The young man rarely practiced listening anymore and no longer heard the Bird of a Thousand Lights. He feared he no longer even remembered what she sounded like.

He continued hunting and gathering food for the old woman, but it was becoming increasingly difficult. She was feeding him less and less, excusing this by saying she had to conserve it all for the winter. His strength waned, and even his sight seemed to be weakening as he noticed the world growing dimmer. It was harder and harder to find the way out of the forest glade where the old woman dwelt and he even got lost in the forest. Frightened, he returned to the glade.

The next day he sat in the woods exhausted, desperate to understand what was happening to him. He tried listening, but his practice was barren. In anguish, he prayed to his master for help. Immediately his master answered him, but the young man couldn't believe what the old man told him to do.

"Your life is in jeopardy," the master said. "The old woman has you under her spell. She will weaken you until she can kill you and eat your remains." The young man was stunned. The master continued, "You must set yourself free at once. Go back to the cottage tonight and do exactly as I instruct you." What the master then told him to do shocked him even more.

He staggered back towards the glade thinking "I must be going crazy and imagining my master's voice. That poor old woman is so humble." He saw her standing in the cottage door and dragged himself across the glade toward her. As he approached her, she raised her glance from the ground and for the first time ever she looked him in the eyes. His soul recoiled in terror! Never before had he seen such malevolence as there was in her eyes. She smiled an evil smile at him. His heart sank. But in that moment he knew his master was right, his life was in danger.

At dinner that night he avoided her look and ate none of the meager portion she served him. He feigned illness, not wanting to arouse suspicion, and thanked her for cooking for him. She barely hid her growing delight at his weakening condition. He knew he must act quickly to save himself.

It was a clear, dark, moonless night and he retired early. The young man struggled not to fall asleep, though he pretended to be so when the old woman checked on him before she went to bed. She smiled as she stood above him thinking, "He's nearly mine." He lay there dead still. Her presence was so powerful, so oppressive he nearly passed out. He battled to remain conscious yet unmoving. He remembered his master's voice and clung to it. She finally left him and he reviewed what his master had told him to do. After a few hours, when he was sure she rested in the land beyond dreams, the young man, following his master's instructions, crept out of the cottage, leaving behind the jacket, pants, and shoes the old woman had given him.

Quickly he set the cottage ablaze. It went up like a torch, dry tinder and thatched roof bursting into fire, flames mounting to the sky! The blazing inferno lit the forest glade. Suddenly, above the snapping roar of the flames he heard the old woman's cackling laugh! She shrieked in delight! He turned away from the fiery spectacle unable to look any longer. Unexpectedly from behind him, light flashed so brilliantly that the dark forest turned to day; even the firelight paled in comparison. Wheeling around he thought he saw a bird and wondered, was that the sound of wings taking flight that he heard? But now all that could be seen was the burning cottage, nearly reduced to ashes. Gone were the old woman's strange laughs and gone were the binding clothes she had him wear.

He sat down, leaning against an old oak tree, sighing deeply, wondering what on earth he had been through. His mind stilled as he watched the last of the fire burning down. Then it crept upon him, taking him unaware, until he was immersed in that glorious call from the divine Bird of a Thousand Lights. Its beauty enveloped him, carrying him into an unimaginably sublime ecstasy. She seemed so close to him, the call more powerful than ever he had experienced it. His soul drank deep from the outpouring of her divine beauty. Months had passed since he last heard her call. Like a good mother, the graceful song stayed with him, soothing him, nurturing him until he fell asleep.

Later, when he came back to his senses and opened his eyes, he could see perfectly once again! His vision had cleared and the path out of the glade stood before him. As dawn broke, the forest came alive with the sounds of its inhabitants. The young man felt invigorated heading down the path deeper into the forest. He realized now how much the old woman's clothing nearly crippled him. He was quite pleased with himself for having overcome her. Flushed with victory he strode along. Playful little creatures darted in and out of the undergrowth dancing through dappled sunlight.

Several times each day the young man stopped to turn his attention within and listen. He would try to hear the divine call during the day while hiking, cooking, washing, or whatever, but he rarely heard it then. However, the call guided him, sometimes appearing ahead in the distance, at other times off to the left or right of him. In this way he knew whether to turn or continue straight onwards. The young man was sure he was making great progress and patted himself on the back for doing so well.

After some days he began venturing into a much denser and darker part of the forest. The creatures living here were different. Snakes and scorpions crawled out of the decaying vegetation covering the ground. Occasionally growls of predators or cries of animals in their death throes pierced the eerie silence. Fear began taking hold of the young man. The call had led him into this sinister land, but he thought perhaps he had missed a turn. Swinging around, ready to run back, he discovered the path had closed in behind him and completely disappeared. The only way open plunged him deeper into the shadowy undergrowth.

Night came quickly, a night blacker than any he had ever known. Neither the light of the stars nor the moon could penetrate that dark forest. The young man lit a small fire, trying to hold back the menacing blackness. Through the night strange cries and groans, chillingly human, kept him from slipping into sleep. Dawn came slowly, as if it could barely push back the night. Darkness loosened its grip but never let go of this realm; even full daylight remained a murky gray. That morning, before setting out, the young man was shaken when he looked into the brush and saw a pair of eyes staring malevolently at him. The young man took off running. His frightened confused mind kept seeing those eyes. Why did they look so familiar? Terror quickened his frenzied pace.

He ran for miles, his heart slamming against his ribs as he ran harder and harder. Feet pounding the earth, he crashed his way through brush and vegetation. Fiery gasps of breath shredded his lungs. About to collapse, he broke out of the undergrowth into a clearing at the edge of a crystal clear lake. Stopping just short of falling into the lake, he listened for his pursuer. In the silence he breathed easier.

The lake reflected the blue sky above and the trees overhanging its edge. Deep springs fed the cool waters that touched the young man's face as he knelt to refresh himself. A draft of water soothed his throat. He dunked his head and the chilly water washed away some of his fear. His mind began to clear as he watched the ripples on the water's surface where he drank settle, until once again the lake mirrored the surrounds. It was too late when he saw the reflection of the tree-limb arching overhead with the vicious beast that stalked him ready to pounce on his back. Just as he caught sight of it, the beast leaped down dragging them both into the water. They struggled furiously at the waters edge. The beast was about the same size as the young man and stood like a human with fur covering its crude features. As they fought the young man became more and more desperate, fearing for his life. Finally he threw himself into the lake, swimming away from the creature as quickly as he could. The primitive man swam after him, staying right behind him.

Light coming from the depths of the lake caught the young man's eye. He thought, "Maybe I can lose him diving down there." Taking a full breath he dove deeper and deeper but the beast remained right behind him. Farther and farther down they went. The young man's lungs felt like bursting. Searing pain and fear kept him from passing out. Now, too far from the surface and too far from the light in the unreachable depths, his breath exploded out of his lungs. The unstoppable reflexive inhale sucked water into his lungs. He was stunned. There was no pain, quite the opposite! "My God, I can breathe this water!" he realized. The water was breathable, energy surged back into his body. So shocked was he that he nearly forgot about his pursuer. Turning to look back at him he noticed something equally amazing. The beast's features had softened. The hair covering its body had lessened, thinned. But the young man continued trying to swim away from it as quickly as the beast swam after him. They were swimming around in circles, and after a while it was difficult to tell who was chasing whom.

Exhaustion finally forced the young man to stop. In their circular chase they had moved closer to shore. When the young man stood up in the shallows and turned around, he was stunned by what he saw. The beast had lost all its brutish features and now looked like he could be his older brother. The young man caught sight of his own reflection in the water and was equally surprised by the changes in his own appearance. He had lost his boyish soft looks. He saw he now had the beard of a man, the muscled arms of a man and the hairy chest of a man. As he surveyed these changes in his body, he also noticed he felt different, more solid, more mature, more complete in some way he couldn't quite grasp. He now realized that the man who had looked like a beast could be taken for his twin.

The magical waters of the lake had washed away whatever ill will there had been between him and the other man. Still standing in the shallows our man asked the other fellow, "Who are you and how did you end up in the dark forest?"

"I was abandoned here when I was a small child and I grew up alone amongst the animals and wild things. I had forgotten I was human until you came along. Even at first I thought you were only something to hunt and eat. It wasn't until we dove into the water that I recognized you as a human and remembered I was human also. I felt such a longing to touch you and be touched by you that I kept pursuing you."

He came forward and they embraced with deep emotion. There they stood in the lake hugging each other and sobbing in one another's arms.

They camped beside the lake that night. In the morning the forest man said he was leaving in search of a community he could be a part of. He longed for the company of people. Before departing he gave our man a present, his only possession from childhood. It was a gold ring with a black square stone, in the center was a small, round, brilliant diamond.

"I don't know how to thank you. It's an extraordinary gift, I will always treasure it."

"What is your name?" asked the forest man.

"Jerome."

"Would you mind if I took your name for myself?"

"Not at all, I would be honored to have you bear my name."

They said their good-byes and the forest man departed for the city with his new found humanity and name.

Jerome heard the Bird of a Thousand Lights calling him once again. His quest took him over a beautiful ridge of mountains. From the top of the ridge he could see a town with its surrounding farmlands in the valley below. The call led him there.

The townspeople were very friendly and greeted him with unusual interest. He heard some of them whispering to each other, "Is he the one?" He was different from them, taller, fairer, and his blue eyes attracted a great deal of attention. No one had ever seen blue eyes before. The towns-people told him he should meet the elders right away. They brought him to the hall of the elders where he was first fed and then given some time to rest before being introduced to the elders. As Jerome rested he reflected on what was happening. He was certain that the call had directed him to this locale, but he didn't want to put himself in jeopardy as he had done with the old woman in the forest. With some anticipation he awaited his summons to meet the elders.

Finally it came and he was led into an octagonal shaped hall with very high ceilings supported by massive tall posts made from smoothly rounded tree trunks. It was quite dark at the periphery of the room. There were no windows; the only opening beside the doorway was a hole in the center of the roof that looked out at the stars. Directly below was a circular pit, stone lined, with a fire blazing in it, the only light in the sacred meeting place. The hall was empty except for the circle of eight elders seated on the ground around the fire.

Jerome was welcomed into the circle and directed to sit facing the fire. He sat alone near the fire within the circle of elders encompassing him and the flames. He told the elders about his search for the Bird of a Thousand Lights and what he had encountered so far. He told them that it was the Bird's call that had directed him to their town. He wanted to know why people were so interested in him and why did they wonder aloud if he was the one. "What one?" he asked.

During his narration of his journey some of the elders were saying to each other that it fit the legend, while others said they didn't think so. When Jerome asked his questions the elders responded by saying, "We will answer all your questions, but first please show us your hands." Jerome did so and immediately one of the elders said, "See, he doesn't have the ring, he can't be the one."

Jerome said, "The ring? Do you mean this one?" He pulled out the leather thong around his neck which had the ring on it that the forest man had given him. The elders passed the ring around, examining it. There was silence as the import of this last sign was recognized by them.

The oldest of the revered group said, "Yes, this is the one, my son. Now let us explain to you all that we know." They told Jerome of a beautiful princess who had been abducted and imprisoned by a rogue warlord. She was in a cave under a mountain that was now protected by the waters of a fairy spirit. The fairy came to save the princess from the warlord by flooding the land around the mountain. The entrance to the cave was under water and no one who entered those enchanted waters ever came out again. However, the fairy said that one day a man would come who could gain access to the cave and rescue the princess. She said the only man who could do this would be one who has faced the darkness and discovered light. He would have a ring to prove it. "You are that man," the elders told Jerome.

He couldn't believe it. It sounded too fantastic, but then so did his other encounters so far on his journey. The elders asked him if he would make the attempt to free the princess. He told them he really didn't want to get mixed up in their legend. He just wanted to continue his search for the Bird of a Thousand Lights, but he added, he would consider it and give them his answer the next day. That night he did his practice of listening and clearly heard the Bird's call nearby. As the sound of her song faded Jerome suddenly heard his master's voice: "You must take on the task of freeing the princess and you must succeed at all cost." Jerome felt deep gratitude for his master's instructions and vowed to fulfill them. The tone of the master's voice and "at all cost" sounded ominous to him. He offered a prayer for the strength to succeed.

In the morning Jerome told the elders he would do all that he could to set the princess free. They led him to the top of a low ridge where he saw the solid rock mountain rising out of the waters, which formed a broad moat around it. Alone he headed toward the mountain and the fairy spirit. As he approached the enchanted waters the fairy rose up out of them. She was exceptionally beautiful and didn't appear at all fearsome.

Jerome bowed to her, greeting her respectfully and said, "I've come to set the princess free."

"The one who finally succeeds will marry her," she told him. "Others have died in their attempts. What makes you think you are any different?"

"I have the ring which the elders told me proves I'm the one to set her free," he said, trying to hide his shock at hearing he was to marry the princess if he rescued her. He thought he would save her and then go on with his search for the Bird of a Thousand Lights. But he had made a vow to set her free and he was determined to fulfill it. He told himself he'd deal with the marriage issue later. Jerome held up the thong with the ring on it.

Looking at the ring, the fairy said "Perhaps you're the one, but you will have to prove it. First you will have to bring me the Great Tree which grows in the highest mountain pass. If you fail it will cost you your life."

He was beginning to understand what was at stake when his master said, "at all cost." Jerome set off on the journey that months later would take him to the roof of the world. There in the highest mountain pass grew a mighty tree with roots that went deep into the earth and branches so high aloft that clouds got caught on them. Clearly there was no way that he could bring that tree back to the fairy. He would fail to fulfill his vow and he would die without having seen the Bird of a Thousand Lights. In despair he sat down at the base of the tree. Detaching himself from his feelings, he turned his mind to listening and quickly attuned himself to the call. He took comfort in the Bird's mystical presence.

Later, when he came out from his meditation he found a little creature scurrying around the rocks and roots of the tree. With no one else to talk to, he told the creature about his dilemma and impending doom. Much to his surprise the little creature answered him. It told Jerome it had a seed from the tree that he could easily bring back. The creature said all he had to do was plant the seed next to the water's edge and it would quickly grow into a mighty tree. Jerome was delighted and asked the creature for the seed. Jerome reeled when it told him he could have it but it would cost him the thumb from his right hand. He again remembered what his master said. Since he was left-handed, Jerome figured he wouldn't miss his right thumb too much. Jerome held out his right hand and the creature bit off the thumb, scurried away with it and returned with the seed.

Jerome bandaged his hand as best he could and made the long journey back to the fairy. He told her he brought what she had asked for.

She laughed, "I don't see any tree."

He took the seed out of his pocket and planted it near the water's edge. The soil moistened by the enchanted waters made the seed sprout, and in just three days it grew into a huge towering tree. As the tree grew it drank the waters from the moat and the level began to drop. Here and there rocks and shallows began to appear in the waters.

"Very good, you've fulfilled my first request. Next," she said, "you must bring me the royal swan from the Lake of Knowledge."

The call from the Bird of a Thousand Lights led him on the long journey to the vast hidden lake that looked like a clear freshwater sea. The magical swan was a white regal bird that stood taller than him and could speak. Jerome asked the swan to accompany him back to the fairy, but the swan refused and flew off on its magnificent wings. Jerome felt defeated and took refuge in silence, turning his attention to the call. It was his master's voice that filled his awareness, telling him to ask the swan for one of its eggs. When the swan returned, Jerome did just that.

The swan agreed with one condition, "Hold out your right hand," the swan said, "it will cost you your pointing finger." Jerome complied and the swan snapped it off with his great beak. Jerome took the egg, wrapped his painfully damaged hand and returned to the fairy.

The fairy asked him where the swan was. When he set the egg down near the water's edge it cracked open and out sprang a large signet. It put its beak into the water and began drinking. Jerome and the fairy watched as it grew into a majestic swan in only three hours. By drinking the water from the moat the swan had lowered the level even farther. The opening to the cave could now be seen above a stretch of sand on the far shore. A broken line of rocks a hundred yards or more long stuck out of the water forming a set of jagged stepping stones leading toward the cave. The rocks were slippery, steep sloped, and far apart. The fairy again congratulated Jerome for fulfilling another of her requests.

"Your last task," she told him, "is to see if you can make it across the water, jumping from rock to rock; but before you try, be warned: if you slip and fall into the water, it will burn you up in an instant."

The young man threw a stick into the water and watched as it hit the surface, hissed, smoked and was gone.

Jerome readied himself to go, praying for his master's help. He wrapped himself in the shawl his master had given him and leaped for the first rock. Landing hard on it he cut his hands as he grappled to stay on the rock. He had to rely mostly on his left hand. He continued to make his way across until he hit the last rock before the shore in front of the cave. He lost his footing as he landed and began slipping into the water. His right leg went in up to his ankle, and searing pain shot through his body. He managed to pull himself up atop the rock. He had lost his right foot. Only one leap remained and with every once of his strength he hurled himself at the shore, passing out in pain even as he lunged through the air. He crashed onto the sandy shore like a lifeless rag doll. Before awakening, his awareness melted into the sound of the Bird's mystical call, soothing him and moving his mind beyond the pain of his body.

When he returned to ordinary consciousness he began crawling and hobbling toward the cave. Entering the cave, his eyes fell on the most beautiful woman he had ever seen. Immediately his heart opened to her. Jerome reached for her and tried to take her hand, but some invisible force blocked him.

"Do you have the ring?" the princess asked.

"Yes," he said, pulling out the necklace.

"Put it on your left index finger," she told him. "Now reach toward me with that hand. It will break the spell."

Jerome made a fist of his left hand, and with the diamond facing forward, hit the invisible wall. A cascade of sparks leaped from where it struck, breaking the spell and setting the princess free. She embraced Jerome and he was so overwhelmed by love that for a moment he didn't feel the pain in his leg.

The princess helped Jerome back toward the enchanted waters and the fairy. The fairy was overjoyed to see the princess, and as a boon to Jerome, she restored his leg and fingers. Jerome was awestruck by her powers, though the princess wasn't at all surprised by what she could do. The fairy gave them her blessings and gathering up her waters, she disappeared into the earth out of view behind the mountain.

The princess told him she had been imprisoned there for years waiting for him to arrive. Now it was time to return to her kingdom, where her father and mother, the King and the Queen would be anxious to see her and meet their future son-in-law. He knew now that he wanted to marry her, though he worried about how to continue his search for the Bird of a Thousand Lights. The princess reassured him that he would certainly be able to fulfill his vow to find the great Bird. There was something delightfully mysterious about the princess. He wondered what secrets she held.

One of those mysteries he unraveled as they journeyed back to her homeland. During the first night he awoke to find a lovely bird that shone with the light of a full moon perched on a tree nearby. The princess was nowhere to be seen. After several more occurrences like that on subsequent nights he finally figured out that it was she who became transformed into the mysterious bird. When he asked her about it she confirmed that it was true and he might as well know it now since he would be marrying her and would discover it eventually. She told him she had the power to turn herself into a bird anytime she wanted, though she enjoyed it most at night. There was also something about her voice that caught his attention. She just laughed when he asked her about it. "Everyone tells me I have my mother's voice," she said.

They finally reached the royal palace and the princess told Jerome to wait in one of the outer chambers until she came to get him. She went to see her mother and father who were overjoyed to see her. She told them about Jerome, how he had rescued her and how he had discovered part of her hidden nature. He knew nothing about the King and Queen. They wanted to meet him right away, though the King said he would not yet reveal his human form to Jerome. The Queen did the opposite, she chose to reveal only her human form to him.

The princess went to retrieve Jerome from where he was waiting. She told him how delighted her parents were that he had freed her from the cave. They looked forward to having him as their son-in-law. There was only one more condition to fill, which would be explained to him by the King and Queen.

Jerome was disconcerted by what the princess had told him. Given all that he had been through so far he couldn't imagine what other trials could await him. The princess brought him to the inner chambers of the King and Queen. He met the Queen first and was taken by her powerful presence and extraordinary beauty. He was afraid of her and kept a respectful distance from her. The Queen was very cordial and warmly received his hesitant courtesies. She asked him to tell her all he had been through since leaving the city and entering the forest. He was surprised that she knew about the city and his having left it to begin his quest for the Bird of a Thousand Lights. He hadn't told the princess about that part of his travels.

He loosened up as he related the tale of his journey. Just as he came to the end where he rescued the princess and accompanied her to their palace, the King suddenly entered the room, flying through a huge pair of open doors that led to a balcony overlooking the palace grounds below. Jerome was totally undone by the King's entrance. He flew in as an eagle, an enormous black eagle with wings spanning sixteen feet or more. He stood over eight feet tall and looked right through Jerome with piercing eyes. The Eagle King let out a penetrating call and Jerome had all he could do not to run away in terror. He stood before the royal Eagle, his legs shaking, unable to speak. The Eagle's golden beak and talons flashed in the sunlight. The princess stood by his side and tried to comfort him. She told Jerome that her father was pleased with him and sometime in the future he would reveal his human form to him.

The Queen said, "First you have to endure one more test of your worthiness to marry our daughter and inherit the kingdom. One the eve of your birthday, in three days time, the King will take you to an old hermit's cave where you will spend the next twelve months alone, walled in the cave by rocks and left with a store of food. At the end of the year the King will set you free. If you have proven your worthiness, you will marry the princess. If you fail, you will die."

The Eagle King let out another nerve-shattering cry before flying out. Jerome watched, too stunned to think, as the Eagle rose higher and higher into the sky on those powerful black wings, eventually disappearing in the blue firmament. The Queen had left quietly while he was absorbed in watching the Eagle King. The princess took him by the hand and led him to his room. The sound of her voice and the touch of her hand steadied him. When she left he retreated into his practice of listening. He heard the mystical call of the Bird of a Thousand Lights and then he heard his master's voice saying, "Give yourself entirely, hold nothing back." He felt ready.

At midnight on the eve of his birthday the princess led him back to where he had met the Eagle King before. This time Jerome was unshaken by the King's powerful presence. The Queen was nowhere to be seen. He was prepared for what was to follow. The Eagle King flew over Jerome, grasping him by the shoulders with his talons, he took off out of the palace. Jerome bore the pain of the talons piercing his flesh and lifting him skyward. As they cleared the palace towers they were joined by some other extraordinary bird that was just above Jerome and the Eagle King, out of Jerome's sight. The other bird gave off such light that the entire way to the mountain cave was illuminated. When they reached the cave the Eagle King flew deftly up to a hole at the top of the wall and dropped Jerome through. With his huge talons the Eagle King picked up a large boulder that all but filled the entrance hole, leaving just a slit open. With a piercing cry and a flash of light, the Eagle King and the unseen one were gone.

Jerome turned to his practice of listening and was dismayed not to hear her divine call or his master's voice. He felt his way around the cave and found something soft to lean back on. Before falling asleep he thought he heard a faint rustling sound from the back of the cave. He decided to wait until sunrise to explore his new home.

When dawn arrived, the bit of light that entered through the slit permitted him to vaguely see the dimensions of the cave. The roof appeared to be about eight feet high at the front of the cave and it sloped downward into the dark at the rear. The back wall, if there was one, was lost in darkness. The sidewalls were about 12 feet apart and angled in toward each other, going back into the darkness. There was a pile of coarse blankets for bedding and warmth and tins of dried biscuits and dried fruit for food. A bucket with a small ladle sat on the floor, catching drops of clean water falling from the ceiling toward the rear of the cave. The overflow ran back in a little channel worn into the rock before disappearing into a crack in the floor. Farther back another crack opened a little wider and was covered by an old board. It looked like the place that served for eliminating waste. The roof of the cave was only about four feet off the ground back there and it was very dark. It was impossible to see how much farther the cave extended. Jerome crawled and then slithered on his belly until the space became too small for him to proceed. He still didn't reach a back wall but he did hear the rustling sound more distinctly. In the dark nothing could be seen and he crawled back out.

Jerome examined the food stores and given that there wasn't much, he devised a plan for rationing it. Once that was done he figured all he had to do was practice his listening and be patient. This might not be such a bad ordeal after all, he thought. He lay down and entered the listening mode of awareness and again heard nothing. He wondered why and being unable to think of a reason he turned his thoughts to what his master last told him: "Give yourself entirely, hold nothing back." What was he to give himself to? What was he to prove during this trial? What did it mean to succeed? He had no answers and fell asleep.

When he awoke, the sun was setting. Darkness spread forward from the rear of the cave, reclaiming the last patch on the wall where the last fiery ray of the sinking sun had shone. Lying still, he could hear the rustling sound once again. He was curious to see who he shared the cave with. He waited a long time until he judged it must be nearing dawn. Then he took a biscuit to the rear of the cave and left a line of crumbs leading along the wall to where he sat on a pile of blankets. It wasn't long before he heard something moving in the darkness. As the few rays of dawn able to pass through the slit gave their meager light to his surrounds, he could see what appeared to be a small bird that must have gotten trapped in the cave. His heart went out to the little creature and he didn't want to see it come to any harm. He felt bad that his own confinement in the cave had cost the bird its freedom. Over the next couple of days he coaxed it out until finally it ate from his hand and stayed in his lap through the sunrise. When he could at last see the little bird he discovered it was only an awkward baby, unable to fly. It immediately took to Jerome, snuggling up against him for warmth.

Jerome knew he would have to change his rations in order to be able to keep the bird alive. He cut down on what he ate and began to feed the bird. The creature became a dear friend. He shared with it his deep concern that he was unable to hear the call anymore. The call and his master's voice had been with him through everything. Now he felt achingly alone. The bird looked at him with knowing eyes and rubbed his head and beak against Jerome's neck as if to comfort him. Jerome was grateful to have the bird's company. In time Jerome discovered a quiet contentment in the silence that had replaced the voice of his master and the mystical bird's call. That sweet silence sang its own song of peace and stilled his restless soul's searching.

As the weeks went by the bird got bigger and bigger. It became apparent that it was growing larger than Jerome had ever expected. He cut his rations even further and continued to feed his dear friend. Months passed by and Jerome weakened terribly. When the time for him to be set free from the cave was only weeks away when the food ran out.

The princess was beginning to anticipate the return of her beloved and their wedding day. In her heart she visited him often. His birthday would be here soon, the day her father would bring him back to her.

Finally the day arrived, and in the predawn hours the Eagle King flew with his consort to the mountain cave. With one great cry from the King all the boulders tumbled away from the entrance. From the cave a piercing shriek answered and out flew an enormous black eagle, nearly as great in size as the Eagle King. There was nothing to be seen of Jerome. The trio flew back to the palace and into the royal chambers, where the princess waited excitedly. The King and Queen assumed their human forms while the eagle stood there looking at the King. The Queen went up to the eagle and embracing him she whispered in his ear. Suddenly the eagle transformed into Jerome. He immediately ran over and embraced his old master, the King, whom he hadn't seen since he first entered the forest. The King held him to his chest and praised him for succeeding on his quest. During their flight back to the palace he had seen the Bird of a Thousand Lights; she was the Queen. The princess came over to him and they embraced. Their wedding was just hours away. It was also his birthday, and he was given a new name, the name the Queen called him by as she whispered in his ear, the name that allowed him to return to his human form.

That night after they were married they both changed into their other forms, he the great eagle and she a Bird of Light. He saw how much brighter she had grown in the year he was gone. One day she would be the Bird of a Thousand Lights. For hours they flew high in the clear night sky, chasing each other higher and higher. To those far below on the ground they looked like two stars, one dark and one light, playing with one another against the backdrop of the heavens. As they began to descend back down to the palace she flew in perfect synchrony right above him, nearly touching his back. His magnificent black form kept her light hidden from the earth below.

A few days later the King and Queen flew with them to the nearby mountains. They passed over the Lake of Knowledge to the Great Tree, landing on its highest branches. From there they could see all the lands to the forest edge and beyond to the city. With his sharp eyes the eagle could see his former twin, Jerome, about to break out of the forest as he headed for the city. The King told the eagle and his bride that their domain included all the earth below them. They would keep their true identities a secret from most and reside in the city. Any time they wanted they could fly back to visit the palace that would always be their home. The King said he would rely on them to do his bidding and help maintain the hidden order of the world. In time the King and Queen would ascend to the next realm, leaving all their responsibilities and powers to them.

When the first part of the vision revealed itself in 1990 I was very excited and I kept wondering when the Goddess would complete it. The initial segment went as far as the transformed primitive man giving Jerome his ring and Jerome in turn giving him his name. Weeks, then months, and finally years went by and all I could do was wonder what would come next. Unexpectedly during a morning meditation in December 1994 the entire vision recapitulated itself and then continued onward. During two more meditations, one in January 1995 and the other in February, the vision came to completion. I was amazed by it in part because, while it is quite archetypal, I could also see how very personal it was. It reflects many of my sadhana issues and my individuation processes.

My mind has been swimming with all the details of the symbols that the Shakti called up from the depths to create this tale. I began planning how I would write about it, excitedly thinking of all the amplifications and associations to the symbols that could be used. It started to look like a whole book in itself, until one morning as I was going into in meditation, a thought passed through my mind about the extensive work needing to be done in order to unravel all the symbolic details in the vision. The Goddess said, "No. Be brief. Let people have their own experience of the vision and discover the meaning of it for themselves." The few pages that follow are my best effort to obey her command!

In myths, dreams, and visions all the details, even the smallest or what, to our ordinary waking-state mind, seems the most insignificant, are symbolic statements of real importance. Since I can't delve into the meanings of all the many symbols that the Great Mother was generous enough to give through this vision, I don't want the omission of any of them to be misunderstood as their lacking significance. My attempt at brevity demands that much of what could be said not be said.

Many of the general motifs of the quest are probably obvious to you. The Bird of a Thousand Lights is the Holy Spirit, Mahashakti, Mother of the Universe. Her song is the irresistible Call of the Divine within us, summoning us home to know God and ourselves fully. Her light is the sublime illumination that reveals all mysteries. She is united with the Eagle King, who is also the grace-bestower and the mystic guide. In the Eastern tradition the royal pair are Shiva and Shakti, the Lord and his Power. The forest is the impenetrable Unconscious, the inner world with all its mysteries and wonders, accessible only to those initiated and instructed in how to negotiate the dangerous journey they are undertaking. Leaving the city, the community of man, in self-imposed exile, the novice makes his or her way into the Unknown, the forest, which immediately tears away the conventional outer clothes, the persona and superficial layers of identity. These have to be sacrificed on the spiritual journey, we have to let them go. Cloaked in the shawl, protected by the powerful practices and wisdom given by the spiritual guide, one is able to proceed.

Departing, going into exile, separating oneself from the common con-sciousness of humanity, is the initial phase of the seeker's journey. Joseph Campbell writes:

> ...[T]his exile is the first step of the quest. Each carries within himself the all; therefore it may be sought and discovered within. The differentiations of sex, age, and occupation are not essential to our character, but mere costumes which we wear for a time on the stage of the world. The image of man within is not to be confounded with the garments. We think of ourselves as Americans, children of the twentieth century, Occidentals, civilized Christians. We are virtuous or sinful. Yet such designations do not tell what it is to be man, they denote only accidents of geography, birth-date, and income. What is the core of us? What is the basic character of our being?
>
> The asceticism of medieval saints and the yogis of India, the Hellenistic mystery initiations, the ancient philosophies of the East and of the West, are techniques for the shifting of the emphasis of individual consciousness away from the garments. The preliminary meditations of the aspirant detach his mind and sentiments from the accidents of life and drive him to the core. "I am not that, not that," he meditates: "not my mother or son who has just died; my body, which is ill or aging; my arm, my eye, my head; not the summation of all these things. I am not my feeling; not my mind; not my power of intuition." By such meditations he is driven to his own profundity and breaks through at last, to unfathomable realizations.[2]

Shortly after entering the forest, the inner world, the young man encounters the old woman. On one level she symbolizes the dark devour-ing aspect of the Great Mother, which is part of the real danger anyone, male or female, encounters entering the Unconscious. The young man goes unconscious meeting her. He abandons his practices, he doesn't listen for his master's voice and he doesn't follow the call.

It's important to understand that as we enter the inner realms we encounter many figures, call them archetypes, symbols, Goddesses, Gods, energies, entities, or whatever, and we must have the steadiness of a disciplined mind to discriminate whether or not to engage those figures. They are potent and can take one totally off the path. For this reason most meditation disciplines demand of the aspirant one-pointed attention to their given practice, ignoring any such manifestations from the unconscious. A mystic guide or spiritual preceptor is needed to assist one in learning which figures are allies, which are enemies to be avoided, and which confrontations must be faced. The young man's master instructed him to stay focused on his practices, but as every meditator knows, things come up from inside that sidetrack us. Our journey may feel derailed at those times. The drama we're playing out in such instances indicates the existence of some complex or other psychic structure in which consciousness is bound. Our journey may have to go through there in order to free the energy and we may need professional help to proceed.

In this instance the old woman also symbolizes the binding, restrictive, and eventually soul-deadening dimension of the mother complex, the remnants of a man's early relationship to his mother, lying in his unconscious. To understand in part how this evolves we have to remember how the malevolent woman got there. She said she was imprisoned in the forest glade by an evil king. This symbolizes the bound state that women, the inner feminine in men, and the Goddess have been in as a result of our patriarchal culture. This imprisonment and abuse of the feminine is reflected in the "glass ceiling" that prevents women from achieving equal status, power, and financial standing in the corporate world; in the plundering and polluting of the earth, a revered physical form of the Great Mother; in the recently reported FBI statistic that a woman is beaten every 12 seconds in the United States, and in countless other acts of rape, abuse, and exploitation.

Moore and Gillette[3,4] have contributed greatly to understanding this topic in their books on the masculine archetypes and the archetype of the

King. They point out that the negative effects of the patriarchal order arise from rulership by an undeveloped, immature king, rather than what would be the case if the king were fully developed and mature. A mature king, concerned about the welfare and prosperity of all his subjects, wouldn't tolerate the oppression and exploitation of women or any other segment of the population. The archetype of the mature king has rarely manifested itself in human actuality. The patriarchal order has become synonymous with its pathological form that is injurious to both men and women. In the vision, this was symbolically expressed through the evil king, a negative form of male dominance, who imprisoned the woman in the forest. The vision also presents an alternative to the patriarchy in the joint rulership of the Eagle King and Queen, the Bird of a Thousand Lights, making this union the ideal that the quest is leading toward.

In the Walt Disney film, *The Lion King*, we see a dramatic presentation of the contrasting results of the rulership of a mature king versus an immature king. Mufasa was a mature lion king under whose rulership the kingdom flourished. However, he had a blind spot. Though he could recognize the threat of evil coming from outside the realm, the hyenas, he didn't recognize or deal with the threat from within the kingdom—from his evil brother, Scar. That blind spot proves his undoing. Scar, in his lust for power and his selfish pursuit of his own comfort above all others, symbolizes the shadow side of rulership and the immature king. Scar plots with the hyenas to kill Mufasa and his son in order to take over rulership of the kingdom.

Mufasa tries early on to impart a higher wisdom about kingship to his son after Simba complains at not being able to go to the shadow lands beyond their borders. Simba tells his father he thought a king could do whatever he wants. Mufasa begins teaching him there's more to being king than getting whatever one wants. He explains the king's role and responsibility to others in the Great Circle of Life, ensuring their safety and prosperity. Simba's immature understanding of kingship as simply being able to do whatever he wants is cute and age-appropriate in a cub, but in Scar, a mature adult, the same attitude turns evil and has a terrible outcome. Scar thinks he can do whatever he wants without consequence, even murdering his brother and his brother's son.

For Simba this attitude also leads to inflation: he thinks he's a brave lion and is deluded about what he can do as a cub. He lies to his mother about taking Nala to the water hole and nearly gets them both killed in the elephant graveyard.

There's another shortcoming in Mufasa's reign symbolized by the outmoded, traditionally subordinate role that his mate, Surabi, fulfills. This contrasts with the relationship between Nala and Simba; she is quite able to flip and pin him while wrestling. Nala isn't dominated by Simba. She serves as the catalyst for breaking him out of his immature, selfish, "no worries" attitude, another form of the immature masculine, different from the tyrannical Scar and more self-destructive than other-destructive.

Simba retreats to that "carefree" place with his new buddies in an attempt to deal with the shamed, disempowered, deflated sense of self that he's left with after his father dies, and Scar hangs the blame on him. He's isolated from his community, the pride of lions, and having abandoned his place in the great circle of life he keeps the base company of a warthog and a meercat. They symbolize the low level of existence we sink tow when we give up our true pride, the royalty of our own Self. Fortunately, they have redeeming qualities also; their loyalty and honesty will serve Simba later.

In his guilt-ridden fall, he finds it impossible to claim his true nature as lion king and instead becomes a mere cat. No longer eating food fit for a king, he subsists on bugs. He tries to elevate that lifestyle to something of value, but when he is finally confronted by a mature Nala the little bubble he's been living in bursts. She still holds the vision of his being the king he's meant to be and won't let him relinquish that truth. The wise baboon Rafiki symbolizes the teacher or guru, the being who brings one to Self-knowledge. Rafiki takes Simba on a dark night's journey to the magical waters where he can see his reflection and experience the presence of his father. In a vision of his father, Mufasa admonishes him, saying, "You have become less than who you truly are"[5] (couldn't the Divine say that to most of us?) and awakens him to his true identity. Simba, with the help of his guru, Rafiki, recognizes who he really is, the true heir to the throne. He also realizes his father is a part of him. At this point he is truly ready to take on the role of king in service of his community. He faces and accepts his shadow, his past, and goes on to confront the other shadow figure, Scar. Simba doesn't make the mistake his father made of thinking he can allow Scar to remain in the community. He tells him he has to leave. That forces the ultimate confrontation, which leads to Simba throwing Scar off Pride Rock to the hyenas below. He overthrows Scar with the help of his Queen, even using the flip he learned from her to overthrow Scar—a deeply symbolic statement in itself. With the help of Rafiki and Nala, Simba gained the Self-knowledge and relatedness to others he needed to become a mature king. One wonders if the closing scene with Simba, Nala, and their new cub, accompanied by the warthog, the meercat, and Rafiki, high upon Pride Rock, facing the Great Circle of Life, symbolizes a new form of rulership where power is shared with the feminine and diverse minorities.

Back to the Bird of a Thousand Lights and the imprisoned feminine symbolized in it. The anger and rage of the collective feminine at being oppressed by the evil, immature king, or patriarchy, may in part be consciously felt by women, but often the greater portion of it lies in the unconscious of women and can come out unconsciously against males around them, including loved ones, i.e. their husbands and their own male children. In the mythic vision the evil actions of the king engender the evil actions of the woman. To deal with her imprisonment and the helplessness that has resulted from her disempowerment, the old woman keeps the young man from his quest, imprisoning him just as she is imprisoned.

He's vulnerable to being caught by her because he was inculcated with the attitude that women have to be helped because of their weakness and lack of power. For many men a woman's voice saying "I need help" has an entrancing effect and they go unconscious. Jerome gives up his quest without reflecting on how it is costing him his connection to his spirit and his master. He can't hear the call as he sinks ever deeper into unconsciousness, the unconscious attitude of having to take care of a woman's needs without regard for himself or whether she is deserving of it. He doesn't see her evil and he pays little attention to the horrible effects her gifts and tasks have on him. She has been robbed of her power and soul and she wants to take his; she wants to devour him. That's the evil intent underlying her actions. Her gifts appear kindly, her pleas seem born of genuine need, but her gifts bind and imprison. Her entreaties are the distorted forms taken by her powers as she uses them to hold, entrap, and suck the life-force from her prey. The tasks she gives him of gathering wood and food symbolize her inability to generate the fire and sustenance she needs to live. Robbed of her rightful domain where her powers could express themselves as true nurturance, creativity, wisdom, strength, perseverance, the power to give form and substance to spirit, and all the other forms the Goddesses powers can take, robbed of her rightful place in the psyche, her powers have taken the perverse forms of manipulation, control and soul-predation. The dynamic of the man being the powerful provider and protector while the woman is reduced to a disempowered, needy, demanding shadow of her real self, having to manipulate in order to get what she wants is played out in countless marriages.

The shoes, pants and jacket given by the old woman to the young man symbolize how men, raised primarily by mothers at this time in history in our culture, receive from women the things to clothe themselves to go into the world—the attitudes, the relational patterns, the ways of acting aggressive, sensitive, and so on. Men are imprisoned by these gifts. What they receive from their mothers is at least in part restrictive, even if the mother, unlike the old woman, is operating from the best of intentions. The gifts from the old woman are poisoned by the rage of being imprisoned by the evil king. The young man partially recognizes this and feels how stiff the shoes and clothes are; he sees how they slow him down and make his work more difficult, but he dismisses his perceptions and feelings because he thinks she means well, and he doesn't want to hurt her feelings. His unconscious, co-dependent, protective attitude cost him his freedom, blinding him to the reality of her evil and keeping her imprisoned in the identity of being too weak to hear the truth. Even the recognition of how binding and impeding the clothes are slips out of his consciousness. Soon he no longer even notices them. He's blinded by the unconscious attitude of seeing all women as positive nurturing figures, and this has made him totally vulnerable to the old woman's evil designs. He doesn't evaluate what he is receiving; he assumes that all milk that comes from the breast is that of kindness. He nearly pays with his life for being unconscious and indiscriminately taking in what this woman puts out There are many men who are vulnerable to women in this way and find themselves hurt, manipulated, disconnected from their quest or on the verge of being devoured by a consciously or unconsciously enraged woman in their life.

The young man is so disconnected from the mature masculine, the good King, symbolized by his own master, that he doesn't even think of turning to him for help until he's nearly totally blind and dead. Then he cries out to the master for guidance and is responded to immediately. The instructions he receives are so aggressive and directed at the evil nature of the old woman, which he has yet to perceive, that he finds it easier to believe he is going crazy than to believe what the voice of the master told him. When he finally sees the woman's eyes and the malevolence in them, he knows he has correctly heard his master and must obey him. The task set by the master demands he take hold of his own courage and his own aggressiveness, dismembered parts of his adult masculinity, and do what is necessary. When the old witch comes into his room he has to struggle not to go unconscious again, for then he will be dead. It takes all his strength to withstand her presence and not go unconscious. Having passed that test he is then able to carry out the instructions his spiritual father gave him and free himself from her clutches.

Many men today have no sense of what it is to be truly fathered, to receive the nurturance and guidance only a man can give a boy. Men are busy working away from home, barely present for the family, doing the two things that society still says are fathering—providing an income and begetting children. In ghettos and broken marriages even the remnant of being the provider is often lost, and all that is left is biological fathering. My father did the best he could, but he had little idea what it was to be a father. His father was an alcoholic whom he had to throw out of the house. When he was only 16 he had to quit school to take over providing for the family. This was back in the 1920s. His many great qualities and strong moral convictions made him an extraordinarily good man, but that doesn't make one a complete father. As much as I thank God I had him as a father and know he was more loving and steady than many other fathers of the kids I was growing up with, that didn't take away the pain of what I missed.

When I see what is happening to the enormous number of boys growing up in single parent families with no fatherly presence at all, I shudder to think what the societal outcome is going to be. Although the negative effects of the absence of a father may be more pronounced in that group, similar effects can be seen in boys growing up in families where dad has all but abandoned wife and children in pursuit of power and material rewards, or where dad has had to sacrifice being present in order to provide the income necessary for the family to survive. Unfathered boys develop a very distorted sense of what it is to be a man, a true progenitor and provider, a true king. Often manhood becomes simply the pursuit of wealth and power, the conquest of women and the siring of offspring. It doesn't matter whether that distorted definition of manhood is played out within the arena of gangs and ghetto life or if it gets dressed in white shirts and ties as it plays itself out in corporate structures and suburban neighborhoods. The tragic result is the same: it gets passed on from one generation to the next, worsening as it expands and deepens. Just as the centuries of imprisonment and abuse of the feminine principle in western culture have created an unconscious rage that turns evil and wells up from the collective level of the unconscious into the individual woman and is turned against males in her life, the unconscious rage in men at being brought up by women and left in a bound, soul-deadened state turns against women. In this context it's terribly alarming, but not so surprising, that rape, abuse, child abuse, and abandonment are rising. The answers aren't going to be found in political posturing about family values. The problems have to be looked at much more deeply than that and the solutions are going to demand spiritual, religious, economic and political changes that will take many, many years to evolve. Will our society be able to meet the challenge?

In The Bird of a Thousand Lights, when the young man finally reaches out to his spiritual father, he receives instructions on what to do. He has to overcome his unconscious positive projection and recognize the old woman's evil intent; he has to take hold of his own power of aggression, his power to move forward and get out of her house immediately; he has to get rid of all the binding and restrictive clothes the evil woman has given him; and he has to set the house ablaze, he has to release all the energy tied up in it. The fire is like the great yagna fire of Vedic rituals to which offerings are made. The sacred fire is the Divine Presence and receives the offerings of one's virtues and negativities, symbolically offered to the Divine through substances like rice and ghee that are fed to the fire. As the offerings are consumed by the fire, by the Divine, all the energy bound in them is released, elevating and purifying those making the offerings.

Men and women have to free themselves from what they've taken in or taken on from the imprisoned feminine, both within themselves and from the outside. We have to offer the limiting structures in our psyches to the fire of Consciousness that allows us to be more fully aware and free. This is the inner yagna, the fire of yoga, the crucible of meditation in which energies are transmuted and released. To the inner fire of Consciousness we offer all the limiting forms of identity that bind us, the attitudes, feelings, habits, and reactions that prevent us from being fully conscious, that prevent the Divine from manifesting fully in us. We have to burn down the structures that imprison the feminine, even if the structure looks benign, like a quaint cottage in the woods. Much to the young man's amazement, when he sets the house on fire with the old woman inside, he hears her laughing ecstatically; she's finally freed. Having offered to the fire the bound forms symbolized by the clothes, the cottage, and the old woman, in the same moment the blinding light of the Queen, the Bird of a Thousand Lights, appears; the unbound form is able to manifest itself. The Great Goddess is pleased by the actions of the young man and nearly reveals herself to him. It was she who was part of the bound form of the evil old woman. Freeing the masculine frees the feminine. Once he sets himself free, destroying the prison and the captive form of the feminine, the Goddess comes to him, filling him with the divine sound of her call. From the state of absorption in her presence he falls asleep, he goes unconscious once again, but when he comes out of it, his sight and strength are restored. The path leading forward lies clearly before him and he continues his quest.

It isn't until the end of the quest that he is able to be in the presence of the Goddess/Queen as the Bird of a Thousand Lights and the King without going unconscious. To get to that point takes the completion of many more tasks that symbolize the spiritual development occurring through the course of sadhana. Next he has to face his shadow, his dark, primitive, unconscious side that appears as the wild beast in the animal and snake-infested dark forest. The beast is a deeper part of his masculinity that he couldn't get to without first freeing himself from the dark mother.

When I told a friend about the first half of this vision back in 1991 he told me I must read Robert Bly's *Iron John*[6]. My attention had been so focused on the study and practice of meditation that I had lost track of the men's movement since the last men's group I was in before I left to become a monk. Encountering the myths, insights, and profound truths that Robert Bly has made accessible to us through *Iron John* touched me deeply. Certainly what he has to say applies here, especially concerning the symbolism of the "wild man" with his wealth of instinctual knowledge and wisdom hidden behind his shadowy visage, treasures which he passes on to the boy whom he initiates into manhood. Bly succinctly describes the stages of initiation that the boy in the Iron John myth goes through, and because of the universality of these stages, several appear in the mythic vision of the Bird of a Thousand Lights. Bly writes:

> There are many sorts of initiation, many models, many sequences of rituals and teachings. All sequences of initiatory stages are linear, and initiation itself resembles a sphere. With that warning, we could look at a linear view of male initiation laid out in five stages. First, bonding with mother and separation from the mother. (We do the first moderately well, and the second not well at all, particularly in the suburbs and ghetto.) Second, bonding with the father and separation from the father. (We often postpone the father bonding until we are fifty or so, and then separation still has to be done.) Third, the arrival of the male mother, or the mentor, who helps a man rebuild the bridge to his own greatness or essence. King Arthur is an example of such a male mother. (This step happens haphazardly if at all.) Fourth, apprenticeship to a hurricane energy such as the Wild Man, or the Warrior, or Dionysus, or Apollo. When he has done well, the young man receives a drink from the waters of the god. (Such a drink is one thing the adolescents are asking for.) And finally, fifth, the marriage with the Holy Woman or the Queen.[7]

The story of Jerome's quest begins with the third stage of initiation, his meeting the old man at the forest fence. Reading *Iron John* and seeing the striking similarities to the themes of Jerome's journey, I was once again impressed by the power of the Goddess to produce the archetypal images appearing in meditations or dreams that correspond to similar ones from myths and legends she authored long ago.

The primitive man was abandoned by his parents when he was a child and grew up alone in the wilds of the forest. He is our shadow side, our disowned, disapproved qualities that our family and culture banished from conscious expression. He possesses the symbol of the Self, the gold ring with the black square stone forming the background for the brilliant diamond at the center. The young man's journey necessarily takes him into the dark realm where the wild man lives. The call led him there and left him no exit. We have to redeem and be redeemed by our shadow. Our spiritual journey isn't simply one of entering realms of light and love. We have to go into the dark inner realms. Later Jerome learns from the fairy guarding the princess that only one who has faced the darkness and found the light can proceed to the mystical marriage, the union of opposites.

The encounter with the primitive man moves from the dark foreboding forest to the life-giving, healing, transformative waters of the crystal clear lake. When we first enter the realm of the shadow it can feel quite scary and impenetrably dark. The young man was frightened by the strangely familiar looking pair of eyes that peered out of the blackness surrounding him. Not on a conscious level, but on a deeper level, we know what is lurking in the shadows of our inner world. We may experience this as a negative intuition about what is there. This kind of partial knowledge, tainted by the fear and hostile rejection of our parents that forced the wild man into the shadow world, exaggerates the fear that often rises in our initial confrontation with the wild man. Panic stricken, the young man takes off running. Many who confront their shadow run to escape back into the world. In the crucible of meditation retreats or ashram living negative qualities boil to the surface and test our ability to remain conscious and present in dealing with them. The less attention we give our shadow the more we project it onto others. Fortunately, the only way open to Jerome leads him deeper into the forest and finally to the magic lake. His entire path through the inner world is guided by grace flowing from the divine pair, the King and Queen, Shiva and Shakti, Lord and Holy Spirit.

Although he may at times feel lost and in danger, he is never outside of their divine realm.

The lake with it's magical waters, inhale-able, inspire-able and transformative, symbolizes the healing side of the unconscious with its light in the depths drawing the young man deeper. Diving into the unconscious is the right course of action for transforming the shadow. In this case the unconscious holds the Light, that is greater consciousness. The unconscious doesn't always present itself in such a beneficial manner. Later when he has to cross the water-filled moat to rescue the princess, the waters there are corrosive; to fall in means certain death. To go into the unconscious at the wrong time is very dangerous. In this instance, a way across the waters has to be raised out of the waters, out of the unconscious, with the help of the Tree of Knowledge and the Great Swan, a symbol of our power of discrimination.

In grappling with his shadow and facing the evil, primitive, and abandoned parts of himself in the life-giving waters of the unconscious, the brutishness of the shadow and immature boyishness of the man are washed away. The shadow gains his humanity and the young man gains a more mature masculinity. In the end they are like twins and embrace one another. The shadow is redeemed and seeks to enter the community of man. Entering the depths of the unconscious, engaging our shadow side, bringing it into the light of consciousness, we see that it has much to give us and we have much to give it. It gives us the hidden strengths and talents that we were pressed to abandon or that went unrecognized as we grew up. We give it a human face, a name, and a conscious life as part of the entirety of who we are. The shadow also gives us its negativities and shortcomings that need transformation or containment. These give the gift of humility, connectedness to humanity, and the ability to see other's imperfections with compassion. The wild man gives Jerome the ring, a symbol of the Self, a sign that he has achieved a new level of wholeness. Jerome gave him his name, which he carries back to the city, the larger community of people in which he will finally assume his rightful place.

The ring is the only possession the wild man has from childhood. As a symbol of the Self, of our Divine wholeness, it means that our connection to the Self is lost early in life with the shadow in the dark forest of the unconscious. Jerome, in redeeming his shadow twin, regains that lost wealth.

It's significant that Jerome's name wasn't revealed until he had faced his shadow and gained his wholeness. Not until we've truly faced our shadow, embraced it, and exchanged gifts with it, do we become whole individuals.

What we've seen up to this point is that the young man separated from his outer parents, and from his society as well, and followed the directions of his guide to gain entrance to the inner realms of the forest. After being stripped of his persona, the outer layers of who he was, he encountered the inner mother, the threatening, devouring aspects of his relationship with the feminine, and his naive indiscriminate relationship to the Unconscious. With the help of his master he frees himself from that complex of energies and proceeds to run into his shadow. With no exit, he was forced to engage the shadow and, receiving the blessings of the unconscious, to do so in a way that was elevating and transformative. He emerges stronger, more mature, and compassionately embraces his twin. With the achievement of this new level of integration and wholeness we learn his name is Jerome. Why Jerome?

I wondered about this at the time. I have no personal associations to the name and can't think of anyone named Jerome. I looked it up in the dictionary and to my astonishment discovered it derives from the Greek *heiros*, meaning sacred or holy, and *onymos*, name. It means "holy name." He is a holy one. One who has entered the inner realms, faced his or her shadow and transformed it, while at the same time being transformed by it, is often revered as a holy or spiritual person. Only such an individual may be a fit candidate for the *heiros gamos*, the holy marriage symbolizing the uniting of the pairs of opposites that marks the ultimate achievement of the spiritual journey. Many people work through their mother and father complexes, many confront pieces of their shadow, but only those treading the path of saints, shamans or enlightened beings so deeply engage the shadow and move on to the state of mystical union. Jerome unknowingly heads toward that destiny. The ring, symbolizing his new-found wholeness and connectedness to the Self, proves his worthiness to engage in the next part of his quest.

The call leads him to the village, where he is recognized by the elders as "the one." This is revealed to him in the sacred space of the elders' temple. Everything about the temple proclaims its sanctity: the doubling of the number four, the number symbolizing wholeness and the Self, in the eight sides, the eight columns, the eight elders; the presence of the sacred fire symbolizing the Light of Consciousness; the only opening placed in the center of the domed ceiling as a portal to the Divine; the columns made from huge trees symbolizing the holy Tree of Knowledge. What he receives in that holy place is of the utmost significance as the symbols point to its coming from the Self. There he is given the knowledge that he is the chosen one and his quest is to save the princess. He demonstrates his newly found wisdom by not immediately committing himself to the task. He has learned to be wary from his past encounter with the feminine principle in the form of the evil old woman. The conditioning by which he had previously responded automatically to a woman in need, is broken. He has learned to take the time to bring decisions and challenges into the sacred space of his practices. In meditation he receives the command from his master to free the princess "at all cost," and informs the elders of his commitment to the task.

Through the princess we're presented with another symbolic form of the feminine imprisoned by the negative masculine, this time a warlord, suggestive of the outmoded form of rogue masculine aggression again confining the feminine.

The princess is being guarded by a powerful form of the earth Goddess. She is the one who informs Jerome that he is to marry the princess after freeing her. He's moving toward the *heiros gamos*, the sacred marriage.

Now he has to prove himself through the successful completion of tasks set by the water fairy. The ring shows he might be the one to set the princess free, but he has to show possession of the powers and strengths the ring symbolizes. First he is sent to retrieve the Great Tree, the Tree of Life.

What does this task say about the spiritual quest? The Great Tree appears in myths and legends around the globe and in the Bible and the *Bhagavad Gita*. The seeker has to find the Great Tree of Life, symbolic of the wisdom that connects the upper reaches of the divine and the lowest reaches of the earth. Finding that wisdom, he has to bring it down from the heights of the mountain pass, down from the exalted states of prayer or meditation, and into the valley where the common people live. The whole tree can't be brought down, but a seed from it can. The seeker brings a seed of it back and plants it near the life-giving waters of the unconscious, not in the high and dry realms of rational thought, but in the damp fertile ground near the realms of dream and mystic vision. To get the seed costs the seeker his right thumb, it cost him his ability to grasp with his right hand. This is the rational grasping of the left brain; linear, logical thinking has to be sacrificed to bring the seed back to daily life. The insights, wisdom, and visions one receives in meditation can't be grasped by the rational mind, nor can they be nourished or integrated into daily life by the rational mind. Supra-rational processes like faith, devotion and intuition guide us in retrieving the seeds of profound wisdom from our practices and helping them to flourish in our day to day living. In the East the thumb symbolizes the ego and its grasping, self-appropriating ways. These have to be sacrificed for divine knowledge.

Next the fairy tells him there's a great swan in the Lake of Knowledge that he must fetch. His strength and perseverance carry him to the distant Lake where he encounters an enormous swan that has the ability to talk. In the ancient *Chandogya Upanishad*[8] there is mention of a swan revealing to a seeker the nature of the Absolute, Brahman. The swan here won't return with Jerome, but when he asks for an egg at his master's insistence, the swan agrees to give him one. Again this symbolizes a seed form of the swan's great consciousness. The egg will cost him the "pointing finger" from his right hand. Jerome makes the sacrifice, returns with the egg, and like the seed from the tree, it grows to full size in a mythical period of time. By drinking the water the swan lowers the level to such an extent, that now there is access to the opening of the cave where the princess is imprisoned. The lowering of the water brought about by the retrieval of the tree and the swan symbolizes a raising of consciousness and a lowering of the dangerous imprisoning level of unconsciousness.

The swan is like the mythical swan of India, the paramahamsa, which is said to have such great powers of discrimination that it can drink the milk alone out of water mixed with milk. The milk symbolizes knowledge of the divine mixed in with all lesser knowledge, the eternal existence of the Self mingled with the ephemeral existence of the world. One who is called a paramahamsa, a great swan, like Ramakrishna Paramahamsa[9], is said to possess such discrimination. He or she can perceive the Real, the True, the Eternal, in everything around them.

After accessing all the knowledge of the Great Tree, one needs discrimination, the ability to discern the right knowledge to drink in and nourish one's mystic vision. The swan is at home both on the water and in the air, symbolizing the fully developed spiritual consciousness that can soar to the heights as well as swim gracefully on the waters of the unconscious; she is able to plunge her long neck into those waters and draw out only that which is good to take into her being. Gaining consciousness costs the forefinger of the right hand. Sacrificing the rational, linear way of indexing, of pointing and differentiating between this and that, what in the East is called the intellect, is demanded of the seeker of higher wisdom. We can't proceed on our quest rationally, we can't follow the Shakti, the Queen, by looking for reasonable directions through the twists and turns of our journey, and Jerome can't follow the master or the call by doing what is reasonable. The sacrifices force Jerome, force seekers, to rely more and more on the left side, the arational, nonlinear, wholistic, nondominant way of perceiving and acting. Achieving this, Jerome is given the next to the last task before winning the princess and the sacred marriage. It's only the penultimate trial. The Eagle King will give the final ordeal.

The third task of leaping perilously from jagged rock to rock across the moat gains him the company of the princess and opens his heart to love for the first time. Though he doesn't know this will happen at the outset, his success also earns him the gratitude of the fairy, which she expresses by restoring his sacrificed fingers and leg. The fairy, pleased by the freeing of the princess, withdraws into the ground, true to her nature as earth Goddess.

The Shakti is pressing me about saying too much. I must end quickly. Perhaps one day she will allow me to write more concerning the rich symbolism she used to create this mythic vision of our spiritual journey. She is only interested in our taking our journey and discovering the divine wonder all around us and within us. She has given these visions to inspire us to fully engage in our quest. She doesn't care about the intellect's fascination with symbolic meaning, though I try to convince her it enables us to better marshal the energies of the mind, body, and spirit to move forward.

To cross the moat and stay out of the deadly water Jerome must rely primarily on the strength of his left side. The task forces him to demonstrate his possession and ability to use the nondominant side and remain above water, remain conscious. It's like the test given to certain meditators of a Tibetan tradition. The aspirant must go out naked during a winter's night onto a frozen lake high in the mountains. Using only the heat given off by their body while performing a particular type of meditation, the aspirant has to dry three wet frozen sheets, one at a time, by wrapping them around his body. His ability to do this demonstrates mastery of the meditation practice.

Jerome's task called for the next sacrifice, his right foot, and for the demonstration of his mastery of pain. His right side disabled, the last leap was powered entirely by his left side. The right foot is a way of going forward in the world, an aggressive, "put the right foot forward" kind of attitude that is again related to the rational, linear way of taking something on and going forward. It won't get one across the moat. It was a fortuitous slip into the waters that took his right foot. Had he leaped using it, he would not have made it across. It takes a leap of the suprarational, intuitive side to land where the imprisoned feminine waits.

The place where the princess is imprisoned is a wonderfully rich, complex symbol. The stone mountain rising out of the waters looks like a great Shiva lingam surrounded by a yoni. The princess is in a cave within the base of the lingam, a feminine hollow deep within the masculine. That which protects her from masculine aggression, the earth Goddess, is also that which imprisons her while she awaits a virtuous man to release her. Presumably by completing the tasks given him by the fairy, Jerome has demonstrated the strengths and purified aggression necessary to prevent a warlord from threatening the princess again, and shown his worthiness to be her spouse. A combination of masculine and feminine guidance allows the seeker, Jerome, to be successful. He receives direct instructions from his master, and he's guided on a more intuitive level by the call from the Bird of a Thousand Lights, the Great Goddess or Holy Spirit.

He hears the Bird's call even as he lies unconscious on the ground after having made that last heroic jump. The call draws his consciousness beyond the pain of his body, enabling him to hobble forward on his left leg alone and enter the cave. His heart opens upon seeing the princess and he's filled with love for her. This marks a dramatic shift in the seeker's experience of the quest. Up until this point Jerome's progress reflected the strength of his commitment and determination, along with the powerful allure of the Bird's call. Feelings haven't had much of an influence except in a deluding, unconscious, obstructive way. His feelings for the evil old woman misguided him in dealing with her. His fear of the wild man threw him into panicked flight. But when he beholds the princess he is filled with love and compassion for her. He becomes excited, he wants to marry her, in contrast to his earlier reluctance, and looks forward to uncovering the mysteries of her hidden nature.

Before he can free her he has to place the ring on his left forefinger. Only the power of the ring thus worn can break the last binding spell imprisoning her. Here the true potency of the ring is revealed. The left side, pointing with the left index finger, empowered by the Self, symbolized by the ring, overcomes the spell. The ring with its black square symbolizing two pairs of opposites, or the four quarters of the world, or the four psychic functions of C. G. Jung, are brought to a point of unity in the Self, symbolized by the round brilliant diamond in the center. Ultimately it is the transcendent, integrative power of the Self that frees the deep inner opposite buried within us. Then we're led to the palace of the King and Queen, Shiva and Shakti, where one last task awaits before the holy union is celebrated.

Before they leave for the abode of the King and Queen, the fairy, another form of the Great Goddess, restores Jerome's fingers and foot. Though we may sacrifice our right side on the inner quest, it is restored to us as we proceed. There's nothing wrong with rational, logical, linear thinking in the realm of waking state consciousness. But in the mystic realms and altered states of consciousness its continued dominance impedes the quest. We have to leave it behind, if only to pick it up again later, more conscious of its limited usefulness.

Earlier it was pointed out that the princess was imprisoned by a warlord, a symbol of an outmoded form of male aggression. The quest demands a new form of aggression. Remember that 'aggress' simply means to move forward. The quest requires Jerome to move forward with perseverance and strength and to have his aggression directed by higher powers, feminine and masculine, the Bird of a Thousand Lights and the master. On our journey we learn to place our aggression, our power to move forward, in service of the Queen, the Shakti, Consciousness, or God. Jerome has had to call upon his aggressiveness to persevere through his master's training, to make it through the thorny barriers at the entrance of the forest, to overcome the dark side of the Great Mother, to survive his encounter with the primitive man, and to fulfill the water fairy's demands "at all cost."

The aggression of the seeker, the spiritual hero, is aimed at securing and retrieving knowledge, wisdom, discrimination and detachment, even if sacrificing the body is demanded. The spiritual hero's aggression is directed toward attaining the highest, and results in upliftment for all. This is not the outmoded aggression aimed at the subjugation and exploitation of women, men, and nature. Instead of his aggression being directed by the profit motive or the drive for power and fame, the seeker submits to the ways of the Call. Instead of standing on the backs of others, he or she discovers the Divine standing in the hearts of all. The seeker trades worldly achievement for spiritual ascendance. This is very different from the ways society teaches men to be aggressive. We must make a shift in how we understand and direct our aggression.

I have to leap to the final task given Jerome by the Eagle King. The Shakti wants this brought to a close.

This test demands the ultimate sacrifice. The King seals him in a cave on his birthday and he won't be let out until his rebirth on his next birthday. Through the Eagle King we see the transformative power of the archetypes of Zeus and Hermes at work. The Eagle King embodies Zeus energy. The stone wall and cave are heralds of Hermes, guide to souls in the process of the most profound transformation. Held in the high mountain cave with no further contact from his master or the Call, Jerome encounters silence and the baby eagle. In the silence he moves to a deeper awareness.

The fledgling bird symbolizes the developing higher consciousness to which he has to give his all. His master's last instructions were to hold nothing back. In the end he literally feeds himself to the eagle. It symbolizes the higher consciousness consuming the totality of one's personhood. The *Shiva Sutras* (II, 8) say, "The body is the offering." Commenting on this sutra, the great 10th century sage Kshemaraja wrote that "the aspirant offers the physical, subtle and causal body to the supreme fire of

Consciousness, the Light of God, and is freed from the ignorance of iden-tification with them. Then he is constantly steeped in the pure Consciousness of being his Self."[10]

Jerome as he was at the outset of his quest no longer exists. He is trans-formed into this new being. The *Mundaka Upanishad* says: "As rivers flow into the sea and in so doing lose name and form, even so the wise man, freed from name and form, attains the Supreme Being, the Self-luminous, the Infinite."[11]

After the ritual time of one year passes, the new being, freed from the cave by the Eagle King and the Bird of a Thousand Lights, is reborn and given a new name. He no longer is the one he was. He is unlike any ordi-nary human being because he has the power to transform himself from his Eagle body to his human body and thus enjoy the lofty realms of the spirit and the earthly realms of human form. This symbolizes entering the cave of the heart in meditation and sealing one's awareness in there for the rit-ual time of one year, one complete cycle, which could be a lifetime, a decade, or whatever period one needs to be consumed and reborn with the ability to move with ease between all realms of existence. He gave himself completely to the Divine and the Divine gave itself completely to him. The human became Divine and the Divine became human. Heaven and earth are joined at the end of our quest.

With the final transformation completed, the holy marriage takes place, the union of opposites symbolized by wedding the Dark Eagle, the newly transformed Eagle Prince, and the Bird of a Thousand Lights, the Princess. Their later return to the world signifies bringing that unity awareness into daily life. The spiritual hero's quest isn't complete without the return. From then on he serves the King in maintaining the hidden divine order. Each of us in our own way has to bring the blessings of what we receive from the states of union we experience into our everyday worldly life, even if it is simply to smile at a stranger and inwardly offer a prayer that he or she may be blessed. People are so ready to offer their venom and curses to others, why not cultivate a practice of quietly offering blessings? Why is it everyone knows how to make a fist and raise a finger to curse and no one knows how to raise their hand in the gesture that confers blessings?

Jerome's sacrifice to the growing eagle symbolizes the permanent shift in consciousness that occurs as our Eagle-vision consumes through meditation, through our practice of sitting in the cave of the heart, our ordinary consciousness born of limited identity. This final task demands of Jerome the quality of supreme compassion. It reminds me of a story I heard about a great saint who was the embodiment of compassion and dharma, righteous action. He was out walking when a quivering little rabbit ran to him and took refuge at his feet. A hawk was hunting the rabbit. Out of compassion he saved the rabbit from certain death. However, the hawk was very upset. He was terribly hungry and argued that he was just following his dharma as a hawk and hunting what was rightfully his prey. The saint felt compassion for the hungry hawk as well. Taking a knife, he cut a piece of flesh from his body equal in weight to that of the rabbit and fed it to the hawk. He willingly made the sacrifice for the sake of compassion and dharma.

Jerome's sacrifice brought me back to my memories of the sannyasa ceremony, the ancient Vedic ritual for initiating one into monkhood, in which I was originally going to take the vows of a monk. Due to a change in fate, I was present only to serve the needs of the Brahman priests and those being initiated. The ritual is a profoundly powerful ceremony conducted around the sacred fire, the yagna, to which one offers, through mantras and various ritual materials, one's entire mind, body and spirit. In the ceremony you also perform your own funeral rites, signifying the death of who you were and freeing you of any karmic obligation in the future when your body dies. The ritual goes on day and night, ending with the initiates walking into a river in the predawn hours to release their bodies in death, freeing their consciousness to merge in the Absolute. Just as they enter the depths of the river, the presiding monk calls them back to a life of serving God and humanity. Later, the initiates are given a new name, which is a name of the Divine. Ritually they have renounced their limited identity and merged with the Absolute. Thus they are given a name by which the Absolute is known.

It was a great blessing to me to have been permitted to serve at that ceremony. I had accepted that the outer form of monkhood wasn't my path in this lifetime, but I yearned for the inner freedom that comes from renunciation. I was determined to take an inner form of sannyasa. During the ceremony I recited in my mind all the mantras and made all the offerings to an image of a blazing fire, the fire of yoga deep within me. By the end of the ceremony it felt like "I" was gone. When we went to the river I started to walk into the river with the initiates. In the dark somebody held my arm and gently pulled me back. Afterwards all the initiates went to the great meditation master's house to receive an ancient Vedic form of mantra diksha, initiation by mantra, and their new names. I was sitting close to Baba, the master, as the new monks came up to him one by one. They were radiant with Shakti and their freshly shaved heads glowed. In a manner that had been done for thousands of years, the guru would draw a new initiate near to him and, throwing a silk shawl over their heads, he would whisper the mantra in the monk's ear, thus giving a very powerful form of mantra diksha, initiation by mantra. Baba was ecstatic as he gave the highest truth over and over to these open-hearted souls. I was near enough so I could hear his melodious voice saying, "Aham Brahmasmi!," an ancient mantra from the Vedas declaring "I Am Brahman," "I Am the Absolute." Over and over again I heard him say "Aham Brahmasmi, Aham Brahmasmi, Aham Brahmasmi, Aham Brahmasmi". "I am the Absolute, I am the Absolute, I am the Absolute." I started to become drunk on the awareness of "I AM THE ABSOLUTE." My body swayed, tears ran down my cheeks, my spirit danced in ecstasy as I merged into the Absolute. Then all movement ceased, Consciousness alone remained.

A few hours after the ceremony had concluded I went to get something to eat. As I looked around the dining area everything looked far away, as if I were looking at the world through the wrong end of a pair of binoculars.

Even sounds from people talking nearby seemed distant. I was having difficulty negotiating being in my body and getting it to move through space. I finally managed to get some food, hoping it would help ground me in ordinary reality, but I sat down and just stared at it for some time. My consciousness kept leaving my body and expanding into the universe. At one point as my awareness returned I found my body feeding itself quite nicely and I was pleased to see it remembered what to do with the food and how to move the hands and mouth appropriately. For a couple of days when people called my name I didn't automatically recognize it as me. I felt as if I didn't have a name or an identity. It caused some awkward moments, and I literally had to begin repeating to myself "I am Lawrence" to remind myself of who I was in this particular form. I could see why they gave the initiates, the swamis, new names, names of the Absolute. The ritual has the power to propel one's consciousness into unity with the Absolute. The initiate then spends the rest of his or her life attempting to prolong and sustain that awareness while living a life of service.

Jerome sacrificed himself to the Divine Consciousness symbolized by the Eagle and became one with what he gave himself entirely to. He lived the rest of his life serving the Divine in the world.

The sacrifice of holy ones is apparent in every spiritual tradition. In Christianity it is believed that Jesus sacrificed his body out of compassion for humanity. The *Upanishads* also proclaim that the body is the offering.

At the end of the vision of the Bird of a Thousand Lights, when the King and Queen flew with the Eagle Prince and the Princess to the top of the Great Tree, my awareness joined that of the Eagle Prince. The Eagle King and the Queen were perched just above and behind me while my bride was at my right side. My talons gripped the tree branch. I could feel through the tree and its roots and branches a deep, intimate connectedness to the earth and the wide domains of land, water, sky and heaven that I surveyed from my perch. The whole magnificent realm was an extension of me, an expression of my being. The experience was filled with a complex mix of expansiveness, loving compassion, and a profound sense of responsibility mingled with a detached completeness in myself, supreme power, and divine wisdom.

The *Chandogya Upanishad* says: "In the world of Brahman there is a lake whose waters are like nectar, and whosoever tastes thereof is straight-way drunk with joy; and beside that lake is a tree which yields the juice of immortality."[12] In the vision the Shakti brought me there.

When I later meditated on this scene again, I was surprised to hear the ecstatic laughter I had heard 13 years earlier. It was Kali's divine laugh. She had invited me to join her those many years ago in the play of creation and dissolution. I wasn't able to. Back then I was too stuck wanting to be her son and have her rescue me from creation and from all that goes with taking on limited forms. I only found joy in the dissolution and merger. Now it was clear she had been inviting me to be the King, to be Shiva, her husband, her co-creator, and give up being her dependent child. As my awareness merged with the Eagle atop the Tree of Knowledge, I regained the feeling of being connected to every color and shape in the regions of the earth, water, and sky. I could hear my beloved Kali's divine laughter and I began to laugh and cry simultaneously. I felt the unbounded ecstasy of total freedom and at the same time I felt the acute suffering and severe bondage of the spirits caught in the drama of creation. Between those two poles were many shades of hope and despair.

From their lofty position atop the Tree, the Eagle King, the Bird of a Thousand Lights, the Eagle Prince and his Princess—these four radiated Power and Light that fell equally everywhere, just as the sun gives itself to all inhabitants of earth. What an individual did with the Power and Light revealed whether he or she was a seeker of the highest wisdom or still a seeker of lower orders of knowledge and experience. The ones who were seeking something higher reflected more of the Light back and could eas-ily be distinguished from seekers of the lower orders who absorbed the Light, appearing dull and dark in comparison. Yet even these spirits had an unmaskable beauty and dignity about them. All were lovely to behold.

The return of the Eagle Prince with his wife, the Bird of Light, into the world to assist in maintaining the divine order wasn't going to require heroic deeds in the world. They weren't going back to preach, exhort, or establish a new religion. Their place in the universal drama wasn't focused on "doing" anymore; it was a matter of simply being and of radiating love and wisdom as effortlessly as the sun radiates light and warmth. They were embodiments of what it is to be a Conscious knower of the truth, a knower of the play of shadow and light in the drama of creation, a knower of the true relationship among all created things, a knower of the true divine nature of every thing, a knower of the true relationship between Creator and created. By simply being such a one, each of them serves the Divine, the King and Queen. Being the embodiment of wisdom they became chalices for the Divine to quietly pour Grace into our world of existence.

Through the vision of the Bird of a Thousand Lights the Shakti revealed more of what we may encounter on our quest. The universal mythic themes depicted here may resonate with the unique forms those themes take in each of our lives. As you contemplate your own quest you will discover how the themes in your life are similar or different, which themes find greater or lesser emphasis in your life, which one's you've already encountered, and which you can look forward to meeting on your path. May you enjoy the full Light and Grace of the Divine on your journey!

Chapter 5

To Know and To Serve

Teach me, my God and King,
In all things Thee to see
And what I do in any thing
To do it as for Thee.

George Herbert[1]

The words of Joseph Campbell from The Hero with a Thousand Faces aptly summarize what the Goddess has shown to be the seeker's quest, the spiritual hero's journey:

> ...[T]he first work of the hero is to retreat from the world scene of secondary effects to those causal zones of the psyche where the difficulties really reside, and there to clarify the difficulties, eradicate them in his own case (i.e., give battle to the nursery demons of his local culture) and break through to the undistorted, direct experience and assimilation of what C. G. Jung has called "archetypal images." This is the process known to Hindu and Buddhist philosophy as viveka, 'discrimination'.
>
> The archetypes to be discovered and assimilated are precisely those that have inspired, throughout the annals of human culture, the basic images of ritual, mythology and vision....[2]

The hero, therefore is the man or woman who has been able to battle past his personal and local historical limitations to the generally valid, normally human forms. Such a one's visions, ideas, and inspirations come pristine from the primary springs of human life and thought. Hence they are eloquent, not of the present, disintegrating society and psyche, but of the unquenched source through which society is reborn. The hero has died as a modern man; but as eternal man—perfected, unspecific, universal man—he has been reborn. His second solemn task and deed therefore (as Toynbee declares and as all the mythologies of mankind indicate) is to return then to us, transfigured, and teach the lesson he has learned of life renewed...[3]

...The passage of the mythological hero may be over-ground, incidentally; fundamentally it is inward—into the depths where obscure resistances are overcome, and long lost, forgotten powers are revivified, to be made available for the transfiguration of the world.[4]

The standard path of the mythological adventure of the hero is a magnification of the formula represented in the rites of passage: *separation—initiation—return...*
A hero ventures forth from the world of common day into a region of supernatural wonder: fabulous forces are there encountered and a decisive victory is won: the hero comes back from this mysterious adventure with the power to bestow boons on his fellow man...[5]

The return and reintegration with society, which is indispensable to the continuous circulation of spiritual energy into the world, and which from the standpoint of the community, is the justification of the long retreat, the hero himself may find the most difficult requirement of all. For if he has won through, like the Buddha, to the profound repose of complete enlightenment, there is danger that the bliss of the this experience may annihilate all recollection of, interest in, or hope for, the sorrows of the world; or else the problem of making known the way of illumination to people wrapped in economic problems may seem too great to solve...

The composite hero of the monomyth is a personage of exceptional gifts. Frequently he is honored by his society, frequently unrecognized or disdained. He and/or the world in which he finds himself suffers from a symbolical deficiency...[6]

The two—the hero and his ultimate god, the seeker and the found—are thus understood as the outside and inside of a single, self-mirrored mystery, which is identical with the mystery of the manifest world. The great deed of the supreme hero is to come to the knowledge of this unity in multiplicity and then to make it known.[7]

Through the mythic visions the Shakti, the Goddess Kundalini or Holy Spirit, reveals how she leads us as seekers, heroes of our own spiritual quest, to the goal of knowing the Divine and returning to a life of serving the One. We saw this through the Queen's journey in "Ascent to Union," through the father, son and daughter in "The Golden Spoon" and through Jerome's quest for the Bird of a Thousand Lights. At the successful completion of the quest, the seeker serves by becoming a Light-bearer, one who brings a higher order of knowledge back to the city, back to the community of earth. We come to know God in the only way that God can be known—through union, through merger in the Absolute. Thereafter, the transformed, enlightened being lives out the remainder of her or his embodied existence serving the Divine in whatever he or she does, their mind and body used the Divine to manifest a more perceivable Presence. That Presence may or may not be recognized by most of humanity, nor does it matter. When the Divine wants to be known, it reveals itself to whomever it chooses. The *Katha Upanishad* says: "This Self cannot be attained by instruction, nor by intellectual power, nor even through much hearing. He is to be attained only by the one whom the Self chooses. To such a one the Self reveals his own nature."8 The quest ends in our serving the Divine and experiencing the delight of union with the Divine, not necessarily in recognition by others of what has been attained.

For many centuries knowledge of the Kundalini was a closely held secret. Awakening of the Kundalini occurred after either a long discipleship to a master, or after many years, perhaps lifetimes, of rigorous practices aimed at purifying the physical and subtle body sufficiently to allow the seeker to gather enough energy to attempt awakening the Kundalini through yogic means. I wonder if something in humanity has shifted because knowledge of the Kundalini and mystic states of union are widely accessible and people are experiencing spontaneous awakenings of the Kundalini. Without demanding the traditional prolonged discipleship, mystic guides capable of awakening the Kundalini are giving away the golden means for entering the depths of Consciousness and providing the wisdom necessary to follow the Goddess's inscrutable ways. The Goddess is directly making her presence known more and more powerfully in many arenas, including the women's and men's movements, politics, and Goddess worship groups. Perhaps this indicates how much the Divine One wants to be known in this age of Kali. The Kundalini is the Creator's power of Self-revelation and she is helping people attune themselves to the Call.

At the same time as knowledge of the Kundalini is becoming more widespread, there's an increasing danger that people who aren't prepared for the potent unleashing of energy that accompanies Kundalini awakening will experience difficulties. The purificatory process initiated by the Shakti produces what are called kriyas, literally movements of energy, which may be experienced physically, emotionally, mentally, and as shifts of consciousness that open our awareness to sounds, lights, and visions from subtler inner worlds. Physical kriyas during meditation may be experienced as the body spontaneously goes into hatha yoga postures or yogic breathing, which may be very rapid or slow; different physical sensations may arise: heat, cold, tingling, numbness; and other forms of physical movement may occur without the meditator intending it or willing it to happen. All forms of kriyas are manifestations of the movement of the Shakti, and mystics of every tradition report experiences of them.

Emotional kriyas take the forms of all the different types of feelings we can have, from profound sadness to sublime ecstasy. As kriyas happen in meditation, the meditator attempts to remain a Witness, detached, allowing the energy to do its work and run its course. An attitude of gratitude is beneficial. We can cultivate an attitude of appreciation for all that the power of grace is doing to allow us to experience fully the presence of the Divine.

Mental kriyas may be experienced as racing thoughts, cessation of thoughts; insights and understandings; sluggishness of thinking, or spaciness. I had to struggle to remain detached during some of these kinds of kriyas. They hooked me on a level that I identify with. I've had to be particularly vigilant not to let my meditations be governed by pleasurable runs of intellectual gymnastics or flights of intuitive understanding. Since I do think the Shakti wants to purify the instruments of the intellect and intuition by running energy through them, I regularly give myself time for contemplation and studying the scriptures and the writings of mystics from various traditions. Perhaps this will work for you. In this way we allow our meditations to be free of even sublime thoughts, which are only distractions when we're in the presence of the One.

The Shakti also produces spontaneous shifts in consciousness to what yoga considers subtler realms where divine sounds called *nada* may be heard and visions may appear. There are also times when the Kundalini moves our consciousness into states of union with God. As sublime and beneficial as these experiences are, they can be deluding if one develops a false or pseudo-enlightenment from them. Just because I occasionally go visit some place doesn't mean I've taken up permanent residence there. The power of grace can move our consciousness into the Divine Presence anytime, allowing us to become acquainted with our Self. Such experiences don't signify our enlightenment.

Kriyas of any type can be distracting, impeding progress if we become focused on them instead of on the Consciousness that illumines and produces them. Often spiritual teachers will show an attitude of disdain for kriyas or tell the student to ignore such phenomena. This is good medicine to help counteract the numinous attractive quality many of the kriyas can have. Once someone complained to Baba that he really wanted to see lights in meditation and felt frustrated that he couldn't. Baba said, if you want to see lights look at the chandelier, if you want to see God, welcome whatever form He appears in during your meditation. The same Consciousness makes up one's thoughts, feelings, sensations, insights, intuitions, images, sounds, lights, or whatever else may be experienced. In practicing meditation our task is to direct our attention to the Experiencer, not the experience. "Be the seer not the seen," as I quoted the Shakti saying earlier.

Kriyas, movements of the Shakti purifying the subtle and physical bodies, can also be disturbing if they interfere with one's normal, waking state, reality-related, ego functioning. In such cases people may find themselves in danger of being psychiatrically diagnosed, medicated, or even hospitalized. This is where a paradigm clash can have tragic consequences for the seeker whose consciousness is opening to altered states that may be confused with psychosis. The Association for Transpersonal Psychology (www.atpweb.org) is a resource for individuals in crisis to find the proper care without unnecessarily pathologizing their experience.

Because of the attendant risks of Kundalini awakening, the yogic texts always emphasize studying only with an adept master. While I was in undergraduate school I studied with a "yogi" who claimed to be able to awaken and guide the Kundalini. After several months of intense hatha yoga exercises and forceful pranayama practices I began going into altered states uncontrollably, perceiving what seemed to be parallel realities coexisting in time and space with ordinary reality. This was profoundly disturbing to me. I immediately went to the "yogi" and I was shocked to see the surprise and confusion on his face. He had no idea what to do. I stopped the practices and never saw him again. Gradually over about two months the experiences subsided and ceased. I advise people to be very cautious in choosing someone under whose guidance they will approach the Kundalini.

The movements of the awakened Kundalini are aimed at removing from the physical and subtle bodies any blocks impeding the Shakti from moving freely throughout and manifesting the fully expanded Consciousness of one's true Self. Like Captain and Will we can align our intention with that of the Shakti by actively taking steps to clean up our lifestyles. The *yamas* and *niyamas*, the restraints and observances prescribed by Patanjali, are excellent practices that ground one in a way that allows one to experience the Shakti without becoming dysfunctional. Patanjali's *Yoga Sutras* are essential reading, and there's an excellent translation with commentary by Swami Prabhavananda and Christopher Isherwood, entitled *How to Know God.* The five restraints are: not injuring any being, truthfulness, not stealing in any way, sexual continence, and not coveting anything. The five observances are: purity, contentment, self-discipline, study of scriptures and chanting, and devotion to God. The harmony with one's Self and one's environment created by devotedly living the restraints and observances enables one to experience the purifying work of the Shakti to be in accord with one's daily life.

In this context we can understand these words of the Lord from the *Bhagavad Gita*:[9]

> One should lift oneself by the Self alone; one should not lower one-self; for this Self alone is the friend of oneself, and the self alone can be an enemy of oneself.

> The Self is the friend of the self for him who has conquered himself by the Self, but for him who has not conquered himself, this Self stands in the position of an enemy.

The Shakti is the power of the Self that stands like an enemy in opposition to the habits, attitudes and desires—the "unconquered self"—that continue to block or impede the manifestation of higher Consciousness. Many people after experiencing Kundalini awakening find bad habits falling away, healthier interests and tastes developing, and they find new ways of approaching problems. Who can resist the Shakti? She will be victorious. Why not surrender right now? The Sufi poet-saint Rumi said, "Don't run off babbling—there is no escape from God."[10]

Let the Self conquer the self and attain wisdom and virtue. The *Katha Upanishad* declares: "The senses of the wise man obey his mind, his mind obeys his intellect, his intellect obeys his ego, and his ego obeys the Self."[11] The conquered self, the obedient ego, gives the One her unwavering attention, ever ready to fulfill the will of the Divine. The *Brihadaranyaka Upanishad* says "…[L]et him know the kingdom of the Self and that alone. The virtue of him who meditates on the kingdom of the Self is never exhausted: for the Self is the source from which all virtue springs."[12]

After the awakening of Kundalini, one's experience of the ensuing transformation depends in part on one's ability to quickly and gracefully come into alignment with the will of the Divine. Often this process is neither quick nor graceful. I've worked with people who, regardless of how much they've purified their way of living, still went through very trying experiences after Kundalini awakening. Some individuals had histories of undiagnosed mental disorders that were made more obvious by the Shakti, but others simply had to go through whatever purificatory process the Shakti prescribed. From the yogic perspective even mental disorders are simply patterns of samskaras in the subtle body, patterns to be transformed by the Kundalini.

Imagine you are given an extraordinary one-of-a-kind car designed especially for you. It's a sleek, high-performance, and rugged model. Suppose you go on a long trip, driving your new vehicle through deserts, swamps, muddy ruts, and off the roads up into the mountains, having numerous collisions along the way as you crawl up to one high point and crash down from another. After having great fun you turn your vehicle back over to the one who built it to be repaired. Is there any wonder that she has to hammer, bang, scrape, polish, and replace things to return the vehicle to its original high-performance condition? The physical and subtle bodies combine to form a vehicle for Consciousness. Through her actions, her kriyas, the Shakti makes our vehicle fit to serve God.

My belief is that the awakened Kundalini does only what is necessary for freeing the bound consciousness of the individual in order to allow one the experience of unbroken unity with the Divine. In so doing she doesn't necessarily act within the constraints of what is socially or psychiatrically defined as normal. In fact, she has to break the socially constructed bars that hold shut the doors of perception that must be opened for us to truly see—to see God in ourselves, in others, and in the world around us. The seeker undergoing such radical renovation often needs a new context and a support group for understanding and integrating the experiences he or she is having. Often the spiritual tradition and one's mystic guide provide these.

The long-term effects of Kundalini awakening are extraordinarily comprehensive and deeply transformative. In my doctoral study[13] of individuals practicing a form of meditation based on the awakened Kundalini, all those in the research study had 10 or more years of experience doing that form of meditation. They reported undergoing a total of 169 types of changes. These covered a broad span of seven categories of change: physical, emotional, mental, relational, conceptual, attitudinal, as well as changes in values and priorities. It was the experience of those studied that virtually every facet of life was impacted in a positive way through the awakening of Kundalini. Thus, the outcome of the kriyas, the movements of the Shakti, is total transformation.

Each spiritual tradition has its own language and practices for engaging this divine power of revelation. As I was contemplating the Kundalini yesterday a poem came to mind:

Sri Kundalini Shakti!
You delight in appearing clothed in many dresses.
Your lovers perceive your presence behind all your disguises.
You are the Amitabha and compassion of the Buddha,
The Holy Spirit, Sophia and Mary for the followers of Christ,
And the wine of ecstasy drunk by the Sufis.
You are the power in the yogi's diverse practices,
The devotion of bhaktas,
The sword of discrimination and the pure knowledge of Vedantins.
Your are the Shekhinah and her Source for the Kabbalist,
And the Tao of the Taoists.
Whatever our path to God, the power that carries us forward and the
    Consciousness attained
Are alluring forms taken by you to draw us to the realization of the Self.

Seeker, choose a path that most suits your temperament and give it
    your full attention.
Enjoy all the ways the Mother
Will reveal herself and her Spouse
To you
            along
                the way.

Each spiritual tradition focuses on certain forms of the Kundalini's
manifestations and rejects others as distracting or unimportant. It's as if
they're saying, when a woman appears in a blue dress welcome her and let
her in, but if she comes in a red dress, bolt the door and hide. The
Goddess doesn't mind. She has more dresses than we can imagine! In this
way some paths focus on insight and awareness while dismissing experiences of inner lights and sounds. On the other hand the ancient path of
Laya Yoga focuses on the inner experiences of lights and sounds as a means

to union with the Divine. Devotional paths, like Bhakti Yoga or the path taken by many Christian mystics, value the rapturous feeling states that accompany contact with the Divine and serving God, often caring little about what may be revealed of the Divine through the refined intellect. Whatever aspect of the path or whatever aspect of the Divine One that a spiritual tradition adores, it owes the revelation of that to the Goddess.

For mystic traditions the path to the Light includes a descent into the Dark. God's universe encompasses both the light and the dark, even though some religions try to exclude darkness from his realm. The darkness has two levels. One is personal, the individual level of shadow, and the other is collective, a transpersonal level of darkness. Everyone on his or her quest confronts the personal level. Facing the collective level of darkness seems to be a rarer experience. Since we can't predict what we will have to face on our journey, it is best if we are informed about both.

The personal level of darkness we've touched on already in the symbolic encounter of Jerome and the primitive man. Shadow work involves uncovering and integrating the disowned or abandoned parts of our self. Psychotherapy and 12-step recovery programs can be great aids to sadhana when it comes to dealing with shadow material. We have to face the unconscious ways that anger, power needs, various kinds of desires, and self-esteem deficits govern our lives. As we practice Witnessing the various mental, emotional, and physical patterns these things take in meditation and in daily living, we shed light on our shadow. This doesn't always resolve the difficulties these patterns create. We may need help in applying the spiritual discipline we're practicing to those situations, or we may need the help psychotherapy can provide in uncovering old patterns and creating new, healthier ones.

During meditation, past actions of our shadow may come up that we weren't previously conscious of but for which we must make amends. Once I bought a used car from my employer with the agreement to pay her over time the balance I owed her. Every month I made payments on the loan and in 18 months it was paid off. A couple of years later in meditation I was told by an inner voice that I had missed a payment that hadn't been detected. I made a mental note of it and went on meditating. When I dug up my check register from three years earlier I discovered that one month while she was in Europe and I was on vacation I had indeed missed a payment. Of course it had happened back at a time when I was angry with her. When I realized it I immediately went to her, apologized, and paid her. She was a Jungian analyst and enjoyed hearing how it had come up in meditation.

Our shadow is made up of the repressed, denied, and unconscious parts of our psyche. Spiritual practices can also create shadow. For example, let's say I'm attempting to practice ahimsa, non-injury, and I eliminate many of the ways I was previously harming living beings. I become a vegetarian, I say only "nice" things to people and I become quite "spiritual." (I'm being a bit facetious, but I'm sure many of us have seen genuine, yet comical, attempts of people, including ourselves, to do this and other practices.) Unconsciously, I begin to think of myself as nonviolent, I identify with being peaceful and loving. With such ego-identification comes ego defenses. I may unconsciously blind myself to the ways that I am still injuring others or deny the violent impulses that are arising within me. I'm creating shadow by disowning the darkness that doesn't fit with practicing ahimsa. Have you ever been around some really "spiritual people" and you feel like screaming and acting outrageous? You may be picking up and containing some of their disowned shadow energy. As that energy looks for expression, it joins your shadow and amplifies thoughts, feelings and impulses that ordinarily remain below the level of awareness.

A better way of practicing nonviolence is by remaining openly conscious of whatever comes up spontaneously—"good" or "bad" impulses—and choosing to cultivate only the patterns of thought and action which won't harm ourselves or others. By remaining fully conscious, accepting, and attentive of whatever arises inside, we don't create as much unconscious shadow. We need to be conscious of our shadow, inviting it to show itself and learn from it. Feedback from others about our dark sides is invaluable in working with our shadows. We need to consciously choose to contain, limit or transmute the energy tied up in it. Shedding light on our shadow doesn't mean we will suddenly eliminate it. It means we reduce the risk of its taking possession of us and getting us to act out in the ways it wants us to. We can see shadow possession occurring in many male religious figures and gurus who appear in the news because of their sexual acting out. These are often the same ones, who from the pulpit, rail against sin or make a show of purity and continence before their followers. "The devil made me do it!" is a familiar cry. Yes, and this devil is part of you, part of your shadow. The more we recognize those dark parts of ourselves the more balanced and focused we can be without the disruptive effects of shadow impulses. The more we distance ourselves from shadow, projecting it onto other individuals or groups and denying its existence within us, then the more apt we are to eventually succumb to shadow impulses.

Uncovering shadow material is by no means limited to turning over the compost pile of our psyche. In the shadows there are hidden gardens of creativity, devotion, strength, sensitivity, compassion and more, waiting to be brought into the light of our consciousness. In the Protestant church and prevailing scientism that I was reared in there was no attention given to devotional attitudes and practices. When I was introduced to such things through Eastern traditions, my first response was to think that ecstasy and devotion were hyped reactions of feeling types that had nothing to do with me. Yet when I finally set my enormous doubts aside and engaged in a devotional ritual, my soul responded with a huge, "YES! I LOVE GOD AND I LOVE FEELING LOVE FOR GOD!" While chanting Sanskrit mantras I found myself swept into ecstasy. My body swayed and tears of joy ran down my face. Through that, I was able to reclaim an entire emotional, devotional way of relating to the Divine. This opened up more feeling-directed and loving ways to relate to people as well. We can look forward to finding such hidden gems in the darkness of our shadow work.

Shadow work in sadhana can bring up past-life experiences that are relevant for progress in this life. It's important to understand that the guiding power behind what comes up, when it comes up, if it comes up, and whatever form it comes up in, is the Shakti, the power of Self-revelation. I don't decide to go looking for past-lives or past events in this life. I trust the Shakti, the great power of Divine Consciousness within us, to bring up what is necessary. I trust she will present it in the form that I can best deal with and at a time that is right for my development. The sequence and forms of these things are unique to each individual. Past-life experiences are a part of meditation for some people, while others don't have such recollections. As I mention various possible experiences of the journey, the point is that these are merely possible, not necessarily what you will or should experience. As we hear of other people's experiences, we don't have to make up a spiritual shopping list of what we want in meditation. "Oh, I'll have one of these and one of those, but none of *them*, thank-you!" Instead, we Witness with equanimity whatever occurs in our meditation. If a meditator were to publish a book with two thousand blank pages describing the countless hours spent simply Witnessing, would we buy it? Would we be able to take in the profound impact of those blank pages?

When past-life recollections come up they may be fleeting images or entire scenarios relived as if in the present. Once while I was staying in an ashram in India and training to give very powerful guided meditations on the Divine I was confronted with potent unresolved material from a past life. It all began during the training sessions I was in with a small number of other meditation teachers. Suddenly I began having difficulty speaking many of the meditation instructions aloud. These were new courses we were being trained to give and the meditations were very devotional and directly addressed God. You can teach meditation in nonspiritual, stress management ways, or as concentration exercises, or directed toward a more abstract concepts such as Universal Consciousness, the Absolute, the Void, or mindfulness. These antiseptic forms often appeal to rational

Westerners who have easily triggered religious buttons. The new courses I was being trained to give were clearly devotional, and sought to open our hearts to God in every moment. As I began to give the meditation instructions, I developed a choking tightness around my throat and difficulty breathing due to a sensation of pressure on my chest. At times I could barely speak. I had routinely spoken to large audiences and never had any such difficulty. Something was being triggered, but I had no idea what. One of the monks helped me begin to free my voice despite the continued sensations of tightness in my throat and chest. At last I got to the point where I could speak intelligibly, but I could still feel some deeper block. Then, the day before I was to give the course for the first time, I had a stunning meditation experience.

As I sank into meditation I found myself in a completely different time and place. I was in rural Spain several centuries ago and I was a simple Catholic priest who lived in a local monastery. I was assigned to travel a circuit of distant small communities, taking care of the people and celebrating mass with them. I loved God and preached to the people about God's presence in everything and everyone around them. The country folk liked being able to feel close to God as they tended their flocks or took care of their home-life. I felt ecstatic as I walked through the countryside from village to village. It seemed particularly easy to feel God's presence in nature. I didn't feel poor, though all I owned were my rosary, Bible, and well-worn monk's robe. I was genuinely serving God and this filled me with joy as my footsteps took me back to the monastery. I was totally unprepared for what would happen next.

As soon as I entered the gates I was summoned to the abbot's office. Two stern visiting priests were there with him. One of them read charges of heresy against me. They demanded I confess and seek atonement for my grave sins and crimes against the Church. I was almost too shocked to speak. Finally I said, "There must be some mistake. I'm just a simple priest who loves God and serves Him in the countryside. I love the Church, I love Jesus. Somebody is mistaken." They misquoted some of my words to people. When I tried to explain, they weren't interested in listening. All they wanted was a confession. I refused to confess and tried arguing further. Eventually they said they had a way of making me confess.

I was seized by the ankles and dragged down several flights of stone steps, my back and head scraping the stones along the way, until we came to a cellar room. There I was held down on my back, arms and legs spread, as an old oak door was put on top of me. Next, stones were placed on top of the door, adding to the weight pressing me down. I was being crushed. I could barely breathe. I screamed in pain, feeling my ribs crack and break. Finally they took one of my screams as a confession and dragged the stones and oak door off me. I was passing out from the agony as they dragged me back up the stairs to the abbot's office again. Placing a pen in my hand they moved it to sign my confession. I was barely able to remain conscious. I was bleeding from my back, my head and my chest. Next I was told I was sentenced to death by hanging for being a confessed heretic. They said God would be merciful with me since I had confessed my sin. I was dragged out to the courtyard where a rope with a noose tied in it hung over a large beam. Unfortunately the poor monk who had to tie the knot didn't know how a hangman's noose was supposed to be knotted or that it was meant to break the neck of its victim and mercifully hasten their death. He had just tied a simple slipknot. When they pushed me off a makeshift platform the rope tightened around my neck and I slowly choked to death. Thus ended that life. I was stunned. I could still feel the rope biting my throat.

As my awareness began to return more fully to my body, a compassionate voice spoke to me from within, saying, "That was then, this is now. You are surrounded by love now. You have nothing to fear." At the same time I felt totally embraced by love and flooded with Light. All the constricted feelings from the torture and hanging which had been lodged in my neck, throat, and chest began to melt away. Silent tears ran down my face as I experienced soft warm waves of love wash through me. "You are surrounded by love, you have nothing to fear. . . you are surrounded by love…you have nothing to fear," echoed over and over in my awareness. The next day as I gave the course, I had no problem speaking with deep love for God.

In addition to dealing with our individual shadow, we may have to deal with the shadow sides of groups. On a collective level the shadow shows itself most clearly in hostilities between groups or nations. It appears in the irrational, indefensible attitudes and actions that one group displays toward another as they project their shadow onto them, making them the enemy, the reason for their suffering or plight. The atrocities and attempts to annihilate the opposing group mimics in exaggerated form what often occurs within us as we attempt to deal with our shadow. People often try to beat their dark side out of existence instead of relating to it, redeeming it, even appreciating parts of it. When the repressed unconscious energy of the collective psyche threatens to overwhelm the group, the group unconsciously selects a scapegoat to project all its negativities onto. Then all the energy of the group is externally directed to what's wrong with 'them' instead of facing what's wrong with themselves. One example of the collective acting out of shadow possession is the situation in Bosnia and Kosovo. Each group projects onto the other the worst and most unconscious of their own qualities, then in a vain attempt to purge themselves of such hated things, they seek to eliminate all others from the opposing group, as if by the magic of getting rid of the external enemy through "ethnic cleansing" the remaining group would be purer and more elevated. To Bosnia could be added Rwanda, South Africa, Hindu-Muslim conflicts, Middle East conflicts, racial conflicts, and on, and tragically on. The United States has been so focused on external threats that it lost sight of shadow forces within itself. The Oklahoma City bombing painfully thrust this into collective consciousness. The militias and hate groups within our own borders are containers for part of our collective shadow and give expression to it. Political leaders don't know how to respond in a way that truly relates to these shadow forces. They can't be ignored, nor can they be wiped out of existence. They must be contained, understood for what they are. Their energy must be redeemed and freed from the constricted hateful forms they are bound in.

In sadhana the collective shadow can be encountered in meditation, visions, or dreams involving archetypal dark evil figures. On some level these dark forces are quite real. The Catholic Church continues to deal with satanic possession and perform exorcisms. Many other spiritual traditions also have rites and rituals for dealing with evil manifestations. Saint Teresa of Avila used to roust devils from suffering souls. She also had her own encounters with evil:

> I was in a chapel when the devil appeared on my left side, looking most horrible. I noticed his mouth in particular, which was fearful to behold, since he was speaking to me. A great flame seemed to be issuing from his body, bright and translucent. He said to me, in terrible tones, that although I had escaped from his clutches he would get me again. I was stricken with terror and crossed myself as best I could, whereupon he disappeared but was soon back again. This happened to me twice. I did not know what to do. There was some holy water nearby, so I threw it in his direction and he vanished for good.[14]

I've counseled individuals who have experienced satanic cult abuse, spirit possession, or spirit harassment. As much as a part of me would like to believe evil spirits are just figments of our psyches, I've had to acknowledge that they have some level of reality and they have undeniable effects on people. I don't pretend to fully comprehend on what levels of reality they exist, though I am certain that on the highest level even their twisted forms dissolve into the Divine. It wasn't until I actually encountered an evil presence in meditation that I finally accepted the existence of such things. It's very different to encounter this archetypal, collective level of evil than it is to face our own shadow. C. G. Jung wrote, "...[I]t is quite within the bounds of possibility for a man to recognize the relative evil of his nature, but it is a rare and shattering experience for him to gaze into the face of absolute evil."[15]

It was October 1982 and I was in an ashram in India during a special ceremonial time marking the recent mahasamadhi of the meditation master Swami Muktananda. *Mahasamadhi* is the Indian term used to describe the time that a great being leaves his or her body, forever merging into the Absolute, while the physical form dies. All day and all night a beautiful Sanskrit chant was being sung by hundreds, at times thousands, of devotees, a chant that means "I bow to the Lord whose nature is the bliss of freedom." I had been there for three weeks doing my *seva*, my work offered as service to God, chanting, and meditating. I was feeling extraordinarily centered, grounded, and at peace with myself, my life and how everything was unfolding. I would chant for hours before retiring at night and get up at 3 A.M. to meditate. It's quite hot at that time of year, so at night I slept on the roof atop a parapet at a corner of one of the buildings that overlooked the courtyard below, where the continuous chanting was going on. I rigged up some mosquito netting over a thin mattress and felt blessed to fall asleep listening to divine chanting as I gazed at the stars of the Milky Way overhead.

One night I went up to my little rooftop bed, flashlight in hand because there were no lights anywhere, with the chant drifting up from the courtyard, and prepared to lay down under the netting. Suddenly, out of the corner of my eye I caught sight of what looked like a patch of blackness against the dark of night. A shiver went through my body and for a moment I was seized by fear. I wielded around with my flashlight and found nothing. Turning my attention back to the sounds of the chant, I told myself I was safe within the hallowed walls of the abode of a saint, and crawled under the mosquito netting into bed. In no time I was asleep. I woke in the dark predawn hours ready to meditate after completing my morning ablutions. I meditated seated on my mat up on the rooftop. For the first time in my life I was completely terror stricken by what I encountered in meditation.

As I went into meditation, expecting nothing unusual, lulled by the chant rising from the courtyard, I felt myself descending through space to what appeared to be a cheap, old motel and bar and grill on a deserted strip of highway somewhere in midwestern America. I was present as a center of consciousness, a disembodied awareness, witnessing what was going on. At first, everything seemed rather ordinary. It was late afternoon, around 5 P.M., with plenty of sunlight outside. There were five or six people at the bar, men and women, including a couple of salesmen having drinks. At the tables were seated a young family with two children, a girl about eight years old and a little boy around five. A middle-aged couple was seated nearby. The bar and dining area were dingy and poorly lit. Sun came through the big windows by the dining area and helped to light that portion of the room. Looking out, you could see the deserted highway and endless fields of stubble, the remains of harvested crops.

The sky began to fill with dark black clouds moving rapidly toward the place. Nobody seemed to take notice. I could see the wind picking up outside as the thick clouds approached. With the advance of their darkness came an oppressive feeling of an evil presence. I had never felt anything like it.

This is when I began to get scared. Usually in meditation I could just return my awareness to my body and ordinary consciousness, but this time I was locked into the vision with no way to escape.

Darkness descended over the bar and grill, permeating the room and the people within it. There was still physical light, though the sun had been overshadowed. The murky interior lighting allowed me to see well enough throughout the bar and dining areas. The feeling and the atmosphere of the whole place changed. People became nasty and angry with one another. In a matter of moments fights broke out, bottles were broken and used as weapons, the parents argued with and then beat the children, and it got worse—much, much worse. I was horrified. I could feel the most evil, powerful, black presence imaginable. In fact it was beyond my imagination. It had no shape or form. It was present as an overwhelmingly powerful malefic force, the distilled, concentrated essence of evil. It took possession of everyone and forced them to beat, rape, mutilate, and hurt each other in the most gruesome, ghastly ways.

I was watching in absolute horror when it detected my presence. I felt it turn its attention toward me, pressing its evil power against me. It wanted to invade me, take me over and possess my life force. This was the beginning of a battle of energies or wills in which my very existence was at stake. At first I prayed to God, Jesus, saints, siddhas, and yogis, but I felt no allies, no divine intervention coming to my aid. The dark force mocked me and enjoyed the impotence and despair that began to arise in me. I saw those feelings as cracks in the boundary of my selfhood that it would exploit to invade me. I began to do the only thing I could think of, and that was to meditate on the supremely inviolate Self, beyond good and evil. If for even a microsecond I took my attention away from the Self and put it on the evil one, it fed on that and grew stronger. If I denied it power, if I denied even its existence, then I could stay focused on the Self. I had to refuse to believe it had any power or existence, even while the most ghastly images and sounds were assaulting my inner senses, and an oppressive, evil force pressed itself upon me from all sides, including above and below. I couldn't even allow myself to feel or sense in any way that I was in a battle or struggle for survival. This took all my powers of concentration and all my energy. Hours passed in this totally intense state of focused awareness. Finally a degree of steadiness in my awareness of the Self came and I relaxed. Suddenly I found myself back on the rooftop in India. My body trembled. The sun was rising as the chant continued. I looked at my watch and three hours had passed. I wondered what on earth had just happened.

I took a deep breath and sighed as I closed my eyes for a moment to try to recover a little. I was drenched in sweat and felt as though I had been through the ordeal of my life. A voice came up from within and said, "You must go back. You can't leave those people at its mercy. You must choose to go back." I couldn't believe it, but in my heart I knew it was true. It wasn't until sometime later that I realized it this was all for the sake of my spiritual development and not for the sake of any others, though I don't know if I would have gone back except for the belief that in that moment others were in danger.

I opened my eyes and looked around at the beautiful sunrise. Birds flew over rice paddies in the distance, the chant continued to fill the air; it was all so serene. I tried to anchor part of my awareness in that as I mentally prepared myself to descend to that other level of reality. I closed my eyes and gave my assent to return. Immediately I was back in that sleazy joint witnessing the horrible acts the evil force was making these people do to one another, even the children. I had to be totally dispassionate and centered in the Self. I shut out awareness of everything but the Light of the Self. From that place of awareness it felt as though I gradually expanded the sphere of my awareness like an expanding cloud of Light, which at first was fairly small and pressed all around by malevolence. I was pushing the sphere of awareness out so as to embrace more and more of my surroundings, and pushing back the evil presence. At first it felt like an enormous struggle to win one millimeter at a time. While doing it, I had to keep absolutely focused on the love and light of the Self. To even consider the presence of an "other," to give a split-second of attention to a feeling of struggle or to the resistance opposing the expansion of my sphere of awareness, gave it power. Then I discovered, much to my amusement, that I wasn't "doing" the expansion of the sphere of awareness at all, it was just happening by the power of the Light. The struggle was an illusion. The only thing that took my effort was to stay focused on it. Eventually the cloud of Light that held my awareness had expanded sufficiently to embrace all the people there. Just as suddenly as the evil force had descended, it retreated. The black clouds gathered themselves up and blew away over the horizon. The people all returned to normal and carried on as if nothing had ever happened. My awareness shifted and I was once again conscious of my body being atop an ashram roof in India.

I came out of meditation and looked at my watch. Another three hours had passed. I felt completely wrung out. I was pouring sweat, my body trembled and it was a struggle to make it to the showers. Letting the water wash over me and chanting mantras as I showered helped me to regain my center. I ate a little and then searched out one of the senior monks, a swami, to tell him what had happened. He said I must have encountered an archetypal level of evil. What was also very interesting, he said, was that just a few weeks earlier, before the revered meditation master had died, he told a few people of a visitation he had in the night from three dark evil spirits. The master laughed and told them he said a mantra, sprinkled a few drops of water on his bed, and the evil spirits fled. I wished that my battle with the fourth of that party had been so easy. It made me aware of another dimension of the difference between one of great attainment and one of little attainment. I wondered how often and on how many levels saints of every tradition carry out their part in the drama of the clash between the forces of Light and the forces of Darkness, even while enjoying a transcendent awareness beyond the pairs of such opposites.

For hours after my ordeal I felt unsettled, as though something was yet to come. My mind felt clear and strong but my body was weak and shaky as I went about my work. It was a very hot day, and in the afternoon I went to take another shower. I was pulled into a meditative state as I silently repeated my mantra while the water ran over me. A voice spoke to me from deep within myself telling me I couldn't let that power remain loose on the face of the earth. I was told I had to call it to myself and the Shakti, the power of grace, would transmute it. I was shown how I had been protected all along, even though I felt alone. The experience was given to me to force me to take firm hold of Self-awareness and to know the power of being established in that awareness. My protectors surrounded me and would have intervened if I had been unable to do what needed to be done. Now that dark force had to be summoned.

I went to a window that looked out over a wide river valley with mountains in the distance. I scanned the landscape, I knew it was coming. Hot dusty air, mingled with the smell of water buffalo walking along the rural road below, blew in my face. A dust devil, like a harmless miniature tornado, came into view moving from the river toward the building where I was looking out from the third floor. It was unusual, for it reached nearly four stories into the air, and several people on the street below pointed to it as it moved forward, picking up bits of paper and debris along the way. It didn't look dark or powerful, but I could feel the evil presence in it. This time I was totally unmoved by it. No fear arose. I was confident the Shakti could handle anything, and it was comforting to know there really were protectors around me. The vortex of wind and energy struck the building exactly where I was standing and all its whirling movement ceased. In that instant a blast of wind came through the window, hitting me full body. It felt as if a dense, heavy, cannonball of energy struck me in the stomach. I was knocked back and landed in the shower that was still running. The energy had entered me; all I could do was sit on the floor of the shower. I fell into a profound state of meditation in which the Shakti appeared as pure white Light with the quality of unconditional, boundless Love. That Light began embracing the dark ball of energy. A while later I came out of meditation. For several days I could barely eat anything. My stomach and intestines were a wreck; it felt like my body was trying to digest that cannonball. The energy was being released from its dark form and not by me. At the same time I experienced more energy, physical and psychic, than I ever had. I struggled to remain grounded. The mantra *Shivo'ham*, meaning "I am the Auspicious One, I am the Lord, I am Shiva," would spontaneously arise and seize my consciousness. It brought with it feelings of unbounded power and capability. I became totally fearless.

During this time, as part of my efforts to keep my ego from getting inflated, I talked to myself about the difference between my Divine Self and my ego-self. C. G. Jung spoke about the danger of inflation that comes if the ego falls into the Self, identifying itself with the Self. The Christian mystics often combated inflation by contemplating what they believed to be their nature as wretched unworthy sinners. To me that approach creates too much distance between God and self. My ego/self wanted to identify with the Divine and possess for itself the qualities of the Divine. I had to speak very compassionately to my little self, reassuring it that it was part of the Divine and could enjoy certain times of being immersed in the Self, but that it also had a very important role to play in service to the Divine. For that it had to accept its limitations and boundaries until the body dies and our time on earth is completed. Then the final merger and dissolution of its boundaries can take place. Talking to myself in this manner, along with a readily available awareness of my obvious shortcomings, helped to maintain the necessary discrimination between my ego-self as servant and my Divine Self as master. Also at times like these the Divine seems to provide a person who's a real critic, or someone who rubs us the wrong way, or situations where we just lose it or fail. These are all very helpful and grounding. After some weeks the high level of energy moving through me lessened, though it left me feeling like I had been rewired for higher voltage.

C. G. Jung said that in order for us to realize our completeness we have to walk with God and wrestle with the devil. We have to experience the Divinity in us and around us. We also have to go toe-to-toe with our shadow, our personal devil, and perhaps some of the devils of the groups to which we belong, the collective devils.

Another part of the collective shadow is visible in how society makes human beings so small, so petty, as if our purpose in life was to buy things we don't really need, make things that will break in the prescribed period of time, and seek happiness in Walmart or Nordstroms. When we face our Creator and the Creator asks "What have you done with the sacred gift of a human birth?" what will we answer? Will you be able to say more than you were a consumer, will you be able to say more than you took the place appointed to you by a political and economic system that views the quality of life in material terms? I ask myself, will I proudly say to our Creator that I participated actively or passively in the destruction of thousands and thousands of God's children, the countless species that have become extinct since humanity substituted its order for God's order? What if an aspect of the collective shadow, like the fallen angel Lucifer, is actually part of human nature—the part of us that is too proud, arrogant, and self-intoxicated with our power over nature to surrender to the will and order of the Divine? Instead of knowing our true greatness, which comes from our essential unity with the Creator and all of creation, we substitute a false greatness, as if we were lords of the planet, free to exploit and destroy all of creation. It may not be very pleasant to look at things this way, but shadow work entails looking unflinchingly at everything.

If we look at the fundamentals of the devil myth we can glean the dynamics by which something turns evil. This great archangel became arrogant, intoxicated by his own power, and saw himself as above or outside the realm of the Divine. He didn't feel he had to adhere to the Divine Order; he felt he didn't have to be surrendered or obedient. Thus he no longer considered the use of his power in the service of the Divine, only in the service of his own agenda. Power, arrogance, self-intoxication, placing oneself above or outside the Divine Order, no longer giving prime consideration to what that order is or what the will of the Divine is and substituting one's own vision and will—these transform an element of light into something that bedevils us. Take the power of reason for example. Especially in the last couple of centuries the power of reason has reigned in the West. The scientific method and deductive reasoning developed as potent means for applying the power of reason to the natural world, yielding great success. We seemed to gain power and control over many diseases that plagued humanity; we gained power and control over fire, water, and air for the production of electricity and mechanical energy. Wonderful inventions, medicines, and understandings of the workings of nature have come from the use of reasonable methods of investigation and development. Thus reason has accrued more and more power. The split came in part with the notion that one could be an objective observer, outside the system or separate from the phenomena being observed for purposes of prediction and control. Now quantum physics has shown that there's no such thing as a detached objective position, the very act of observation changes the thing being observed. Observer, observed and act of observing are inextricably bound together. This understanding has a long way to go before it trickles down to our everyday understanding. For the most part we think it reasonable to take an objective look at something in order to reasonably understand it, to be able to predict what will happen and, if necessary or desirable, control it.

In many arenas this is a great strategy. But the dark side of it is when reason no longer knows its limits, when everything is approached reasonably, when reason substitutes its order for the Divine Order. It's one thing to say there are certain phenomena in the universe that are approachable through reason and its mode of inquiry, the scientific method. It's a very different thing to say that only those things that are approachable by reason and scientific inquiry are real and valuable. The mystical, the intuitive, and the arational are devalued and invalidated. No wonder there's such spiritual hunger in the industrialized world. That's the arrogance, the self-intoxication, and the delusion that the successful use of reason and science can lead to. It can seem perfectly reasonable to approach nature rationally and scientifically for control and exploitation, stepping back from nature and assuming it exists to serve us. Whose order is the power of reason serving in that case? Reason can take a very different direction if we start with an intuitive, unitive experience of our connectedness to everything and a more humble perspective of seeing ourselves as servants of a Divine Order. Then we can put reason and scientific methods to work in a role of sustaining the health and diversity of this marvelous planet created with us as one of its many inhabitants.

The quest demands that we set aside the dominance of reason. In fact, the quest is a very unreasonable thing to do! It's a journey in which you don't know where you're going, how you'll get there, or even if you'll get there, and all along the way unreasonable demands and ordeals will beset you. You might have to surrender your way of reason to an intuition, a dream, a vision, a master, a call, a bird, an inner voice, or some other manifestation of the mystical, spiritual dimensions of reality. To our mind of reason *mystical* has become a dirty word, something to be dismissed, shunned, or left safely in the grave of a saint. By our collective reliance and focus on the power of reason alone we've made the mystical, the spiritual, the magical, sink into our collective shadow. The hero's journey takes us into that realm to redeem it, to bring its treasures back to the rest of humanity. We're in desperate need of it.

Confronting the dark sides of ourselves and our groups is part of the purifying process that the awakened Kundalini or the Holy Spirit, performs on our subtle and physical bodies. As she refines those vehicles or instruments of Consciousness, they become better suited to serving the Divine. When, how, and in what ways they will serve are up to God. To know and to serve the Divine: this is for me the ultimate expression of our humanity, our purpose for living. To be satisfied with anything less is to ignore the will of the Divine. It's up to each of us to discover the ways in which the Divine is revealing Itself to us and the manner in which we are best suited and called to serve. Our journey is one of discovery and expansion. Discovering and expanding the ways in which we perceive God's presence, discovering and expanding the ways in which we serve Her.

Confronting the archetypal or collective level of evil occurred to me without my seeking it. We don't seek particular experiences, but trust that the necessary ones will find us. The Kundalini Shakti is the power of transmutation. She transmutes lower bound forms of energy, samskaras, into higher, freer forms of Consciousness. All our karmas become means for her to reveal the Divine. I don't know what karma or intention brought me face to face with that dark force, but the Shakti seized upon what was happening to me and used it to further my sadhana. She transmuted the energy and released contracted forms of consciousness in me. In sadhana we don't have to look for experiences because the Goddess and our karma provide all that is necessary for us to realize the Self. However, people who aren't in touch with this inner power, who aren't receiving her guidance, often seek through various means experiences of energies, higher consciousness, or God. In doing so they may be opening themselves to energies or forms of consciousness that can be negative, evil, or possessive of their self.

Many people are experimenting with accessing other energies or realities through ouija boards, visualizations, homemade rituals, and nontraditional meditation and concentration exercises. It's great that so many people are interested in going beyond the boundaries of what has been thought of as the limits of human consciousness in exploring realms that were once seen as the sole province of rare mystics or saints of long ago. In our rush to leave behind the constraints of traditional spiritual forms or the powerlessness of familiar rituals, we mustn't neglect to observe the safeguards that they provide. In the ritual practices, prayers, and meditations of the great religious traditions and ancient lineages of Buddhist or yogic masters, there is built-in protection for aspirants. These practices invoke the protective powers of saints and sages and they specifically invoke only the highest, purest, God-force. Keeping this focus prevents the unwanted intrusion or invasion of negative or evil energies. One person I worked with felt like she was being threatened with possession. She had been doing a meditation practice she had read about, one of simply sitting with her eyes closed and opening herself to the universe, visualizing her whole being as open to the energy of the universe, as if everything in the universe were benign or good. She had thrown the door of her soul open and invited in any presence in the neighborhood. What came in was decidedly unwanted.

The same meditation exercise might be done within a different context, one that consciously invokes the protective power of God, or Jesus, or the saints or sages of your tradition, focusing one's intentions only on the highest, with the result being a sublime experience. It's not that you should seek only within the practices that traditional spiritual paths offer, even though if revivified they do include all that is necessary; but if you do explore outside the protective sacred circles they offer, then you need to be conscious and vigilant in invoking the protective power of the Divine and you need to consciously call upon only the powers or energies that uplift, heal, or move one forward with love and compassion to union with the Divine, or toward better serving the Divine. In this way you proclaim and assert your choice to be protected and you focus your intention only on the highest.

Like most people doing sadhana, I often don't know what specifically is being purified or transformed as the result of any given experience. Afterward you usually can detect a new understanding or some shift in energy, or an expansion of love to embrace more of the universe. One of the changes I was aware of after encountering that evil power was a pulsing energy radiating out of my hands that became intensified when I was around sick people. A few months later I began having experiences in meditation of healing energy pouring out of my hands. A past-life experience came up of having been a healer. Another past-life experience showed me how I had become so involved in taking care of others that I had completely lost track of my sadhana and failed to fulfill my higher purpose in that life. I realized it at the end of that life and vowed never to allow it to happen again. That was enough to convince me not to "do" anything with what was happening and just allow it to unfold while I kept meditating on the Self. I wasn't going to pursue doing healing work.

A couple of years later I was a full-time graduate student in a Ph.D. program at Temple University in Philadelphia and working full-time as the vice-president and assistant executive director of a residential psychiatric treatment center in Connecticut. I still had a lot of energy. My wife was doing her residency program in pediatrics at Children's Hospital of Philadelphia. I commuted back and forth between Philly and Connecticut, alternating a few days stay in one place and a few days in the other.

One morning while I was in Connecticut a new type of meditation experience occurred. I saw the figure of a young woman standing before me, unclothed, when a bright light came on behind her and illumined the inside of her body like an x-ray. My attention was drawn to a large black spot covering one of her ovaries. The image lasted for some time and then disappeared. I went on meditating and afterwards wondered what that was all about. The woman was a newly hired junior staff person whom I hadn't even been introduced to yet. She was working for a couple of months during her college summer break and that was about all I knew of her.

The next morning the same experience repeated itself while I was meditating. This continued for several days with an increasing sense that something was very wrong with her that needed attention. Finally, after about a week, a voice or a presence came into my meditation with the x-ray picture and told me I had to tell her what I had seen, that it was very serious, but it could be healed. The voice gave me a visualization procedure for her to do. She was to image Light pouring onto the dark spot and I was to tell her this would heal the problem if she did it daily. I came out of that meditation wondering if I should try to ignore the whole thing. I couldn't imagine how I would even begin talking to her about such a thing. By then I had found out she was from a small town nearby, she had little or no knowledge of yoga, meditation, altered states, or any of the things that might give her a context for understanding or accepting what I might say to her. She avoided the chanting and meditation groups I did, which told me she wasn't even interested in such things. However, the next day in meditation the voice made it clear I really had to speak to her because her life was in danger.

I made an appointment to meet with her and she arrived very nervous. As I began explaining a little about why I wanted to talk to her she was very relieved. She thought getting called to a meeting with me meant she was in trouble and would be fired. We laughed and it broke the ice. She knew I was into meditation and yoga though she admitted she didn't know much about such things. I talked with her about meditation and how it opens us to expanded knowledge, wisdom and consciousness. Before I related my recent experiences I sought her permission to ask a very personal question which she was free not to answer. She told me I could, so I swallowed my disbelief that I was actually doing this, and asked if she had noticed any problems with her ovaries or any other gynecological problems. She was startled and said yes. In fact she hadn't menstruated in two years. She said the doctors didn't know why. I related my experiences to her and told her about the visualization she could do to heal herself. Much to my surprise she said she wasn't interested. Flippantly, she told me she was happy not to have a period and considered it easy birth control. I was a bit taken aback. I told her I hoped she might reconsider, since it was her health that was at stake. She made it clear she didn't care about what I had told her. She wasn't in any pain so it didn't seem important. I accepted it. What else could I do? I had done my part informing her; the rest was up to her. I changed the subject and we chatted a while longer before parting.

I felt quite clear afterward, confident I had given it my best, and I assumed that would be the end of it. However, the next morning the x-ray picture of her reappeared. This was followed by an extraordinary Light energy, filled with love, pouring through me into the image of her. The energy put me into ecstasy. It was the same Loving Light that I've experienced in the presence of the Goddess, my Lady of Light. It lasted for about half an hour. When it stopped I went on meditating, simply witnessing all the levels of reaction my mind and body had to the presence of the Light. The same thing happened the next day. This time I saw that by the end of the time the Loving Light poured through me into her form, the black spot had turned gray. It had lightened. Several more days passed, with the same thing happening. Each day, the spot grew lighter until it disappeared. On that day I went to breakfast as usual, but this time I met the young woman on the way in and she pulled me aside.

"Have you been doing anything?" she asked accusingly.

"No, why?" I replied.

"I had my period for the first time in two years this morning."

"Oh," I said. "Let me explain what has been happening, though it wasn't my doing." We were both amazed.

She wanted to know more about meditation and what kinds of experiences I had over the course of my practices. I told her most of the time my experience was simply that of sitting and attempting to remain conscious. I mentioned a couple of experiences of merging into the Light that had radically transformed my sense of who I am. Although nearly two years had passed since my encounter with the evil power, it was still very fresh in my mind. I had told very few people about that one, but I felt compelled to tell her. After I related a somewhat toned down version of the experience, she shared with me that she was being terrorized by what appeared to be some kind of evil spirit. What repeatedly happened to her was that this screaming, horrible looking face would suddenly come at her. It was a very real looking vision of just a head, no body, racing toward her own face. Sometimes it happened as she opened a closet door, other times it came screaming out of the clothes dryer as she opened the door, or it came out from under her bed. She never knew when it would occur next. She hadn't told anyone about it because she was afraid people would think she was crazy. It had gotten so bad she was afraid to sleep at night and she was afraid to be by herself. At least in talking with me about it she felt less alone and relieved that I didn't think she was crazy. I began praying for her. Praying is one of the most powerful actions we can take to aid someone.

A couple of nights later I was in our apartment in Philadelphia when I awoke at about 4 A.M. and sat up in the dark. Out of the blackness a screaming, contorted face came right toward my face, swerving at the last moment to pass over my shoulder. I wasn't the least bit afraid. It was nothing compared to what I had encountered before. I was able to see it quite clearly and to me she—it was a she—looked as though she was terrified herself. Her eyes looked petrified.

The next day I called the woman in Connecticut and told her what I had seen. My picture matched what she had seen, though she had never described the particulars of the face to me. I continued to pray for her. A couple of days later in meditation the face appeared to me again. This time she came at me as she had previously, but then she stopped just a couple of feet in front of my face. She was quiet. As I looked into her tortured eyes an overwhelming feeling of love and compassion came up inside me, compelling me to reach out and stroke her face. I did it, and tears ran down her cheeks. In a flash she was gone. I offered a prayer for her. I never saw her again.

A few days later when I was back up in Connecticut I told the young woman what had happened. She was pleased to tell me that for the last several days she had not been terrorized by the face. As far as I know she remained free of it. Had everything ended there it would have been great. But, I had lessons to learn about becoming deluded by wrongly identifying with the power that had moved through my mind and body. I had helped the young woman. Now she was going to help me learn a few things.

The energy of Light and Love that had poured through me in the first healing incident seemed to dissolve certain boundaries between us. During the times when the energy was flowing I experienced merging in the energy and in her. After those meditations stopped there were still times when the boundaries between myself and her seemed to melt. For instance, on a several occasions during the workday when I needed to reach her for business reasons, I discovered I could see through her eyes and know exactly where she was on the 56 acre grounds of the treatment facility. The first time it happened I was about to go looking for her where she was supposed to be out in the gardens with a work crew. I happened to close my eyes and stretch as I was getting up from my desk when I saw a clear image of the kitchen. Just for the fun of it I called the kitchen and there she was, having just come in for a drink of water. In the parapsychological literature this phenomenon is called "remote viewing" and is being researched as a demonstrable psychic phenomenon. It was unusual to me and I assumed it had to do with some channel of consciousness that was opened when all the energy had passed through me.

What was especially confusing for me, as I was new to such energies back in 1984, was the intense love. It made me begin to doubt my marriage. I began to wonder if what I was feeling toward this young woman wasn't more real than what I felt for my wife. Fortunately, the young woman had better boundaries and a more grounded sense of herself than I did at the time. It took me a long time to understand the universal quality of this love. It wasn't directed or attached to the individual in the way we ordinarily experience love. In a sense it wasn't at all relational. When the sun shines on us it doesn't have a personal relationship with us, no matter how much we benefit from the light and warmth it gives. Similarly, this universal energy of Light and Love shines on or through us, but it isn't relating to us personally in the ways we are familiar with. When I could separate out what my relationship was to the young woman, apart from that transpersonal love, I came out of the deluded state.

While I was floundering trying to deal with that energy, perhaps as part of my effort not to get lost in it, I attempted to take control of it. I tried to "do" a healing as if I could direct and control the energy. What a mistake! A couple of months had passed and the young woman complained to me about having constant abdominal problems, poor digestion, cramps, and nausea. She said it had been occurring on and off for years. In my deluded, inflated state, I told her I would try to heal it for her. I devised my own healing meditation and attempted to make light pour over her and into her. In my ignorance I hadn't prayed to the Light or to a Higher Power or God to heal her and then let it go, leaving it up to God. Instead, I offered a prayer and then tried to do it, I tried to make it happen, to make Light pour through me by visualizing it happening. It didn't occur spontaneously. What did happen was I got really sick and spent nearly two weeks in bed recuperating.

I learned my lesson and from then on I never "did" another healing. The energy has moved through me at times and I've remained clear about the boundary between me and that Divine power. At other times I've prayed for and invoked the healing power of the Divine and watched it work its wonders. Recently my Lady of Light has made her presence known to me again. She has revealed herself to be a form of the Goddess, what she called "the Feminine Face of the Tao" and has begun instructing me on offering myself and my hands as conduits for healing energy. By offering myself in service to Her my focus remains on the highest and I remain uninvolved with what happens. I didn't do that in the previous life or earlier in this life when I became enmeshed in taking care of others. I was entrapped by "doership." In addition to showing me the pain created by that attitude, the Shakti made it clear that the only way to be free of it is through serving only the Divine.

Learning the paramount importance of offering our actions in service of God was further impressed upon me by an event that happened in a business situation. I was given the responsibility of identifying and solving the problems staff members were having in a small acute care unit. Everything we do is part of our sadhana, and I wanted to approach this task from the highest, to be able to do what my meditation teacher had always said to do—to see the Divine in others. But, no matter how I looked at those people, no matter how I squinted my eyes or turned my head, they didn't look like God! I saw character defects, lack of training, bad attitudes, but not divinity. For days I kept contemplating how does one see God in others, how do I apply such a lofty teaching to this situation? I couldn't figure it out, but one day in meditation I received an insight, a corollary to seeing the Divine in others: serve others as God. Serve the Divine in others, now that I could do! In order to make it concrete for myself I invited the whole staff over to my house for dinner. I would serve them dinner as if I were serving Her, my Beloved Divine.

I was filled with enthusiasm for making dinner for God. Almost the entire staff accepted my invitation; it may have helped that I had a reputation for being a good cook. It was planned for a Friday evening. I went shopping and bought all the food for the meal. While I was shopping, I talked to myself about God coming to dinner. Would God like this or that, what would God like to drink, what kind of desert would God like?

That Friday I took the afternoon off in order to cook all the food myself. On the way home I went to the florist and bought flowers for God to enjoy on the dinner table. While I was cooking I chanted the names of God. I baked fresh bread for God, kneading the dough with mantras. I made soup, salad, vegetables, and I baked a pie from scratch to serve to God, á la mode of course! I was dancing around the kitchen cooking and singing in ecstasy!

Finally the time came for my guests to arrive. They came in. Some were a little awkward being at the "bosses" house for the first time. This passed quickly. A beautiful tape of chanting played in the background. Inwardly, I welcomed each one as God and did all I could to attend to their needs and comforts. We sat down to eat and I went to the stove to ladle soup for them. As I turned to bring the first bowl of soup to the table I was stunned: where each person had been sitting a moment before, now all I could see were golden orbs of Light. God had come to dinner! Tears of joy and gratitude began streaming down my face. Quickly I turned back to the stove. I knew that somewhere in those Lights were my staff and they wouldn't understand my tears. I looked back over my shoulder and I could see their forms re-emerging from the Light. The dinner party went very well indeed! In addition, a good deal of the disharmony resolved itself. Organizational changes had to be made, but we had a new foundation for relating to one another. I certainly had a new way of viewing them.

Serving others as God is the most sublime way of organizing human endeavors. It is the way we walk the path of our quest as well as an expression of our journey's end. It is both the means to, and the fulfillment of, our great purpose in life: to know and to serve God.

The experience of serving my staff made two other lessons clear to me. One was the necessity of taking an insight or inspiration gained in meditation and making it concrete, making it real in everyday life. Knowledge and wisdom, however gained—through personal insight, from a teacher or from scriptures—must be made manifest in our simplest acts to be of any value. Secondly, ritual is a powerful means for doing that. Essentially I had created a ritual for serving God. It was similar to rituals I have seen performed in India, where a statue of the Divine is related to as a living form of God, bathed, clothed, and served meals with all the love and caring attention one would naturally give to God if He stood before you. In such a ritual all the energies of our body, mind, and heart are focused on serving God. This results in our direct experience of the Divine Presence. The ritual practice didn't so much transform my staff as it did my vision, my ability to see the Divine in my staff. Where else can we perform such consciousness-altering rituals? Our home, our office, and our places of worship are temples where the Divine awaits our loving attention. The ritual may be the routine act of making breakfast, dressing a child, serving coffee, conducting a meeting, or greeting others, to which is added the conscious offering of it to the Divine and whatever else it takes for you to invoke and experience the Divine at that moment. We can create the daily rituals that will engage our heart and soul and bring us back to the living presence of God. We don't have to wait for a priest or holy person to invoke God for us, we're empowered by Her to do it for ourselves and as often as we like.

Our society is in crisis and I believe the root of most of its problems is the split between the individual and the Divine: between the individual and the Divine within, and between the individual and the Divine as the earth and her inhabitants. This split-off, dissociated state of individuals and of the groups we make up—family, government, businesses, and nations—can only be healed or made whole through living ritual and the quest. Rituals invoke the awareness of unity consciousness, connectivity, or communion in the moment, giving a new point of reference, while the quest, of which ritual is a part, creates permanent transformations in our awareness. Most of our leaders have quested for power and fame, sacrificing spirituality. They can't lead where they haven't been. They're reduced to looking at opinion polls for direction. In the *Bhagavad Gita* the Lord says: "Whatever a great man does, other men do also; whatever standard he sets, the world follows that."[16] Those whom our culture has elevated to the rank of "greatest" have barely begun their journeys. Many have hardly examined their own shadow until the press forces them to. Our religious leaders, though most are good, pious individuals, haven't succeeded on their own spiritual quest. They may have studied the quest of others from their tradition, but most haven't been down the road on their own. They deliver undigested truths. The rituals they try to perform are often hollow and powerless to effect a change in consciousness. There are very few who can inspire us to set out on our own journey. Doing so is the only way we can effectively deal with the crisis. We have to go on our quest, we have to encourage others to go on their quest, and we need to seek out those who have been down the road. Joseph Campbell wrote in *The Hero with a Thousand Faces*:

> [A] transmutation of the whole social order is necessary, so that through every detail and act of secular life the vitalizing image of the universal god-man who is actually immanent and effective in all of us may be somehow made known to consciousness.[17]

> The modern hero, the modern individual who dares to heed the call and seek the mansion of that presence with whom it is our whole destiny to be atoned, cannot, indeed must not, wait for his community to cast off its slough of pride, fear, rationalized avarice and sanctified misunderstanding. 'Live,' Nietzsche says, 'as though the day were here.' It is not society that is to guide and save the creative hero, but precisely the reverse. And so every one of us shares the supreme ordeal—carries the cross of the redeemer....[18]

Our individual good and our collective good depend on our engaging in our quest. It's an inward journey, so we may go nowhere physically. However, at times we may feel quite distant, and people around us may notice and react to our changes. We need to support and encourage our spouses, our loved ones and friends to go on their quests. We also have to ask for the support we need from our loved ones and from the Divine. The quest demands a tolerance for uncertainty. Uncertainty can be very stress-ful for ourselves and people close to us. The uncertainty is born of the questioning we must do along the way. We have to have the courage to ask the big questions and not accept society's shallow answers. Notice the 'quest' in 'question.' Why am I here; what's the purpose of life; what's the purpose of *my* life? Is my work harmful to others, my environment, or myself? What did I come to learn? What did I come to heal? What chal-lenges did I come to meet? Who did I come to love; how do I become large-hearted and more inclusive in love? These are the types of questions we need to have the courage to ask and we need the strength to tolerate the uncertainty they bring as we notice how much of what we do and believe doesn't really answer them.

There's an old saying, "When the seeker is ready the teacher appears." The Divine is looking for those souls who are tired of being split-off from their Creator and Creation. The Grace-Bestower, the power of Self-revela-tion, is waiting to hear that we are ready to awaken to God's presence and that we wish to be able to follow the will of the Divine. The Goddess lis-tens intently to the prayers rising from a heart yearning for Her company. She will provide you with the quickest way possible to Her palace door. Give up the notion that you know a shortcut!

At the same time we have mountains of evidence that many "masters" are frauds abusing their power, turning earnest seekers away from the Divine. Some argue that the honored tradition of the master/student or guru/disciple relationship must be abandoned because of the abuses that occur within it. I don't think this is possible because of the basic structure of our psyche reflected in the guru/disciple relationship. The psyche appears to be organized with the transcendent Self, the Divine, as its sole ruler. The Self is the only true master. The ego and the other psychic instruments are to serve that Divine Self. This basic structure replicates itself in the outer world, where we project it and live it out unconsciously. For most of our history we enacted this projection of the inner ruler in the relationship between Kings and their subjects. We finally realized that the power structure of Divine Kings was too easily corrupted and that kings don't embody the Divine, nor do they have the capacity for acting solely in accord with the will of the Divine.

Just as we have projected the outer rulership of the Divine onto kings, we project the inner rulership of the Divine onto masters or gurus. We are creators, we create and learn through projection. We need to do this, we do this precisely so we can encounter and relate to the Divine from which we are so alienated internally. Once we've encountered it outside we can begin to realize its presence inside (and later we can dissolve the inside/outside duality). If the teacher is good and can carry the projection, the transference, while assisting the students' development of their ability to connect with the inner Divine independently of the teacher, then the relationship has served its highest purpose. If it ends in some lesser outcome then the relationship has served the learning needs of both souls.

Democracy evolved as a way of empowering people while decreasing corruption and the abuses of absolute power. In a democracy we substitute rulership of the majority for rulership by a King or Queen. This is a great improvement for accomplishing the tasks of worldly governance, though we're still a long way away from having the majority be enlightened and attuned to the will of the Divine, much less the representatives of the majority. But the democratic model doesn't fit the inner structure of our psyche that we deal with in sadhana.

Within our inner world the Self isn't symbolized by a group or a committee. The transcendent Self shows up in dreams, myths and visions as a king or queen, a wise old man or woman or as an animal. Nor does the democratic model transfer to accomplishing the tasks of sadhana, of our soul's journey. Refining the mind and teaching the ego its proper place as servant of the Self aren't developed by it being part of an inner committee, nor is the shift in self-identification from ego/mind/body to whole Self achieved through democratic means.

Another task for the evolving soul is developing the discrimination to differentiate between a true spiritual guide and a false one. We do this by experiencing for ourselves, over numerous lifetimes, various aspects of both sides of the guru/disciple relationship and in the process we evolve, developing the ability to pass on what we've learned before we leave behind the cycles of reincarnation.

During this evolutionary process the soul matures. Along the way its level of maturity will be reflected in the type of teacher, master, or guru it seeks as well as the type of teacher or master it will present itself to be. Thus the soul's age is another important factor in understanding the guru/disciple relationship. The soul's age will also be reflected in its way of understanding and conceptualizing the nature of the Divine as well as in its ways of relating to the Divine. A first grader relates to teachers and authorities differently than a graduate student. Their needs for structure and rules are different, too.

Although we must seek ways to minimize the abuses that can occur within the guru/disciple relationship, some basic form of that relationship will always exist, continually recreated from the basic structures and imperatives of the soul. The relationship is an archetypal one and even finds expression in the *Star Wars* saga, with Luke Skywalker as a disciple of Yoda on a quest to become a Jedi Master. Equally archetypal is the dark side of the guru/disciple relationship and the abuse of power, power used for the sake of subjugation, exploitation, and self-aggrandizement. The wise master uses power only in the service of love, compassion, wisdom, and upliftment.

It will continue to be true that when the seeker is ready a teacher or master will appear. And with that teacher comes the challenge for the soul to be able to judge the quality, the ethics, the intent, purity of heart, the power, and the truth of that teacher and his or her methods. Often souls in their early stages of seeking are so motivated by pain and weariness that they leap to follow whoever promises relief from suffering. It's as if they are saying, "I'll do anything, just save me!" They enter the relationship as a passive, helpless recipient, which is fine if the guru has truly attained a state of love, wisdom, and power. Such a one will empower the powerless.

If, as is too often the case, the guru/teacher has little or no attainment, then additional suffering ensues. After a few painful lifetimes the soul develops increased discrimination. We want to and are obliged to pass on that lesson to younger souls, even as we are prepared for the certainty that many will only learn it through experience. On the soul's journey the development of discrimination is simply one of the requirements it must fulfill along the way.

There is a form of democratization that could support the development discrimination and protect both teachers and students. When I lived and worked in a therapeutic community we had a policy that anyone could compassionately confront anyone else for attitudes or behaviors that violated the community's values and rules. There were regular groups where this was encouraged. Everyone from the executive director of the psychiatric treatment center to the most mentally ill patient had the right to speak out about what they perceived to be a wrongdoing by someone else. It would be healthy for spiritual communities to have a similar policy and means for implementing it. It would help the leaders to keep from becoming inflated and empower the group and individuals making up the group to be accountable for what goes on in the community.

Just as lightning strikes only when a charge is built up in the ground as well as in the clouds above, for the lightning bolt of grace to discharge into the ground of our soul and set it ablaze, we have to build up a charge through our longing, through our intention to know and to serve the Divine, and through the practices we do. Intense yearning for the highest, contemplation, meditation, chanting, serving others, living with caring attention to the Divine presence in everything and everyone, offering all actions consciously and repeatedly to the Divine, living ritual, worship, acts of devotion to the divine—any of these done with commitment, passion, and delight, build the charge in our soul. Also, going into the dark, doing the courageous inner shadow work builds the charge. Our spiritual practices harness and concentrate our intention and yearning making them manifest in our feelings, thoughts, and actions. These communicate our readiness to receive Grace. I've met people who have had experiences of awakening doing many different practices. To keep up with the awakened Queen, to learn to follow her and have our will truly surrendered to the Divine, takes a set of practices done over a sustained period of time and guided by one of wisdom, a friend of the soul, the Celtic *anam cara*.

Your path is unique and your experiences of the Divine, of the Self and of the light and shadow, will be just as they need to be for you. Who can say why the Divine chooses to reveal herself in one form to one person and in a different form to another? What is important is that we respect and honor all the different forms, religions, and spiritual traditions through which the Divine manifests. We can recognize the unity of God's Love and Presence in all of them. For me they are gifts of God's power of Self-revelation, the Holy Spirit, the divine Kundalini Shakti. She creates so many paths, bridges, techniques, insights, and perceptions in her relentless pursuit of revealing God to humanity. It's all part of her play of revealing God to God. Who wants to waste their breath arguing about whether the Divine should be called Brahman, Allah, Yahweh, the Void or Consciousness? Let's leave that to those who thrive on divisiveness. For Lovers of God all that is important is how to fully give our hearts and our hands in service of the Lord. How can we align ourselves with the will of the Divine to manifest love and compassion in each moment? Ask yourself how can I do that in relation to my wife, my children, my co-workers, my environment and all others?

St. Teresa taught: "The highest perfection does not consist in feelings of spiritual bliss nor in great ecstasies or visions nor yet in the spirit of prophecy, but in bringing your will into conformity with that of God."[19] All the phenomena manifested by the awakened Kundalini work to create this perfect union of our will and the will of the Divine. Through her miraculous workings she purifies the mind and opens the heart to the Love and Light of God.

We can't do it without the aid of grace. We're dependent on the power of Self-revelation to know God and to know how to serve God.

Who else can reveal the path to us and open the door of meditation on the Divine? The Shakti wants us to share Her delight in seeing Her Lord at all times, in all places. *Let every meditation be a revelation and every moment a meditation!*

The Goddess Kundalini also delights in showing the way. She shares her ecstasy equally with everyone wanting to tread the path; even those who eschew bliss, in the end, will drop into the ocean of her nectar. The most serious ascetic is made to laugh and giggle in her lap. Why wait until the end, climb into her arms right now! Offer a heartfelt prayer to whichever of her forms you most love. She's listening to you right this instant.

Ralph Waldo Emerson wrote: "This energy does not descend into individual life on any other condition than entire possession. It comes to the lowly and simple; it comes to whoever will put off what is foreign and proud; it comes as serenity and grandeur."

One day as I was wondering how this book would end I went into meditation and the following poem was presented to me as the answer.

<< OM KALI MA >>

Oh Seeker!
You wish to build a mansion of happiness in which to dwell for all your
        days.
Upon what foundation will you raise your mansion?

You wish to build a palace of peace, a place of refuge for all times.
Upon what foundation will your palace rest?

You wish to build a temple of love with fountains of devotion to cleanse
        you of all impurities,
Upon what foundation will your temple find steady support?

You've built castles of joy on the shifting sands of the senses,
How long have they stood?

You've sculpted tranquil inner landscapes from personal
        accomplishments and professional degrees,
Can they withstand the ravages of time and the scorn of others?

You've searched through a desert of relationships for the site of love's
        shrine, the wellspring of devotion.
What have you found but teardrops and dust?
Your endeavors have amounted to naught.
You cannot create the Eternal; only the ignorant and the proud try.
Through the Grace of the Master, know the Truth.

With reverence listen to the Self of all:
My dear one, haven't you heard?
The doors to the mansion of happiness have been thrown open to
        welcome you!
Leave behind the poverty of the five petty realms,
Follow the ecstatic ones who have crossed the bridge of grace to the
        abode of the ever-blissful Self!
Turn within and discover the divine mansion of the Infinite!
Innumerable rooms of pure joy await you!

My dear one, haven't you heard?
The palace of peace is before you—just the other side of time.
Leave behind the delusion of doing and not doing,
Follow the ecstatic ones who have crossed the bridge of grace and found
        repose on the throne of contentment.
Turn within and discover the palace of the Self!
You are the rightful Lord of the realm of Eternity!
Sit on your throne and enjoy unwavering peace.

My dear one, don't you remember?
Love's shrine has always been your true home.
Leave behind the wants and needs of mind and body.
Follow the ecstatic ones who have crossed the bridge of grace never
        more to return.
Enter the Temple of Love and discover where Lover and Beloved have
        gone.
Turn within, dance along the path of love shown by the Master.
It will take you directly to the abode of God.

Appendix

The following is a summary comparison of traditional Western psychology and yoga psychology, and a basic overview of the psychology of yoga. The majority of this section first appeared in my doctoral dissertation.

Western psychology is a paradigm, as is yoga psychology. Our culture is steeped in psychology, to such an extent that most people aren't aware of it. At another time or in another culture if someone was behaving badly or strangely, their actions would have been explained by influences from the stars or the planets, or blamed on demons or possession; in some cultures it would have been attributed to spells and witchcraft. In our culture if somebody is acting strange or in a way we don't like, we'll speculate about painful childhood experiences, upbringing, and family influences, or what they've been rewarded for and learned from peer groups. Our explanations are psychological. We operate from a psychological paradigm, and for this reason it's important to take a moment to look at a few of the basic assumptions of traditional Western psychology. These are assumptions that you may hold without being aware of it or without having consciously examined them recently. They are assumptions and beliefs about how our mind and consciousness operate that may clash with those of yoga and other Eastern and Western spiritual traditions. When different paradigms come into contact, such as our implicit Western psychological one and a spiritual or yogic one, there can be a clash that results in misperceptions and misunderstandings. Understanding one's own paradigm and the assumptions of the other paradigm can help reduce the misperceptions and miscommunications between the two.

Kuhn[1] pointed out that a paradigm includes the system of beliefs, concepts, values, and techniques of investigation that dominate the thinking of a community—scientific, yogic, religious or other—during a given period in its history. Over time the basic assumptions of the dominant paradigm become implicit and unconsciously order one's thinking, perception, and theories of the nature of reality. For example, who thinks of gravity and the laws of gravity as a mere theory that may be false? Due to the successful nature of the theoretical constructs of gravity they are taken for granted to be "real" and not just theory. Kuhn indicates that in the history of science the bringing together of two disparate paradigms for comparative study or integration often results in "paradigm clash." The implicit, unrecognized basic assumptions of the dominant paradigm lead to incorrect deductions and conclusions when examining the competing paradigm. Eastern, yogic, and transpersonal paradigms on the one hand, and traditional Western psychological paradigms on the other, are in such a clash[2]. Unless the underlying assumptions of each system are understood and taken into account during any comparisons, paradigm clash and resultant distortions or false evaluations ensue.

Traditional Western psychology refers primarily to the psychoanalytic and behavioral schools of psychology. It is in contrast to those schools of thought that yoga psychology differs the most. The other main schools of psychology are the humanistic and transpersonal. Yoga psychology is more similar to them and nearly indistinguishable from transpersonal psychology on the level of basic assumptions. Yoga psychology throughout this book refers to the system codified by Patanjali and applied through the non-dualistic schools of Advaita Vedanta and Kashmir Shaivism.

In comparing paradigms, a general principle is "that to try to examine the larger model or set from the perspective of the smaller is inappropriate and necessarily produces false conclusions."[3] The multiple states of consciousness model held by spiritual disciplines or consciousness disciplines, including yoga and other traditions of meditation or prayer, is considerably broader than the traditional Western one in its view of the range of functioning of human consciousness. Thus when the Western model is applied to yoga or the consciousness disciplines they may seem pathological or nonsensical. I had a Freudian-trained psychology professor who became apoplectic at my mentioning higher states, out-of-body, near-death, or past-life experiences because in his view all such experiences were invalid and pathological. From his perspective consciousness was a function of biological processes, unable to exist apart from the body and ceasing with death. This is what happens when the smaller more restrictive model, in this case Freudian psychology, is applied to phenomenon included in the larger model. From the perspective of yoga psychology the traditional Western paradigm is a useful model within its limits, but mustn't be misapplied to states of consciousness outside its scope.

Traditional Western psychology is in an analogous relationship to the consciousness disciplines as Newtonian physics is to Einsteinian physics: it is a subset of the broader, more inclusive model. Transpersonal psychology is a paradigm that attempts to encompass and integrate the entire range of human functioning, from the most sublime states considered by the consciousness disciplines to the most restricted pathological states delineated by traditional western psychology.

Four central points highlight the differences in the basic assumptions of the paradigms of the yogic or consciousness disciplines and traditional Western psychology:

(1) whether or not our normal, waking state of consciousness is optimal or suboptimal.

(2) whether or not true higher states of consciousness exist.

(3) whether or not higher states of consciousness are attainable through training.

(4) whether or not verbal communication is adequate for the communication of knowledge, especially that knowledge gained from higher states of consciousness.[4]

The consciousness disciplines hold that the waking state is suboptimal, that higher states of consciousness are attainable, and that verbal communication about them is limited. Traditional Western psychology holds an opposing position: the waking state is the optimal state of consciousness; other states are either suboptimal, irrelevant, or pathological, and intellectual analysis based on verbal encoding of experience is the highest form of knowledge.[5]

Traditional Western psychology reflects the materialistic philosophical position characteristic of the physical sciences prior to the impact of quantum physics. The materialist perspective is particularly evident in Freudian and behavioral psychology. Both look to the material, the biophysiological, to explain the nature of human beings. Freud wrote: "all our provisional ideas in psychology will some day be based on an organic substructure."[6] Thus they assume that who we are is limited to and defined by our physical body. Traditional Western psychology seeks to explain the subtle in terms of the gross, assuming that the gross, physical level of reality (physiology, brain chemistry, sensory functioning, etc.) causes the subtler phenomena of consciousness (awareness, emotions, ideas, intuitions, etc.). Thus the range of valid human experience is limited in such psychologies to those related to material existence. Altered states of consciousness, mystical states of union and ecstasy, trans-body or out-of-body experiences, post-death experiences, and other forms of transpersonal experiences are either dismissed by traditional Western psychology as pathological, regressive, or merely subjective. At times the behaviorists have either ignored or denied the existence of consciousness, viewing it as an epiphenomenon of biological functioning. The newer Western psychologies, humanistic and transpersonal, have been greatly influenced by Eastern psychology and integrate Eastern psychological concepts into their frameworks.

Yoga differs from Western psychology in its assumptions about:
1) the nature of the universe.
2) the nature of consciousness.

3) the nature of a human being.

4) the levels of functioning of the human mind.

5) the foundations of human suffering.

6) how relief from suffering is gained.

You might find it interesting to take a moment and reflect on what your ideas and beliefs are concerning these six areas.

From the yogic perspective there is only one "stuff" of this universe that is pure unbounded Consciousness, what we might call the Infinite Spirit of God. It is therefore monistic, not simply monotheistic. In the yogic tradition "pure" means untainted by any limiting form and untainted by any duality, that is no pairs of opposites, no subject-object split, no self and other; all there is the Self of All—God. Yoga asserts that pure Consciousness contracts to become the universe nearly like the physicists' notion of energy taking the form of matter. The nature of the universe is Consciousness, it is a manifestation of Consciousness. Thus, it is the subtle that creates the gross, Consciousness that creates the body and exists independently of the body.[7]

Yoga psychology views healthy human functioning as inclusive of various states of consciousness and experiences that transcend body awareness. Like many spiritual disciplines, it prescribes specific methods for bringing about experiences of who we are beyond our body and our mind. For traditional Western psychology, consciousness can't exist independently of the body, since consciousness is assumed to be materially caused and biologically based.

Yoga holds that:

1) The nature of the universe is that of pure Consciousness, God, manifesting in various forms or levels of contraction.

2) The nature of pure Consciousness is eternal Being, Consciousness, and Bliss. Consciousness identified or tainted by a limiting form reflects the attributes of that form, whether it is inanimate, vegetative, animal, human, or transcendent.

3) The essential nature of a human being is pure Consciousness, God.

4) The mind functions on a variety of levels broadly described by the three states of consciousness recognized by Western psychology (waking, dreaming, and deep sleep) and a fourth, recognized by yoga: the unlimited state of the Self called the *turiya* state.

5) The foundation of human suffering is twofold: the relative cause of suffering and the absolute cause. The relative cause is the lack of certain basic needs such as food, shelter, warmth and so on. Western psychology also holds this view. The absolute cause of suffering is ignorance of the Self, wrong identification, considering our self to be the mind/body complex and not the Self of All, the Divine.

6) Yoga focuses on the absolute cause of suffering, which is relieved only by direct knowledge of our true identity with the Divine. All of yoga is aimed at bringing about the recognition and experience of our true essential nature as pure unbounded Consciousness.

Indeed, working toward Self-realization is viewed as the highest human endeavor and the specific aim of all yoga disciplines. Yoga psychology envisions us becoming as established in the fullness and completeness of our highest Self as we are currently established in the limited and wanting nature of our bound self. How different is Freud's vision of successful psychotherapy as "changing the extreme suffering of the neurotic into the normal misery of human existence."[8]

Yoga psychology recognizes the three common states of consciousness and a fourth state, the turiya state, of superconscious Self awareness. Compared to the turiya state the waking state is severely limited, if not a state of delusion. Turiya is the ever-present pure I-consciousness of the Self, Witness of the three usual states of consciousness. It is the ultimate state of Consciousness, the rapturous state of perfect unity awareness described by mystics of all traditions. Turiya is the state that subsumes the other three states, illuminating them with Consciousness. Turiya consciousness is experienced by yogic sages as eternal, uncaused, omniscient, and omnipresent. It is indistinguishable from the Self. The real nature of the turiya state is unutterable, unapproachable by speech, words, or the mind.

Ordinarily we experience only an infinitesimal fragment of turiya in the form of a continuous sense of I-ness that persists through all the discontinuity of the various states of mind and consciousness comprising reality. We may intuit that there is something greater about ourselves than we already know, but the true vastness, the infinite expanse of our I-ness, our Selfhood, is beyond the reach of our imagination. Attempting to know the Self with the mind is likened to attempting to illumine the sun with a broken piece of a mirror. It is the Self's irreducible quality of Consciousness that enables the Self to be the illuminating source behind the mind, the senses, and the body. Knowing the pure "I" in its fullness is the aim of yoga psychology.

Eastern disciplines and yoga psychology in particular assert that the highest state and the direct experiential knowledge of that state are beyond the mind, beyond words, and to get to it one must leave behind the mind and rationality. This assertion is in sharp contrast to the basic assumptions of traditional Western psychology, which view reasoning as the highest skill and the written word is the least ambiguous, most accurate way of transmitting our greatest knowledge. Mystics of every tradition become mute when asked to describe union with the Absolute.

Over the course of thousands of years yoga has studied the various states of consciousness available to humans and concluded that our normal waking state is primarily one of delusion similar to the dream state. It comes to this conclusion from the vantage point of what it considers the highest state of consciousness, the turiya state mentioned earlier. From this perspective the other three states of consciousness represent a limiting or a negation of infinite Consciousness.

Yoga Psychology Overview

Yoga maps out three stages or phases in the process of limiting pure transcendent Consciousness into the restricted state of consciousness we are familiar with. These three stages correspond with the three ordinary states of consciousness—deep sleep, dreaming and waking. The deep sleep state is called the state of the causal body, it is the awareness of nothingness. It comes about by negation of the true all-encompassing state of Consciousness of the Self through the Self's power of concealment, Maya Shakti. This Self-negation is called *avidya*—primal ignorance. It's the beginning of the notion of limited individuality, the ego sense, and identification with limitations. Thus instead of experiencing oneself as universal and unbounded one thinks of oneself as a limited, particular individual. It's the negation of one's true nature, the denial of one's true Self, and the identification with a limited part of that Self. It's referred to as the causal body due to fact that this negation of, or dis-identification from, one's true nature, causes all that follows. This is the root cause of the contraction of Consciousness into the limited forms of mind and body as we know them. They evolve from that initial negation of universality.

In the deep sleep state there's only the awareness of no-thingness. The Universal Self has been negated or dis-identified with so we're not conscious of that, yet the world of particulars, the thoughts, desires, and all the details of individual existence, have not yet arisen. This state can be clearly experienced in meditation. We experience it in deep sleep, but as we are dissociated from our fully conscious witnessing Self, the experience of that state is hazy at best. We know we had a deep sleep, we know we spent some time being aware of nothingness, but we never stop to think how that could be. This is a classic Vedantic argument demonstrating the presence of the Self as the Conscious Witness of the mind's various states[9]. How can we be aware of being aware of nothingness? What part of us remains conscious even in deep sleep when we're not aware of the world, our body, or our mind? Who is the one who is conscious as we dream and reports the dream to ourselves? From the yogic perspective the ever-present, ever-conscious Witness is our Self and we can never be truly separated from it, no more than the wave can be divided from the ocean. Our suffering and our quest arise only from our being unconscious of our unity with it. Even in deep sleep the Self is accessible. The ever-present illuminating Consciousness of the Self allows us to experience the nothingness of deep sleep as well as the contents of the other states of consciousness. If we shift our awareness to the Witness, the Experiencer of that state, then we can know our union once again.

From the causal body arises the subtle body and the physical body with their attendant states of dreaming and waking. The subtle body is basically the mind, thoughts, emotions, attitudes and so on. It's the subtle sense of "I" compared with the gross sense of "I" associated with the physical body. The dream state reflects our identification with the mind and the subtle senses of which it is comprised. The subtle body isn't bound by the physical laws governing the physical body; thus the experiences and actions of the subtle body during dreams seem nearly incomprehensible to the mind identified with the physical body in the waking state. However, while in the subtle body one can have experiences that seem "paranormal," out-of-body or post-death. During the course of yogic practices, such experiences may occur, especially in meditation, and are taken to indicate the expansion of one's awareness beyond the confines of one's physical body.

Yoga psychology describes the mind and its workings in great detail. In some ways it corresponds to the various descriptions of the mind and personality developed by Western psychology. It similarly includes concepts of ego, the unconscious, and processes of projection, identification, and conditioning. However, the origin and context are quite dissimilar. Three of the most salient features of the context in which the mind is viewed in yoga are its relation to bondage and liberation, its existence over time, and the condition of the mind in various states of consciousness.

Yoga views the mind as the cause of bondage and liberation. It creates bondage by thinking it is not the Self and that it is this particular, limited individual. Universal Consciousness becomes bound to individual consciousness. That negation of infinite wholeness creates an identity that is wanting and incomplete. Yoga asserts that the mind then creates the senses, the body and the physical world to roam in, searching for wholeness, completeness, a total identity. The Self, that which is omnipotent, seems powerless and seeks to gain power, perhaps by pumping iron or by scaling the corporate ladder. That which is omniscient seems unknowing and seeks to raise its consciousness through therapy, growth groups, Eastern disciplines and courses. That which is eternal seems bound in time and seeks to avoid death and leave a legacy by which to be remembered. The 11th-century sage Kshemaraja, commenting on the *Shiva Sutra* (III, 2): "Limited knowledge is bondage,"[10] explains:

> Limited knowledge of the embodied individual becomes the cause of bondage. Firstly, in practical life we have to do with particulars. Therefore, the empirical individual thinks that particulars are the sole truth of life. He is confined to the differences and distinctions and is unable to grasp the Universal of which the particulars are only a limited expression. Secondly, all the ideas of the individual are derived from sensori-motor perceptions, their images, and thought-constructs, imagination and fancies of the mind...He is unable to believe that there can be a supersensuous reality. So he builds a prison for himself in which he takes the utmost delight to live. Thirdly, he considers his mind-body complex, his psychophysical organism to be his Self. He does not care to know that these are only instruments for the life of the Atman—his real Self on the material plane. So he indulges in gross physical pleasures. The desire for them becomes so strong that he becomes their victim. He does not enjoy them; they enjoy him.[11]

How many times have you felt like a victim of your own drives for sense pleasure, knowing you shouldn't indulge in something, yet being compelled to do it anyway?

The subtle body has as one of its components the unconscious. Yoga views the unconscious similarly to Freud, as the repository of past experiences and the driving force behind much of an individual's current actions and thoughts. The subtle body is held to exist independently of the physical body and doesn't undergo death as does the physical body. It contains the karmic impressions, desires, and tendencies developed over the course of countless lifetimes, not just one lifetime as thought by Western psychology. These impressions, called *samskaras*, stored in the subtle body, determine much of what we do, seek, and experience in this life. Kshemaraja writes "The various desires of such a person are awakened by the force of his subtle body, and he wanders from life to life by acquiring suitable bodies in which these desires can be suitably satisfied."[12] The mind creates the physical body for the purposes of experiencing the results of past actions (karma) and for the fulfillment of desires on the material plane. Those notions concerning the nature of the mind and its existence from one life to the next are in direct contradiction to these basic assumptions of traditional western psychology: (1) the physical body is the only body that we have; (2) death is the inevitable end of human existence; and (3) physical death is the final termination of human consciousness.[13]

The yogic conceptualization of the unconscious differs from Freud's view in terms of how the contents of the unconscious arrive there. Freud held that repression is the process by which most of the content of the unconscious is created whereas yoga psychology asserts that practically every thought, desire, act, or experience leaves its trace regardless of whether or not it's repressed. These traces, the samskaras built up over time, serve as templates or potentialities for the creation of future thoughts, desires, actions, and bodies.

Yoga psychology takes a very practical approach towards remedying the problems of the mind. Given that past impressions have been deposited over innumerable lives, it is impossible to search for all the antecedent causes determining our present psychological make-up. Such a search would therefore be fruitless in terms of stilling the mind and preventing the continued influence of those impressions. Since the basic problem is root ignorance of who we truly are and the subsequent modifications of the mind, that is thoughts, emotions, and the deluded ideas of who we are, then the solution is the stilling of the modifications of the mind and the eradication of the root ignorance. All yoga practices aim at stilling the mind and eradicating the root ignorance. Patanjali, the great sage and codifier of yoga (circa 350 B.C.), writes in his *Yoga Sutras* "When the mind is still then man abides in his true nature."[14] To enable one to abide in one's true nature, yoga examines and classifies the contents of the mind and prescribes remedies, the yogic practices, for reducing and eliminating the thought waves, or modifications of the mind.

All modifications of the mind, called *vrittis*, can be classified as one or a combination of five types and categorized as either painful or non-painful. The five types are right knowledge, wrong knowledge, fantasy, deep sleep, and memory. Painful or non-painful have special meaning in the yoga context. Painful vrittis refer to those thought waves that manifest or sustain the delusion that we are not the Self. Thus sense pleasures, even your favorite chocolate cake or whatever else you take delight in, are considered painful because they reinforce ideas such as "I am the body," "the source of my joy is external," or "my identity is limited in some way." Such vrittis produce desires, seeking after some objects while avoiding others, which keep us bound to the cycle of birth and death. Non-painful vrittis are of either a neutral type, e.g. simply perceiving the sky as you're walking, or of the type that leads towards liberation and identification with our true Self, e.g. thoughts such as "I am not limited to the body, I am not limited to the mind, I am the Self."

Notice that the two categories are "painful" and "non-painful," not "painful" and "pleasurable," or "joyful." It's a very important point. It reflects the yogic insight that modifications of the mind, no matter what type, do not produce joy or love. The qualities of joy and love, called *ananda* in yoga, are infinite dimensions of the Self. Yoga asserts that as we split ourselves off from our innate ananda, our ecstasy, our Self, we then project it onto objects and people, and seek it externally. We build up the belief that joy will really come from eating Haagen-daz chocolate-chocolate-chip ice cream! Our minds become agitated with the desire for it. When we finally walk to the store, come home, and dig into it, there's a moment when the desire ceases, the mind is still, we're in the bliss of chocolate, chocolate chip! *"No!"* says the yogi! We're in the bliss of our own Self (ananda) which we've experienced a reflection of for the moment when our mind was still. The yogic perspective holds that joy and love always arise from within. If joy was really in the chocolate ice cream, then every time we ate it, and no matter how much we ate, we would experience that joy, just as we experience the coldness and chocolateness that really are qualities of the ice cream. We delude ourselves into believing that pleasure, love, and joy are qualities of the world rather than seeing them as arising from the source within and turning our attention toward the Self, immersing ourselves in our innate center of love, allowing it to flow outward as naturally as a rose shares its beauty and fragrance with all passersby.

The process by which we become deluded is essentially a conditioning process very similar to the conditioning processes described in behaviorism. The sequence in the conditioning process is: 1) avidya, the primal ignorance manifest as the identification with the limited self instead of the true Self creates the mental agitation of desire, obscures our real nature and the experience of bliss inherent to it; 2) the desires are focused on a particular object; 3) possession of the object temporarily eliminates the agitation caused by the desires, thus allowing the mind to be relatively still; 4) in that stillness, the joy or feeling of completeness that is our true nature arises within us; this feeling is temporally paired with the object and we erroneously come to believe that the object gave rise to the joy or pleasure. We're particularly susceptible to conditioning because we are primarily identified with our subtle and physical bodies. Our attention is focused on sensory and mental/emotional events and their co-occurrences. The causal body and the Self are beyond the effects of conditioning. In their respective states of deep sleep and turiya, conditioning cannot occur. In deep sleep we're not aware of any physical or mental events, and in turiya we're beyond them. Yoga practices are can be viewed as deconditioning practices aimed at breaking the conditioning patterns established through lifetimes of identification with our minds and bodies. Stephen Wilson, Ph.D.[15] describes the processes by which one becomes a yogi as resocialization and deconditioning processes. Thus research on yogis and meditators has shown that in some states they don't habituate to stimuli or they don't react at all, both of which interfere with the conditioning process. Because of their effectiveness in deconditioning, yoga practices, primarily meditation, are used clinically in application to stress reactivity, psychosomatic illnesses and anxiety disorders. However it must be remembered that the level of deconditioning that they were originally aimed at is deeper and broader than those therapeutic applications imply. Daniel Goleman, Ph.D. writes:

> Asian psychologies have largely ignored psychologically loaded contents of awareness, including psychodynamics, while seeking to alter the context in which they—and all other information—are registered in awareness. Conventional psychotherapies assume as givens the mechanisms underlying perceptual, cognitive, and affective processes, while seeking to alter them at the level of socially conditioned patterns. Asian systems disregard these same socially conditioned patterns, while aiming at the control and self-regulation of the underlying mechanisms themselves. Therapies break the hold of past conditioning on present behavior; meditation aims to alter the

process of conditioning per se so that it will no longer be a prime determinant of future facts. In the Asian approach behavioral and personality change is secondary, an epiphenomenon of changes, through the voluntary self-regulation of mental states, in the basic processes which define our reality.[16]

All modifications of the mind are to be overcome t̹ / intense practice and detachment born of discrimination. In yoga, discrimination is the ability to differentiate between the Self and the mind, between one's true nature and one's assumed, limited nature. With that ability one can detach from the desires and conditioned identity of the mind and body. The intense practice refers to the eight types of yogic disciplines—yamas, niyamas, asana, pranayama, pratyahara, dharana, dhyana, and samadhi— referred to as the eight limbs of yoga. They are aimed at reducing and eventually eliminating all the current modifications of the mind, as well as all the samskaras from the past. These practices and the yogic process they engender purify the subtle body of all the impressions of past lifetimes and eventually destroy the root ignorance of Self, the avidya that causes all else. The practices don't improve the Self or change the Self. The Self isn't bound and the Self can't be liberated. The mind however is bound. Vedanta likens the mind to a dirty mirror; its power to reflect is obscured and distorted. Yogic practices remove the dirt, the vrittis, and then the purified mind reflects the luminous Consciousness of the Self.

The yamas and niyamas are moral and ethical practices of self-restraint and self-regulation. They are: nonviolence, truthfulness, nonstealing, sexual continence, nongreed, purity of body and mind, contentment, austerity, scriptural study, and constant remembrance of the Self and surrender to Divine will. These reduce the vrittis caused by conflict and disharmony with others and oneself and begin to purify one's thoughts and actions.

Asana means a posture that one can sit in comfortably for a long time. Westerners are often familiar with the yoga postures that are taught as part of yoga classes in YMCA's, gym classes, etc. In those settings they are taught as part of exercise and relaxation routines. Their real intent however is to prepare the body for sitting comfortably for a long time in meditation and to further purify the subtle body by influencing the flow of energy through the subtle body. The practice is aimed at reducing the vrittis caused by the body. If one makes the body strong, healthy, and able to sit comfortably, then when one sits in meditation the mind will not be disturbed by sensations, aches, and pains produced by the body. A comfortable, erect posture also facilitates the rising of the Kundalini Shakti, our divine power of Self-illumination and transformation, which traverses up the sushumna nadi (the central energy channel of the subtle body which lies contiguously with the spine), clearing the samskaras stored there, thus transporting one's consciousness to higher levels.

Pranayama refers to the control of our breathing and the vital force, prana, that is related to our breath and our mind. Prana the subtle power linking matter and physical energy on the one hand and mind and consciousness on the other. Regulating the prana influences our mind. Pranayama exercises are enormously powerful and shouldn't be practiced except under the guidance of a qualified teacher. For meditation it's fine to simply allow the breath to flow spontaneously and naturally. As our breathing becomes rhythmic and natural the mind becomes quiet, the vrittis are further reduced.

The last four practices may be referred to as psychospiritual disciplines whereas the previous two, asana and pranayama, are psycho-physical disciplines. Pratyhara, dharana, dhyana, and samadhi combined are what is commonly thought of as meditation. Pratyhara is the withdrawal of the mind from the senses and the outside world and turning the focus of attention within. It eliminates all the vrittis caused by the senses in contact with the body and the outside world. Dharana is the practice of concentrating the flow of attention toward a single object within. The highest object of concentration is the Self or its vibratory equivalent, a mantra such as *So'ham* or *Hamsa* (Sanskrit for "I Am That"). Dharana develops into dhyana, meditation proper, the uninterrupted flow of awareness toward the object of concentration. Dharana and dhyana eliminate all remaining vrittis except the one of the object of concentration. The yoga practices so far described reduce the multifarious thought waves that usually occupy our minds down to just one. As the meditator eliminates the last remaining vritti, the practices culminate in samadhi, where the subject-object split dissolves, leaving only Unity Consciousness. However, to attain this state through the practice of yoga one is warned: be prepared to pursue the perfection of each of those eight limbs over *lifetimes*.

Yoga psychology shows that the mind takes the form of whatever it dwells on, like water taking the shape of any container into which it is poured. Normally our mind is focused on the subtle and physical bodies; takes their forms and identifies with them. Thus consciousness is ordinarily limited to the body and mind and the roles and functions they perform. In the process of meditation the mind is withdrawn from the physical body and directed towards the pure consciousness of the Self. The mind dwelling on the formless Self dissolves its limited nature and becomes one with Consciousness. All vrittis cease and one abides in one's true nature, to paraphrase Patanjali. Repeated immersion in samadhi purifies one of all samskaras, all the past impressions of limitations, and shifts one's identity from the mind/body complex to pure Consciousness. When we're identified with our minds we think of our limited self as the subject?? the knower, the perceiver of objects. During the course of yoga it becomes clear that the body, the mind and all its contents, as well as the states of waking, dreaming, and deep sleep, are objects of perception for some conscious knower. That conscious knower, which is never an object of knowledge is the Self.[17] Ultimately one's identity remains established in one's Self even in the midst of thought and action. Then the process of Self-realization is complete.

Yoga holds that absolutely indispensable to successful completion of the goal of yoga is the spiritual master or Guru. The *Shiva Sutras*, II. 6, state: "The Guru who has attained Self-realization can alone help the aspirant in acquiring it."[18] Patanjali recommends as a practice for the realization of the goal of yoga that the aspirant fix their mind on one who has risen above attachment and passion.[19] The Guru has been considered by Western psychologists to be similar to a therapist, change agent, role model, and teacher. The Guru may play all of those roles to some extent, but the most important function of the Guru isn't captured by such descriptions.

The essential function of the highest Guru knows no analog in Western psychological terms. The fundamental quality of a Guru is the bestowal of grace, known as the ability to awaken the Kundalini Shakti of the seeker. There are lesser gurus of great value who can teach scriptures, prayer, meditation techniques, hatha yoga, pranayama, and so on. The ability to awaken the Kundalini is held by only the most potent gurus of any tradition. There have been great Christian saints whose touch or words inflamed the souls of those who followed them. Similarly there have been rabbis, Sufi masters, Buddhist masters, and yogis with such power. Kundalini Shakti is the term for what yoga considers our dormant, inner, omnipotent, omniscient power of Self by which all the spiritual practices are enlivened and brought to fruition. Kshemaraja[20] in his commentary on the *Shiva Sutras* says the Guru is the grace-bestowing power of God. Many times I heard Swami Muktananda speak about the true nature of the Guru or the Guru principle being the divine power of grace flowing through an individual. "Shakti" is another name for that power. It is one with the Self, the Universal Power of Consciousness. Thus it is not so much the individual who is referred to as the Guru, but the universal power, the Shakti manifesting through an individual. The essential nature of the true Guru is transpersonal, not individual. In this way the true Guru is the inner Guru, the archetypal power of the Self-revelation, the Kundalini, inherent to everyone.

Before going further in this discussion of Kundalini as the basis of yoga, the words Sir John Woodroffe seem especially appropriate:

The bases of this Yoga are of a highly metaphysical and scientific character. For its understanding there is required a full acquaintance with Indian philosophy, religious doctrine, and ritual in general, and in particular with that presentment of these three matters which is given in the Shakta and Monistic (Advaita) Shaiva-Tantras. It would need more than a bulky volume to describe and explain in any detail the nature and meaning of this Yoga, and the bases on which it rests. I must, therefore, assume in the reader either this general knowledge or a desire to acquire it, and confine myself to such an exposition of general principles and leading facts as will supply the key by which the doors leading to theoretical knowledge of the subject may be opened by those desirous of passing through and beyond them, and as will thus facilitate the understanding of the difficult texts here translated. For on the practical side I can merely reproduce the directions given in the books together with such explanations of them as I have received orally. Those who wish to go further, and to put into actual process this Yoga, must first satisfy themselves of the value and suitability of this Yoga and then learn directly of a Guru who has himself been through it (Siddha). His experience alone will say whether the aspirant is capable of success....If the latter enters upon the path, the Guru alone can save him from attendant risks, moulding and guiding the practice as he will according to the particular capacities and needs of his disciple.[21] (parentheses in original)

Though the Guru principle may be archetypal or divine, that doesn't mean the individual who is embodying that principle or carrying the projection of it is infallible or perfect. Even the power to awaken the Kundalini doesn't make one perfect. Such a static notion of perfection as an attainment is deluded. We need to be wary of the limitations, the shadow sides of gurus, which are often hidden or obscured by the brilliance of the light of ancient truths they clothe themselves in. We have to look past the public persona of the guru to see what they truly embody.

Jung would say we have to talk to the pastor's wife or children to see what the pastor is really like. It's often backstage or with the inner circle that the shadow side of the guru is most visible. Unfortunately, those who have the privilege of seeing the teacher or guru at such private moments are least likely to speak out publicly or privately so the guru could get the feedback necessary to transform their shadow side.

Shankaracharya, the eminent 8th century sage of Advaita Vedanta and one of the greatest yogic masters ever, wrote an ecstatic prayer, *Saundaryalahari*,[22] proclaiming the supreme power of Kundalini Shakti. In it he states that all knowledge, all wisdom, all inspiration, all creativity—musical, poetic, literary, artistic—as well as union with the divine Self come through the power of Kundalini alone. For this reason the awakening of Kundalini, the power of Self-revelation, is the esoteric goal of all yogas. Shaktipat is the term for the descent of grace that awakens the Kundalini. The *Kularnava Tantra*[23] states that without shaktipat there is no liberation or Self-realization. The descent of grace may happen spontaneously and unexpectedly, or through the power of a master of the highest attainment. In some cases the Kundalini is awakened through contact with a mystic guide who appears in one's dreams or meditation. Often it is awakened through the spiritual practices learned from a master-teacher. It may even have been awakened in a past life and is continuing to unfold in this life. No one person or practice is the solely available means to the awakening of the Kundalini. The Divine is too generous to put such limitations on its accessibility.

The awakened Kundalini, referred to as Shakti, purifies the physical and subtle bodies of all blocks, the samskaras and hidden mental tendencies and eliminates the primal ignorance, avidya, which causes bondage. The Shakti becomes the motive power behind all the practices of yoga—the yamas, niyamas, etc.—and takes the aspirant to the goal of liberation. The purification work of the Kundalini Shakti results in the unity state of consciousness, where all distinctions between God, Guru, Self, and disciple dissolve. This ultimate state of consciousness is called sahaja samadhi, the natural samadhi that is present at all times, in all places, not limited to sitting in meditation.

It is to this ultimate state that the eternal quest points. Living in that state allows the Divine to infuse all of our activities. It's not an attainment that is meant only for renunciates, monastery or ashram dwellers, but for everyone. In India there is a rich tradition of householder saints, men and women of the highest attainment, who lived family lives and worked as potters, shoemakers, weavers, farmers, and teachers. We need such models of an integrated life of the spirit. Search out the stories of those in your tradition who have realized the highest and lived it fully.

Notes

Foreword

1. Joseph Campbell, *Brahman and Baksheesh: The Indian Journals*, ed. Stephen and Robin Larsen (San Francisco: Harper Collins, 1995).
2. *See: The Gospel according to Sri Ramakrishna*, ed. Swami Vivekananda. Swami Vivekananda wrote of the invaluable assistance he received from Joseph Campbell in the editing of this work; *see also: A Fire in the Mind*, Joseph Campbell's biography by Stephen and Robin Larsen. For more information about the Larsen's unique work and The Center for Symbolic Studies you can visit their website: www.mythmind.com.
3. *See also: Technicians of the Sacred* by Jerome Rothenberg; and Larsen's discussion of this in *The Shaman's Doorway*.
4. From *The Book of Common Prayer*.

Chapter One

1. Joseph Campbell, *The Hero With A Thousand Faces* (Princeton: Princeton University Press, 1973), 3.
2. Campbell, 11.
3. *The Kabir Book*, trans. Robert Bly (Boston: The Seventies Press, 1977), 29.
4. *Wisdom of the Spanish Mystics*, trans. Stephen Clissold (New York: Directions Publishing Corp., 1977), 32.

5. *Saundaryalahari of Sankaracarya*, trans. V. K. Subramaniam (Delhi, India: Motilal Banarsidass, 1980).

6. *Kularnava Tantra*, trans. M. P. Pandit (Madras, India: Ganesh & Co., 1973).

7. Lawrence Edwards, *Psychological Change and Spiritual Growth Through the Practice of Siddha Yoga* (Ann Arbor, MI: University Microfilms International, 1986), unpublished doctoral dissertation.

8. Carl Jung, *Psychological Commentary on Kundalini Yoga, Lectures 1 & 2, 1932, Spring 1975* (New York: Spring Publications, 1975), 18.

Chapter Two

1. Lex Hixon, *Mother of the Universe* (Wheaton, Illinois: The Theosophical Publishing House, 1994), 76.

2. Sir John Woodruffe, *The Serpent Power* (Madras, India: Ganesh and Co., 1973). Sir John Woodroffe's *Serpent Power* is one of the best works on the Kundalini and the subtle-body. I recommend it as the most comprehensive exploration of this miraculous possession of ours.

3. Aldous Huxley, *The Perennial Philosophy* (New York: Harper Colophon, 1970), 11.

4. Hixon, 7.

Chapter Three

1. Lex Hixon, *Mother of the Universe* (Wheaton, Illinois: The Theosophical Publishing House, 1994), 53.

2. *The Song of God: Bhagavad Gita*, trans. Swami Prabhavananda and Christopher Isherwood (Hollywood, CA: Vedanta Press, 1972).

3. Thomas Merton, *The Wisdom of the Desert* (New York: New Directions Publishing Corp., 1960), 47.

4. *The Kabir Book*, trans. Robert Bly (Boston: The Seventies Press, 1977), 24-25.
5. Prabhavananda and Isherwood, 72.
6. *John of Ruysbroeck: The Adornment of the Spiritual Marriage; The Sparkling Stone; The Book of Supreme Truth*, ed. Evelyn Underhill, trans. C. A. Wynschenk (New York: E. P. Dutton & Co.,1916), 122-23.
7. *Shiva Sutras*, trans. Jaideva Singh (Delhi, India: Motilal Banarsidass, 1979), 37.
8. Swami Prabhavananda, *How to Know God: The Yoga Aphorisms of Patanjali* (Hollywood, CA: Vedanta Press, 1969), 50.
9. *The Ruins of the Heart: Selected Lyric Poetry of Jelaluddin Rumi*, trans. Edmund Helminski (Putney, VT: Threshold Books, 1981), 33.

Chapter Four

1. *The Ruins of the Heart: Selected Lyric Poetry of Jelaluddin Rumi*, trans. Edmund Helminski (Putney, VT: Threshold Books, 1981), 26.
2. Joseph Campbell, *The Hero With A Thousand Faces* (Princeton: Princeton University Press, 1973), 385-86.
3. Robert Moore, Douglas Gillette, *King, Warrior, Magian, Lover: Rediscovering the Archetypes of the Mature Masculine* (San Francisco: Harper San Francisco, 1991).
4. Robert Moore and Douglas Gillette, *The King Within* (New York: William Morrow and Co., Inc., 1992).
5. *The Lion King*, Walt Disney Company (Burbank, CA: Walt Disney Co., 1994).
6. Robert Bly, *Iron John: A Book About Men* (New York: Addison-Wesley Publishing Company, Inc., 1990).
7. Bly, 181-82. Parentheses in the original.

8. *The Upanishads: Breath of the Eternal,* trans. Swami Prabhavananda and F. Manchester (Hollywood, CA: Vedanta Press, 1957), 66.
9. Lex Hixon, *Great Swan: Meetings with Ramakrishna* (Boston: Shambala Publications, Inc., 1992).
10. *Shiva Sutras,* trans. Jaideva Singh (Delhi, India: Motilal Banarsidass, 1979), 119.
11. Prabhavananda and Manchester, 48.
12. Prabhavananda and Manchester, 76.

Chapter Five

1. Robert Way, *The Wisdom of the English Mystics* (New York: New Directions Publishing Corp., 1978), 45.
2. Joseph Campbell, *The Hero with a Thousand Faces* (Princeton: Princeton University Press, 1973), 17-18.
3. Campbell, 19-20.
4. Campbell, 29.
5. Campbell, 30 (italics in the original).
6. Campbell, 36-37 (italics in the original).
7. Campbell, 40.
8. *The Principal Upanishads,* trans. S. Radhakrishnan (New York: Humanities Press, 1978), 619.
9. *Bhagavad Gita,* trans. Swami Shivananda (Durban, South Africa: Divine Life Society of South Africa, 1983), 81.
10. *The Ruins of the Heart: Selected Lyric Poetry of Jelaluddin Rumi,* trans. Edmund Helminski (Putney, VT: Threshold Books, 1981), 50.
11. *The Upanishads: Breath of the Eternal,* trans. Swami Prabhavananda and F. Manchester (Hollywood, CA: Vedanta Press, 1957), 20.
12. Prabhavananda and Manchester, 81.

13. Lawrence Edwards, *Psychological Change and Spiritual Growth Through the Practice of Siddha Yoga* (Ann Arbor, MI: University Microfilms International, 1986) unpublished doctoral dissertation.

14. *Wisdom of the Spanish Mystics*, trans. Stephen Clissold (New York: Directions Publishing Corp., 1977), 57.

15. Carl Jung, *Aion* (Princeton: Princeton University Press, 1978), 10.

16. Adapted from: *Bhagavad Gita*, 51.

17. Campbell, 389.

18. Campbell, 391.

19. *Wisdom of the Spanish Mystics*, 76

Appendix

1. *See* Thomas Kuhn's *The Structure of Scientific Revolutions* and Roger Walsh's article "The Consciousness Disciplines and the Behavioral Sciences: Questions of Comparison and Assessment," *American Journal of Psychiatry, 137* (1980), pp 663-73. Much of this discussion of the clash between traditional western psychology and the eastern or consciousness disciplines is derived from Walsh's article.

2. *See* Walsh and Ken Wilber's *Eye to Eye: The Quest for the New Paradigm* (Garden City, NY: Anchor Press/Doubleday, 1983).

3. *See* Walsh, 668.

4. *Beyond Ego: Transpersonal Dimensions in Psychology*, eds. Roger Walsh and Frances Vaughan (Los Angeles: J.P. Tarcher, 1980).

5. *See* Charles Tart's "Some Assumptions of Orthodox, Western Psychology" in *Transpersonal Psychologies*, ed. Charles Tart, (London: Routledge & Kegan Paul, 1975).

6. Fritjof Capra, *The Turning Point* (New York: Bantam Books, 1982), 178.

7. *The Principal Upanishads*, trans. S. Radhakrishnan (New York: Humanities Press, 1978), Taittraya Upanishad, II, 6.

8. Stanislav Grof, "East and West: Ancient Wisdom and Modern Science," *The Journal of Transpersonal Psychology,* 15 (1983),14.

9. *See* Brandt Dayton's *Practical Vedanta: Selected Works of Swami Rama Tirtha,* edited by Dayton Brandt (Honesdale, PA: Himalayan International Institute of Yoga Science and Philosophy, 1978)

10. *Shiva Sutras,* trans. Jaideva Singh (Delhi, India: Motilal Banarsidass, 1979), 128.

11. *Shiva Sutras,* 131.

12. *Spanda-Karikas,* trans. Jaideva Singh (Delhi, India: Motilal Banarsidass, 1980), 167.

13. Charles Tart "Some Assumptions of Orthodox, Western Psychology."

14. Swami Prabhavananda, *How to Know God: The Yoga Aphorisms of Patanjali* (Hollywood, CA: Vedanta Press, 1969), 16.

15. Stephen Wilson, "Becoming A Yogi: Resocialization and Deconditioning as Conversion Processes," *Sociological Analysis 45* (1984), 301-14.

16. Daniel Goleman, Gary Schwarz, "Meditation as an intervention in stress reactivity," *J. of Counseling and Clinical Psychology,* 44, 465.

17. *The Principal Upanishads,* Brihadaranyaka Upanishad VI, 22.

18. *Shiva Sutras,* 102.

19. *See* I. K. Taimni's *The Science of Yoga: The Yoga Sutras of Patanjali* translated by I. K. Taimni (Wheaton, ILL: The Theosophical Publishing House, 1975).

20. *Shiva Sutras,* 103.

21. Sir John Woodruffe, *The Serpent Power* (Madras, India: Ganesh and Co., 1973), 25-26.

22. V. K. Subramanian *Saundaryalahari of Sankaracarya* (Delhi, India: Motilal Banarsidass, 1980).

23. *Kularnava Tantra,* trans. M. P. Pandit (Madras, India: Ganesh & Co., 1973).

Glossary

ahimsa—the practice of non-violence

ajna chakra—a center of consciousness in the subtle body located in the space between the eyes, often referred to as the "third eye."

anahata chakra—a center of consciousness in the subtle body at the level of the heart.

anima:—Jungian term most frequently used to denote the feminine side of men; also can mean the whole of the unconscious or the soul.

animus:—Jungian term most frequently used to denote the masculine side of women.

arati—a devotional ritual performed by waving a flame in circles before a representation of the Divine. The individual flame, a lighted oil wick or candle symbolizes the individual light of consciousness, while the representation of the Divine is the Universal Light of Consciousness.

ashram—a residential center for the practices of yoga, meditation, seva and other practices.

bhakta—an individual on the path of bhakti yoga; a lover of the Divine.

bhakti yoga—the form of yoga emphasizing devotional practices and the path of love.

chakra—a center of consciousness in the subtle body.

diksha—initiation

Hamsa—a very potent mantra for expanding one's awareness of Unity Consciousness. It means "I am That." This mantra is said to be repeating itself with our every breath. The breath comes in with the sound ham (pronounced hum) and goes out with the sound sa. Thus our every breath proclaims the truth of our unity with all.

Kali—The great black Goddess, Mother of the Universe, destroyer of the demons that plague the mind and create delusion.

kriya—a movement of the shakti that can manifest itself through movements of the body, mind or spirit.

Kundalini—the dormant power of Consciousness in everyone which when awakened allows the individual to fully experience their union with the Divine.

laya yoga—the type of yoga which emphasizes practices leading to merger through divine visions, lights and sounds.

lingam—masculine symbol of the Divine in phallic form.

mahasamadhi—the term used for the death of an enlightened being meaning the great samadhi.

manipura chakra—a center of consciousness in the subtle body at the level of the solar plexus.

mantra—words or sounds imbued with the power of Consciousness.

Maya—the power of the concealment, all that appears to be separate from the Divine.

muladhara chakra—a center of consciousness in the subtle body at the base of the spine where the dormant Kundalini awaits awakening.

mumukshtva—longing for liberation.

nada—divine sound perceptible to purified consciousness in certain meditative states.

nadis—conduits for subtle energy, prana or shakti through the subtle body.

nirvikalpa samadhi—level of samadhi or meditation in which the seer, the seen and the process of seeing have all merged in one.

niyamas:—the five observances delineated by Patanjali as part of the practice of ashtanga yoga, eight-limbed yoga, which help to quiet the mind. They are: purity, contentment, self-discipline, study of scriptures and chanting, and devotion to God.

Om—the powerful mantra embodying the Creator, Creation and the act of creation.

Om Namah Shivaya—a very potent mantra for awakening the Kundalini and centering consciousness in the Self. It means "I bow to the Self."

prana—a form of subtle energy which moves through the subtle body, in part flowing into the subtle body with the inbreath and out with the exhalation.

puja—a devotional ritual.

sadhana—spiritual practices done as part of one's path as well as the whole process of spiritual endeavoring.

sahasrara—the center of consciousness at the upper terminus of the sushumna nadi. It is the center of transcendent Unity Consciousness or God Consciousness.

samskaras—impressions left in the subtle body by past experiences.

sannyasa—vows of renunciation taken by a sannyasin or monk in the Vedic tradition.

self—limited individual sense of being.

Self—unbound, unlimited, infinite Consciousness, the Divine.

seva—practice of selfless service offered without concern for personal reward.

shadow—the unconscious aspects of ourselves.

Shakti—the infinite power of the Divine.

Shaktipat—the descent of the infinite power of the Divine which awakens the Kundalini.

Shiva—the auspicious one, God.

Shivo'ham—a very powerful mantra vibrating with the consciousness of "I am Shiva" or "I am God."

Siddha—one who has fully accomplished the goal of yoga and meditation.

So'ham—a potent mantra vibrating with the consciousness of "I am That." A form of the mantra *Hamsa*.

subtle body—the body of our mind, emotions and prana made up of nadis.

sushumna nadi—the principle nadi connecting the main chakras from the lowest, the muladhara, to the highest, the sahasrara, forming the pathway the awakened Kundalini moves up through as it purifies the chakras and elevates individual awareness to its highest Universal Consciousness.

svadhishthana chakra—a center of consciousness in the subtle body located at the root of the sexual organs.

swami—one who has taken the vows of total renunciation in the Vedic tradition.

turiya—transcendent state of Unity Consciousness

vishuddha chakra—a center of consciousness in the subtle body located in the throat.

vritti—a modification of the mind, e.g. thoughts, feelings, sensations, perceptions.

Witness Consciousness—the perspective of the Self, supremely free, all-embracing, Unity Consciousness.

yagna—sacred ritual fire.

yamas:—the five restraints delineated by Patanjali Patanjali as part of the practice of ashtanga yoga, eight-limbed yoga, which help to quiet the mind. They are: not injuring any being, truthfulness, not stealing in any way, sexual continence, and not coveting anything.

yoni—a feminine representation of the Divine in the shape of a female sexual organ.

References

Ajaya, Swami. *Psychotherapy East and West: A Unifying Paradigm.* Honesdale, PA: Himalayan International Institute of Yoga Science and Philosophy, 1984.

Aranya, Swami H. *Yoga Philosophy of Patanjali (3rd ed).* Calcutta, India: Calcutta University. Press, 1981.

Bly, Robert, trans. *The Kabir Book.* Boston: The Seventies Press,1977.

Bly, Robert. *Iron John: A Book About Men.* New York: Addison-Wesley Publishing Company, Inc, 1990.

Bohm, David; Welwood, John. Issues in Physics, Psychology and Metaphysics: A Conversation. *The Journal of Transpersonal Psychology, 12,* 1980, 25-36.

Borysenko, Joan. *Fire in the Soul.* New York: Warner Books, 1993.

Campbell, Joseph. *The Hero With a Thousand Faces.* Princeton: Princeton University Press, 1973.

————*Transformations of Myth Through Time.* New York: Harper and Row, 1990.

Capra, Fritjof. *The Turning Point.* New York: Bantam Books, 1982.

Chatterji, J.C. *Kashmir Shaivism*. Chandigarh, India: Galav Publications, 1981.

Chaudhari, Haridas. Yoga psychology. In Tart, Charles (Ed.), *Transpersonal Psychologies* (pp.231-80). London: Routledge & Kegan Paul, 1975.

Clissold, Stephen. *Wisdom of the Spanish Mystics*. New York: New Directions Publishing Corp., 1977.

Corby, James; et al. Psychophysiological correlates of the practice of Tantric Yoga meditation. *Archives of General Psychiatry, 35,* 1978, 571-77.

Cragg, Kenneth. *The Wisdom of the Sufis*. New York: New Directions Publishing Corp., 1976.

Dattatreya. *Avadhuta Gita*. Translated by Swami Ashokananda. Madras, India: Sri Ramakrishna Math, 1977.

Dayton, Brandt, Ed. *Practical Vedanta, Selected works of Swami Rama Tirtha*. Honesdale, PA: Himalayan International Institute of Yoga Science and Philosophy, 1978.

Edwards, Lawrence. *Psychological Change and Spiritual Growth Through the Practice of Siddha Yoga*. Unpublished doctoral dissertation. Ann Arbor, MI: University Microfilms International,1986.

Glick, Stephen. *An Analysis Of The Change Process In The Guru-Disciple Relationship*. Ann Arbor, MI: Univ. Microfilms International, 1983.

Goleman, Daniel. Meditation and consciousness: An Asian approach to mental health. *American Journal of Psychotherapy, 30,* 1976, 41-54.

Goleman, Daniel; & Schwartz, Gary. Meditation as an intervention in stress reactivity. *Journ. of Counseling and Clinical Psychology, 44,* 1976, 456-66.

Grof, Stanislav. East and West: Ancient wisdom and modern science. *The Journ. of Transpersonal Psychology, 15,* 1983, 13-36.

Helminski, Edmund (trans.). *The Ruins of the Heart: Selected Lyric Poetry of Jelaluddin Rumi.* Putney, Vermont: Threshold Books, 1981.

Hixon, Lex. *Great Swan: Meetings with Ramakrishna.* Boston: Shambala Publications, Inc., 1992.

————*Mother of the Universe.* Wheaton, Illinois: The Theosophical Publishing House, 1994.

Huxley, Aldous. *The Perennial Philosophy.* New York: Harper Colophon, 1970.

Isherwood, Christopher, ed. *Vedanta for the Western World.* New York: The Marcel Rodd Company, 1946.

Jung, C. G. Psychological Commentary on Kundalini Yoga, Lectures 1 & 2, 1932. *Spring* 1975. New York: Spring Publications, 1975.

————*Aion.* Princeton: Princeton University Press, 1978.

————*Symbols of Transformation.* Princeton: Princeton University Press, 1990.

————*The Archetypes and The Collective Unconscious.* Princeton: Princeton University Press, 1990.

Kara, Ashok. The Guru and Therapist: Goals and Techniques in Regard to the Question of the Chela and Patient. *Psychotherapy: Theory, Research and Practice, 16*, 1979, 61-71.

Kopp, Sheldon. *Guru: Metaphors from a Psychotherapist.* Palo Alto, CA: Science and Behavior Books, 1971.

Kuhn, T. *The Structure of Scientific Revolutions, (2nd ed.).* Chicago, Illinois: Chicago Univ. Press, 1970.

Kutz, Ilan, et al. Meditation as an Adjunct to Psychotherapy: An Outcome Study. *Psychotherapy and Psychosomatics, 43*, 1985, 209-18.

Larsen, Stephen. *The Shaman's Doorway.* Barrytown, NY: Station Hill Press, 1988.

Larsen, Stephen. *Mythic Imagination.* Rochester, VT: Inner Traditions, 1998.

Madhavananda, Swami, trans. *Vivekachudamani.* Calcutta, India: Advaita Ashrama, 1982.

Merton, Thomas. *The Wisdom of the Desert.* New York: New Directions Publishing Corp., 1960.

Moore, Robert; Gillette, Douglas. *King, Warrior, Magician, Lover: Rediscovering the Archetypes of the Mature Masculine.* San Francisco: Harper San Francisco, 1991.

——*The King Within.* New York: William Morrow and Co., Inc., 1992.

Muktananda, Swami. *Play of consciousness.* San Francisco: Harper and Row, 1978.

————*Kundalini: The Secret of Life.* South Fallsburg, N.Y.: SYDA Foundation, 1979.

————*Siddha Meditation.* South Fallsburg, N.Y.: SYDA Foundation, 1979.

Ornstein, Robert, ed. *The Nature of Human Consciousness.* San Francisco, Calif.: W.H. Freeman, 1973.

Pandit, M.P., trans. *Kularnava Tantra.* Madras, India: Ganesh & Co., 1973.

Prabhavananda, Swami. What Yoga Is. *Vedanta for the Western World.* Isherwood, C. edit., (pp. 41-46). New York: The Marcel Rodd Company, 1946.

————The Goal of Yoga. *Vedanta for the Western World.* Isherwood, C. edit., (pp.47-50). New York: The Marcel Rodd Company, 1946.

————*How to know God: The yoga aphorisms of Patanjali.* Hollywood, CA: Vedanta Press, 1969.

————trans. *Shankara's Crest-jewel of Discrimination.* Hollywood, CA: Vedanta Press, 1978.

————& Isherwood, C. trans. *The Song of God: Bhagavad Gita.* Hollywood, CA: Vedanta Press, 1972.

————& Manchester, F. trans. *The Upanishads: Breath of the Eternal.* Hollywood, CA: Vedanta Press, 1957.

Radhakrishnan, S., trans. *The Principal Upanishads.* New York: Humanities Press, 1978.

Rama, Swami; Ballentine, Rudolph; & Ajaya, Swami. *Yoga and Psychotherapy.* Honesdale, PA: Himalayan International Institute of Yoga Science and Philosophy, 1981.

Rothenberg, Jerome. *Technicians of the Sacred.* New York: Doubleday Anchor Books, 1968.

Singh, Jaideva, trans. *Shiva Sutras.* Delhi, India: Motilal Banarsidass, 1979.

———trans. *Vijnanabhairava.* Delhi, India: Motilal Banarsidass, 1979.

———trans. *Spanda-Karikas.* Delhi, India: Motilal Banarsidass, 1980.

———trans. *Pratyabhijnahrdayam: The Secret of Self-Recognition.* Delhi, India: Motilal Banarsidass, 1980.

Subramanian, V. K. *Saundaryalahari of Sankaracarya.* Delhi, India: Motilal Banarsidass, 1980.

Sutich, A. Transpersonal Therapy. *The Journal of Transpersonal Psychology,* 5, 1973, 1-6..

Taimni, I.K., trans. *The Science of Yoga: The Yoga Sutras of Patanjali.* Wheaton, Illinois: The Theosophical Publishing House, 1975.

Tart, Charles, ed. *Transpersonal Psychologies.* London: Routledge & Kegan Paul, 1975.

———Some assumptions of Orthodox, Western Psychology, *Transpersonal Psychologies.* Tart, Charles ed., pp.59-112. London: Routledge & Kegan Paul,1975.

Tirtha, Swami Vishnu. *Devatma Shakti.* Delhi, India: Swami Shivom Tirth, 1974.

Underhill, Evelyn, ed., Wynschenk, C. A., trans. *John of Ruysbroeck: The Adornment of the Spiritual Marriage; The Sparkling Stone; The Book of Supreme Truth.* New York: E. P. Dutton & Co. 1916.

Vahia, N. S., et al. Psychophysilogic Therapy Based on the Concepts of Patanjali. *American Journal of Psychotherapy, 27,* 1972, 557-65.

Venkatesananda, Swami, trans. *The Concise Yoga Vasishtha.* Albany, New York: S.U.N.Y. Press, 1984.

Walsh, Roger. The Consciousness Disciplines and the Behavioral Sciences: Questions of Comparison and Assessment. *American Journal of Psychiatry, 137,*1980, 663-73.

————Meditation Practice and Research. *Journal of Humanistic Psychology, 23,* 1983, 18-50.

————& Shapiro, Deane, eds. *Beyond Health and Normality: Explorations of exceptional psychological well-being.* New York: Van Nostrand Reinhold, 1983.

————& Vaughan, Frances, eds. *Beyond Ego: Transpersonal Dimensions in Psychology.* Los Angeles, CA: J. P. Tarcher, 1980.

Walt Disney Company. *The Lion King.* Burbank: Walt Disney Company, 1994.

Way, Robert. *The Wisdom of the English Mystics.* New York: New Directions Publishing Corp., 1978.

White, John, ed. *Kundalini: Evolution and Enlightenment.* New York: Anchor Books, 1979.

Wilber, Ken. *No boundary.* Boulder, Colorado: Shambhala Publications, 1979.

————Psychologia perennis: The spectrum of consciousness. *The Meeting of the Ways* (pp. 7-28). John Welwood, ed. New York: Schocken Books, 1979.

————*Eye to eye: The Quest for the New Paradigm*. Garden City, NY: Anchor Press/Doubleday, Anchor Books, 1983.

————The developmental spectrum and psychopathology: Part I, stages and types of pathology. *Journal of Transpersonal Psychology, 16*, 1984, 75-118.

————The developmental spectrum and psychopathology: Part II, treatment modalities. *Journal of Transpersonal Psychology, 16*, 1984, 137-66.

Wilson, Stephen. In Pursuit of Energy: Spiritual Growth in a Yoga Ashram. *Journal of Humanistic Psychology, 22*, 1982, 43-55.

————Becoming a Yogi: Resocialization and Deconditioning as Conversion Processes. *Sociological Analysis , 45*, 1984, 301-14.

————Therapeutic processes in a yoga ashram. *American Journal of Psychotherapy, 34*, 1985, 253-62.

Woodroffe, Sir John, trans. *Tantra of the Great Liberation: Mahanirvana Tantra*. New York: Dover, 1972.

————*The Serpent Power*. Madras, India: Ganesh and Co., 1973.

————*The Garland of Letters: Studies in the Mantra-Shastra*. Madras, India: Ganesh & Co., 1974.

————*Shakti and Shakta*. New York: Dover Publications, 1978.

————*Principles of Tantra (Vols. 1-2)*. Madras, India: Ganesh & Co., 1978.

————*Inroduction to Tantra Shastra*. Madras, India: Ganesh & Co., 1980.